EXCEL GUIDE FOR SUCCESS:

Transform Your Work with Microsoft Excel, Unleash Formulas, Functions, and Charts to Optimize Tasks and Surpass Expectations [II EDITION]

Copyright © 2023

Kevin Pitch

TABLE OF CONTENTS

Introduction 3

1   What Is Microsoft Excel? 4

2   What Are the File Extensions Used by Excel? 7

3   Excel Dashboard 11

4   The power of sorting and filtering...19

5   Power of Automatism 41

6   Graphs and Charts 49

7   Microsoft Excel Data Analysis..65

8   Common Problems and Mistakes with Microsoft Excel 67

9   Personal Finance Use 71

10 Engineer and Statistician Use of Microsoft Excel...73

11 How Can Business and Management Use Microsoft Excel?..................................75

12 Most Helpful Formulas 77

13 Writing Text in Microsoft Excel 97

14 Using Images and Shapes in Microsoft Excel...105

15 Basics of Data Validation in Microsoft Excel...108

16 Using Pivot Tables in MS Excel 111

17 How to Use a Microsoft Excel Named Range in Formulas, Cells, and Formulas.......119

18 How to Use the Microsoft Excel Lookup Function...120

19 Macros In MS Excel 121

20 Printing 129

21 Excel Shortcuts...135

22 Conclusion...139

Introduction

Have you ever wanted to play "spot the difference" with your colleagues? Or do spreadsheets seem too complicated for you to learn how to use? Do you ever feel like you're drowning in words, numbers, and percentages? Do you ever wish that there was someone to teach you the ins and outs of Microsoft Excel? Have no fear! This Microsoft Excel guide has the perfect solution! In Excel, you can make it as easy or as complicated as you want. For example, you can make a spreadsheet that only includes one column and two rows or create a complex spreadsheet that will take hours to figure out.

How? With Excel, you can create and use lists to store information. You can sort, search and filter that information. You can clean up and organize the data using formulas and functions, so your lists are in alphabetical order, or a list of numbers is automatically converted into a graph. How great is that!

If you're a beginner looking to learn the basics of Microsoft Excel, look no further than this book! This comprehensive reference guide shows you everything you need to know to create worksheets, use formulas, integrate graphs, format data, and create charts. In addition, it's easy to follow the examples, making learning easier and saving you time! The book is an ideal choice for both personal use and business purposes!

Many books claim to be your best Excel ally, but they are just a waste of your time. Unlike other books, this one is highly recommended by people of all levels, from beginners to experienced Excel users. It's also an excellent reference for people who love learning. It's thorough and research-based, ensuring that you learn everything you need to know to master Excel charts and graphs.

As a beginner, you'll find that there are many things you must learn to become an expert in Excel. For example, learning to recognize data patterns and analyze them is essential. Once you have mastered basic Excel skills, you'll be ready to apply more advanced skills, including learning to customize Excel macros. There are also many tips for advanced users.

If you're ready to move beyond basic Excel skills, this is the book. Although not intended for beginners, it assumes you have some knowledge of pivot tables and relationships. It also introduces you to advanced Excel tools. These tools are ideal for those who need to analyze complex data. You'll learn about advanced Excel techniques, such as financial modeling, which is incredibly complex.

What will you learn?

Once you have learned the basics of using Microsoft Excel, you will probably want to take advantage of its advanced features. These include writing formulas and visualizing data. While these skills may seem time-consuming at first, they can save you a lot of time in the future. Advanced Excel features blur the line between spreadsheets and code. One may use the Visual Basic for Applications, a programming language working inside Excel software, to automate tasks, create interactive forms, and coordinate changes among multiple users.

Basic skills are essential for any job, no matter the industry. You should be familiar with the UI and ribbons to create effective charts and reports. Learning to use basic macros, data validation, and graphs and charts is essential for almost every job. If you have a specific job or want to become a more efficient worker, you should take courses and practice on a project. Learning by doing is a great way to gain confidence in using Excel.

Luckily, most companies now use spreadsheets and cloud computing. Microsoft Excel is now available as a web app for mobile devices. Unlike the Excel desktop, the web app has less features, such as functions, pivot tables, and charts. Microsoft has also recently released an all-in-one office app designed to be used for spreadsheets and other office applications. Fortunately, learning to use Excel doesn't need to be difficult. Take it step by step until you're comfortable using it.

Advanced Excel training for employees improves employee productivity. More efficient employees will complete tasks faster, provide better customer service, and produce more work in less time. Advanced Excel training can result in an hour or two saved per employee, which translates to significant extra hours per week for the company. This is an invaluable investment for your career and your job security. You'll be surprised at how quickly you can increase productivity by taking advanced Excel training.

Daily challenges that require Microsoft Excel

Many books and online courses teach the basics of Excel, but true mastery of the program takes practice. Daily Excel challenges provide an opportunity for you to practice. Excel Experiences may include problems like duplicates, inconsistent formatting of cell, or incomplete data. In addition, you can download an exercise file and work out a solution for the problem on your own.

The future of technology

A new research project at Microsoft, called Calc Intelligence, aims to bring intelligence to spreadsheets and end-user programming. Rather than just extending the grid and formulas that makeup spreadsheets, it will extend them to the point where they can do end-user programming. This innovative approach was spawned from the work of researchers who have used spreadsheets as the basis for research into knowledge computing, natural language processing, software analytics, and more.

In 2021, a senior researcher at Microsoft Research Cambridge, Advait Sarkar, envisioned adding extra cells in Excel for formatting and other purposes. Programming language design is a research discipline, and he envisions more streamlined human-computer interfaces.

Adding advanced analytics features to Excel has already changed the way it works. Users can ask it to calculate average sales in each country. This feature is available only to Office ProPlus users. Access, however, has been around for years and hasn't found widespread acceptance.

One way to make Excel even more helpful is to integrate it with enterprise-level databases. Many BI Software applications already add these integration elements, including Oracle Answers. Another example is Qlikview, which supports exporting to Excel. Currently, there is no clear competition for Excel. The feature set of Excel makes it the most comprehensive and versatile spreadsheet software available. Other less popular spreadsheet applications are not fit for real-world corporate use.

While Excel will remain important for general purposes, it won't become a stand-alone big data tool. But, for high-level manipulation and management, Excel is an invaluable tool. It's unlikely to go away anytime soon. For the time being, the future of Excel is bright. So, what should it do to improve? The future of Excel should focus on its strengths. However, it should be simple but powerful.

1 What Is Microsoft Excel?

You can learn about the different features and functions of Microsoft Excel in this book. We will also cover where to buy MS Excel and the different ways to sell it. This section provides all the information you need to make the right decision. If you are considering selling MS Excel, read this section first. It will help you choose the best option for your needs. In addition, it will save you time and energy by giving you the essential information you need.

The Clear Definition of Microsoft Excel

We describe Excel as a spreadsheet application advanced by Microsoft. It is available on various platforms, including Windows, macOS, iOS, and Android. Its features include calculation abilities, graphing tools, pivot tables, and Visual Basic for Applications. In addition, it falls under Microsoft Office suite of software. But what is Microsoft Excel, and what can it do for you? Let's find out.

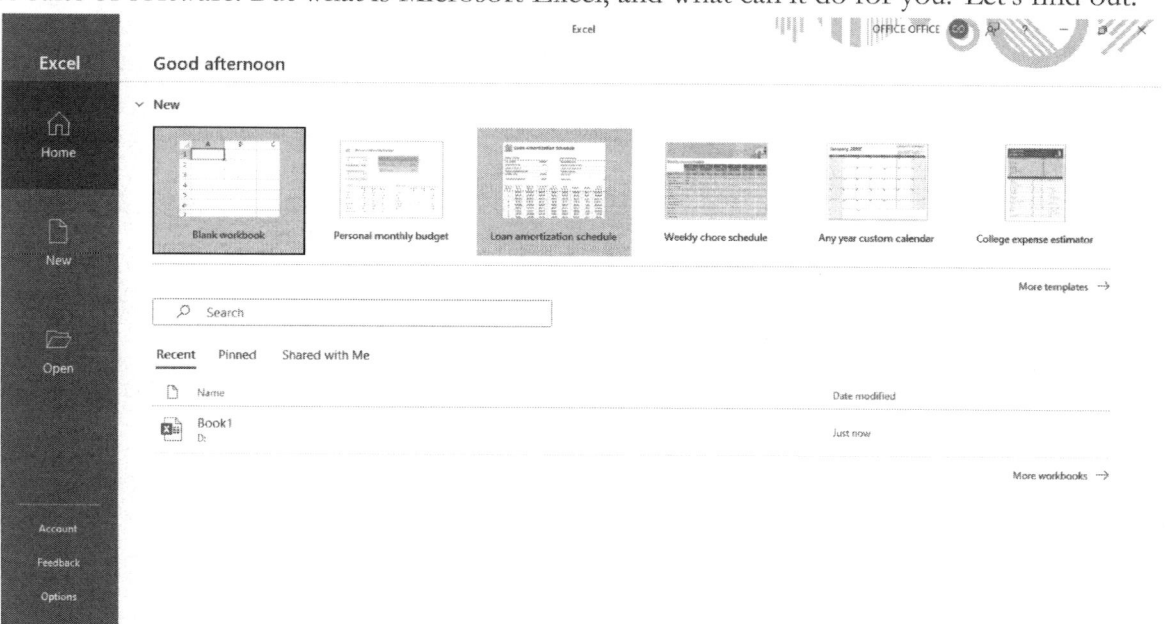

Image 1: The Microsoft Excel platform

Workbook: Every Excel document contains at least one worksheet. Worksheets are grids where you enter information. They can contain large amounts of text, numbers, and formulas. Worksheets can be renamed and have different styles and colors. They can also be organized according to data type entered. The Workbook always contains a worksheet. You can open multiple worksheets simultaneously and switch back and forth between them by navigating tabs.

Hundreds of Calculations: Excel is a great spreadsheet application. You can perform hundreds of calculations using the tool's many functions. It can perform basic math, pivot tables, charts, and more. It can even perform advanced calculations involving large amounts of data. For instance, besides numbers, you can utilize Excel to calculate angles, the tangent of angles, and pi to fourteen decimal places. You can also use this software to perform statistical analysis and report statistics.

Getting Started: Microsoft Excel can be started in either of two ways, depending on your computer setup. For Windows users, click Start button to open Start menu. Next, navigate to the Program Files (x86) folder. Double-click on this folder, and you will see the Microsoft Office folder. Double-click this folder and open Microsoft Office application. There, you've just learned a new application. Alternatively, press the Window button and type Excel in the search box (for the latest Windows operating systems). Click on the Excel icon and the app will launch.

Pivot Table: Another feature of Excel that is often overlooked is the pivot table. These can help you easily and efficiently create complex charts, reports, and calculations. This feature can save you a lot of time by automating the process and reducing the need for manual work. Lookup Formulas: Another helpful feature of Excel is its lookup function, which locates information within a workbook based on the criteria entered. You can write lookup formulas to build dashboards, interactive charts, and even complex mathematical functions.

Chart of Excel Versions

#	Name	Released
1	Version 1	1985
2	Excel 2	1987
3	Excel 3	1990
4	Excel 4	1992
5	Excel 5	1993
6	Excel 95	1995
7	Excel 97	1997
8	Excel 2000	1999
9	Excel 2002	2001
10	Microsoft Office Excel 2003	2003
11	Microsoft Office Excel 2007	2007
12	Microsoft Office Excel 2010	2010
13	Microsoft Excel 2013	2013
14	Microsoft Excel 2016	2016
15	Microsoft Excel 2019	2019
16.	Microsoft Excel 2021	2021
17.	Microsoft Excel 2023	2023

Table 1: Microsoft Excel Versions

1.1   How Does Microsoft Excel Work?

A spreadsheet program is the foundation of Microsoft Excel, which is used to make financial statements and other documents. Anyone can use Excel to create a spreadsheet. To use Excel, click "File" icon on the computer's desktop, and choose "New." You can then decide to create a new workbook in any location. You can also name the workbook and put any relevant information into the cell. After creating a spreadsheet, you can save the workbook to your chosen location.

Many businesses use Excel heavily in their day-to-day operations. They must keep track of many different pieces of information, including inventory flows. Inventory flows need to be controlled to avoid overstocking. Excel keeps track of customer and supplier transactions, important dates, schedules, and dates. Many people use Excel to manage their contacts, keep track of sales and keep track of clients and suppliers. You can even organize your client's sales and financial health with this powerful software program.

You can also enter formatting rules to make data appear a certain way. This will allow you to format a cell for specific text or a range of numbers. For instance, if one types "3/4" into a given cell, it will display as "4-Mar". You may not realize it, but you're entering a fraction. To avoid the "3/4" displayed on the screen, you'll need to format the cell before entering the data.

Learning to use the keyboard shortcuts to save time and make the most of your spreadsheet. While most of us cannot imagine living without a mouse or a touchpad, keyboard shortcuts are essential for our daily tasks. Learn to use the Ctrl + A shortcut to select all the data in a sheet. Then, insert hyperlinks with triangle-shaped button in the upper left corner. Using this shortcut, you can also find information about contacts in a list.

1.2 Where do you buy Microsoft Excel?

If you've been looking for a good office software suite, this the appropriate place. Microsoft Excel is a spreadsheet program that stores data in a special format called a "workbook." Each column and row contains data referred to as a "cell."

If you're looking for a specific Microsoft Office application, you can purchase it separately. Microsoft Excel is part of the Microsoft Office productivity suite. To use Excel's full capabilities, you'll need a subscription to Microsoft 365. This subscription bundles Excel with other Office applications and includes regular updates. A subscription to Microsoft 365 includes Excel as part of a yearly plan and will consist of other benefits, like cloud storage.

What are the possible sell options for MS Excel

In an office, the use of Microsoft Excel is a necessity. Its powerful features make it an excellent tool for managing information on people. Individuals can be tracked using a single column in a spreadsheet. Information such as name, email, start date, items purchased, subscription status, and last contact can all be tracked in one place. Microsoft Excel is widely used by companies and individuals alike for budgeting, analysis, and reporting.

In the corporate world, account managers often require MS Excel skills. This is because they handle records on customers. Microsoft Excel allows them to organize and edit those records. Employees, too, need to be comfortable using the software. In addition, employees with Excel skills are typically required to keep track of their customers' records, making the software indispensable. However, there are several alternatives available. In the case of Microsoft Excel, you should consider the following alternatives.

2 What Are the File Extensions Used by Excel?

What is an Excel extension?

File extensions are a group of letters appearing at the end of a file's name. They are usually two to four or even characters long and can be any length. Excel uses a few standard extensions. This section will cover Excel 2019 to the latest versions. It also covers XLSX files. Here are the most common file extensions used by Excel.

The XLS extension is the oldest file format supported by Excel. The XLS format is the default file extension for Excel versions 2.0 to 2003. It requires more disk space and may contain malicious VBA code. Also, the XLS format has fewer rows and columns than its newer counterparts. The XLS format is not compatible with Excel 97. Whenever you wish to use an older version of Microsoft Excel, you'll need to convert it to an XLS format first.

If you have a file in Excel, the file extension shows you its name and type. Before opening it, you should look for the XLS file extension. Before Excel 2007, it was XLS. The XLS extension was used for older versions of Excel. This format is an archive of XML documents. Unlike the XLS file format, Excel 2007 uses the Office Open XML format to save its spreadsheet information.

XLSB files are a comparatively faster version of the XLSX format. Therefore, they are often used if your Excel file contains VBA macros. Since they are binary files, XLSB files are much faster than those with XLSX or ODF extensions. Regarding file size, the XLSB extension is the best choice for large Excel files. You should use the ODF format if the file size is smaller than 10 MB.

XLS files are Microsoft Excel spreadsheets. They may contain charts, mathematical functions, and other formatting. Excel spreadsheets are often used in business contexts, where they can store financial data and perform calculations. XLSX files use the Open XML standard. Microsoft Excel 2007 and later versions support XLS format. These files can also be viewed using other spreadsheet programs. You can open XLS files with any text editor and view them on your computer.

- The .xlsx extension is commonly used in Excel to store basic data. XLSX is the current and most recent default extension for such an Excel file. This is in addition to XLS, another default extension was used until Microsoft Office 2007.

- The .XLSM is a database that may be used to store VBA code. This is solely designed for usage with macros. With the aid of extension, you can quickly determine if a file contains macros. A second file extension named (.CSV) Comma Separated Values demarcates the data, separated by commas in another file format.

- The .XLSB extensions are used for various functions such as compressing, saving, and opening. If your excel files contain a large amount of data or information, this file extension will help you by first compressing, then saving, and opening them quickly. By selecting File > Save As from Excel menu bar, you could merely save an Excel file in a different file format.

- **XLTX -**An Excel file is kept as a template that can use to create new Excel workbooks.

- **XLTM -** An Excel file with macros that are stored as a template.

- Several file formats are available in the Save As dialogue box, depending on which sort of sheet is active in the document: a single worksheet, chart worksheets, or other worksheets.

- For files that were created in a prior version of Excel or another program but are not yet in the current file format, pick File > Open using the menu bar.

- In Compatibility Mode, the workbook automatically opens when you access an Excel 97-2023 workbook. The use of Excel 2023 file format will enable you to take advantage of the new features that have been introduced to the application since its introduction.

Image 2: Microsoft Excel File Extensions (a)

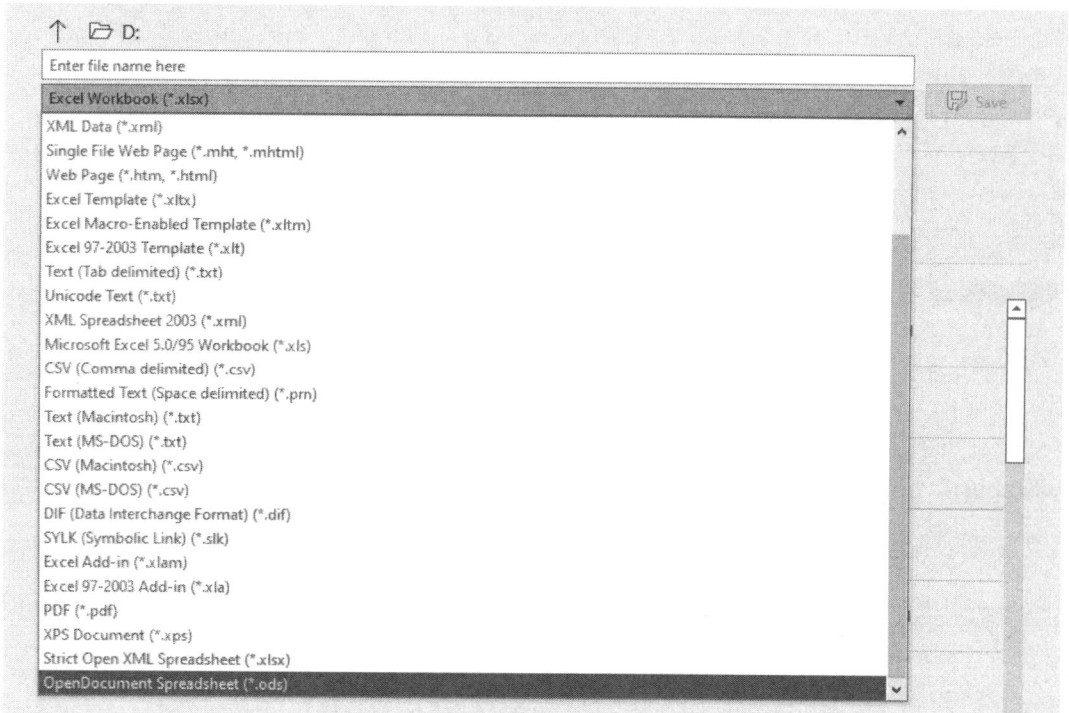

Image 3: Microsoft Excel File Extensions (b)

Where do you download Microsoft Excel Extensions?

If you wish to use a Mac version of Excel, you may wonder where to download the various Microsoft Excel extensions. The extension of an Excel file is essential because it indicates if the file has macros. When you save a document using this extension, it is protected from malicious macros. It is also reliable for security and macros, as it can accommodate large amounts of data. However, this file format can be slow to load and frequently crash.

You can also download the Office Online Extension if you own a Chromebook. This extension allows you to work on Excel files through your web browser. To install this extension, you must have an active Microsoft account. Once you log in, your Excel Online files will be stored on your OneDrive account. This makes it easy to access and edit Excel files on the Chromebook. While this extension isn't a complete replacement for Microsoft Office, it is an excellent option for those who prefer a native Windows experience.

If you can't locate the Microsoft Office Addins folder, you can use the Excel Addin Folder Path file. To find the Addins folder, open Windows Explorer and navigate to the Microsoft Addins folder. Next, click on **Insert,** then select Get Add-Ins. In the Addins dialog box that shows up, choose add-in you need and check the details. You can then click Add, Try, or Buy option.

Once done, you are now ready to use the Excel program with the latest version of Excel.

Once you've installed the new Excel version, you can install the free or paid versions of Excel Add-Ins in the same place. The Office Add-Ins Store is an easy-to-use website that offers a variety of useful Excel tools. It's run in Excel Online so you can access it from either desktop or mobile devices. You can also install the Office Add-Ins in Excel using the Start button.

2.1 Microsoft Excel vs. Google Sheets

If you compare the features of Microsoft Excel and Google Sheets, you'll discover that Google's product is much more flexible and capable. The app's online integration with other Google solutions makes collaborating with others on your spreadsheets easy. Google Sheets' formulas can also connect to other Google solutions, like Google Translate and Google Finance. In addition, Sheets can be used offline. This means that both spreadsheets are equally as useful for small businesses and large corporations. Both programs have their advantages and disadvantages. However, there's no need to choose between the two if you don't have many documents to store. Google Sheets' free version is a boon for people who need to share spreadsheets with co-workers. The latter also offers collaboration features that Excel lacks. But Google Sheets has a lot of advantages that you should consider before choosing one or the other. For small spreadsheets, Google Sheets is the better choice. This free tool allows you to work with multiple users on the same spreadsheet and save it in real-time. Microsoft Excel, on the other hand, does not allow real-time saving. You must save your spreadsheet on OneDrive or SharePoint to access it. Microsoft's online spreadsheet also requires you to share the file via email, which isn't ideal for collaboration. However, the free version of Google Sheets has many advantages that make it a better option for small businesses. While both programs are very similar, one crucial difference lies in the data handling capabilities of each. While Google Sheets' maximum cell capacity is five million cells, Excel can support up to 17 million. This means that Google Sheets' maximum cell capacity is much lower than Excel's. As a result, in addition to better overall performance, Google Sheets' free version is much less user-friendly than Excel's. The same goes for formatting and editing. If you need to share spreadsheets with a team, you'll want to use Google Sheets. The free version allows you to edit and track changes, but you'll need a subscription plan if you want to share spreadsheets with others. Microsoft Excel is available to all Google users, but many people start with Google Sheets and stick with it. Besides, Excel can also be downloaded to your system.

2.2 Microsoft Excel vs. QuickBooks

While these programs are very similar, they serve slightly different purposes. As a result, one is excellent for small businesses, while the other is best for larger enterprises. For example, small businesses can use Excel to manage their finances and monitor cash flow. Still, for larger companies, the features of QuickBooks are far more comprehensive and powerful when specializing in accounting and invoicing. In addition to having extensive functionality, QuickBooks Online is also available on mobile devices. As a result, business owners can easily access most accounting features on the go. In contrast, Excel's mobile app is limited in its capabilities, including the ability to invoice, enter bills, and generate reports. Both programs also offer assisted bookkeeping for an additional fee. Another benefit of using accounting software is that it eliminates the need for manual bookkeeping, saving business owners precious time. With Quickbooks, business owners no longer need to spend hours entering data into spreadsheets; the software will do it for them. QuickBooks is easy to learn and can be used by outsourced bookkeepers. Small businesses can also focus on expanding their businesses instead of managing their books manually. QuickBooks offers many customization options, making it a highly versatile option for smaller businesses. Another benefit of QuickBooks is its ability to manage expenses. It imports data from connected accounts and digital wallets. Users can also create custom expense rules that display expenses when they run financial reports. QuickBooks mobile app lets users attach pictures of receipts to transactions. In addition, the software automatically sorts expenses to maximize tax deductions. With the help of QuickBooks, you can create shareable profit and loss reports and a cash flow statement.

3   Excel Dashboard

There are several ways to explore the Microsoft Excel interface. First, learn how to use the various tabs to access important information. Excel comes with more than a dozen different cursor shapes. You'll learn which ones do what when you explore these shapes. You can also use the mouse to select any cell in the worksheet. Clicking on a cell will make it active. A name box will appear for the active cell. Once you've changed the cell, you can save or change your work.

3.1   What is Excel Interface?

The interface is composed of several components that make up Excel. These components are the Workbook Components and the Ribbon. The Ribbon has commands, groups, and buttons. Each tab has a different function and is categorized based on its usage. For example, the Home tab has buttons for most frequently used functions. The Ribbon also has tabs for Inserting, Formatting, Data, Review, and Clipboard. The Ribbon can be used to move between different sections of the workbook or between individual workbooks.

The user interface in Microsoft Excel has a few key elements. The status bar displays some common information, and the zoom slider controls the size of the worksheet. It can also be customized. Here are some of the other components of the Excel interface. The ribbon contains tabs and other icons that control the application's functions. Once you've chosen a tab, go to its properties and choose a color scheme. You can also adjust the background of the workspace and background color.

The title bar of the spreadsheet displays the name of the active document. The upper-right corner has control buttons that allow you to change the sheet label, share it, and close the workbook. Other interface elements in Excel include the diskette and excel icon. In addition, the menu bar has commands like File, Insert, Page Layout, Formulas, Data, Review, and the Help tab with a light bulb icon. All menus have subcategories to simplify the distribution of information and calculation.

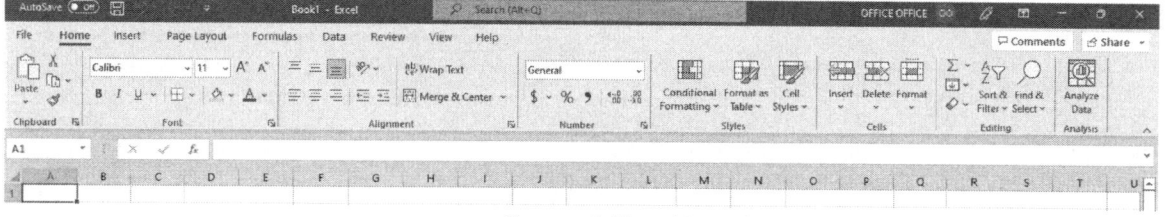

Image 4: Excel Interface

3.2   Tabs in Excel

File

There are various ways to organize the information you store on your file tabs in Microsoft Excel. For example, the Office Tab consolidates actions such as saving and closing multiple files. This tab is also used to organize the files in your Favorites Group. You can also customize the size of the tabs. You can set the length of the tabs to be automatic, self-adaptive, or fixed. The auto-adaptive option displays most file names, and the fixed option shows the same length for all tabs.

All your Excel worksheet operational aspects are here in the File Tab. The INFO section gives you a chance to set a given password to your workbook to ensure no one else can modify it when you are not around.

Use the NEW option under File to come up with a new worksheet. In addition, you may use the keyboard shortcut Ctrl+N or Command+N (for Mac users). The OPEN option allows you to open and work on a previously saved file. Choosing the option will open a directory where you are supposed to choose your file's location. SAVE option ensures that everything you are working on is stored and up to date every time you select the option. Other options include share, print, close, and export.

The Quick Access Toolbar

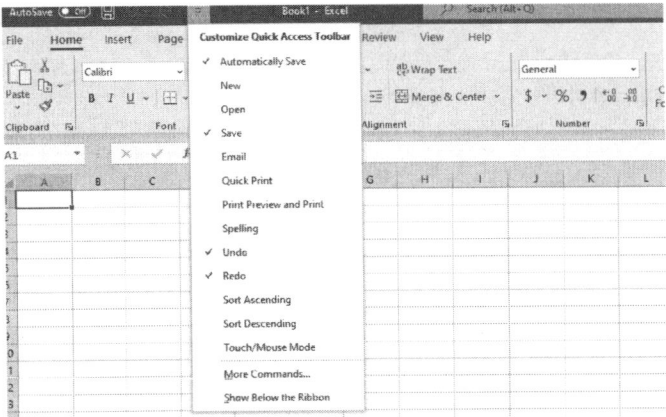

Image 5: Quick Access Tab in Windows

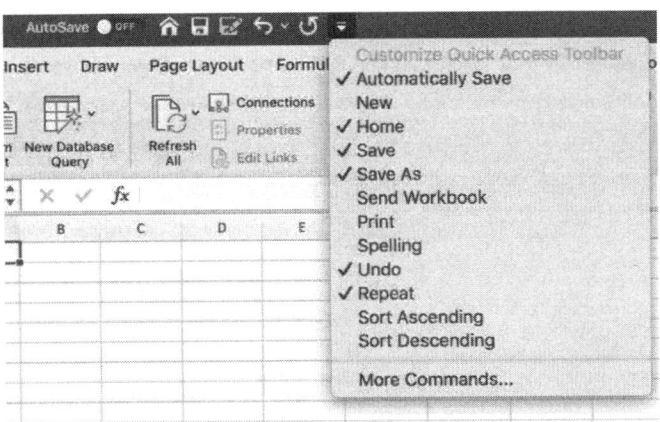

Image 6: Quick Access Tab in Windows in Mac

Quick Access Toolbar (QAT) is positioned to the upper left corner of Excel program. Save, Redo, and Undo are part of the QAT's default commands. Clicking the little downward arrow at the right end of the toolbar brings up a customization dialogue box where you may add or remove icons from the toolbar.

Tell me

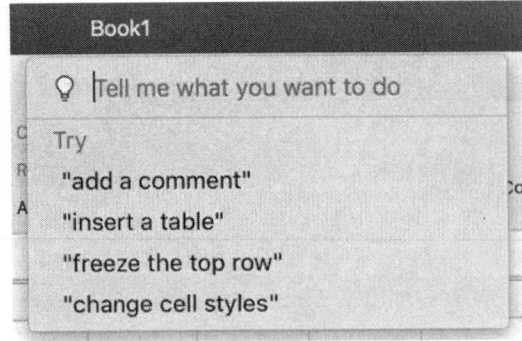

Image 7: Tell me search box in Mac

The tell me search box in the user interface allows for quick and easy locating commands without necessarily going to the ribbon tab or group. Instead, type here any command you wish to use.

Title Bar

The name presently in use is shown in the title bar at the top of excel spreadsheet program. The bar places the workbook's name at the center.

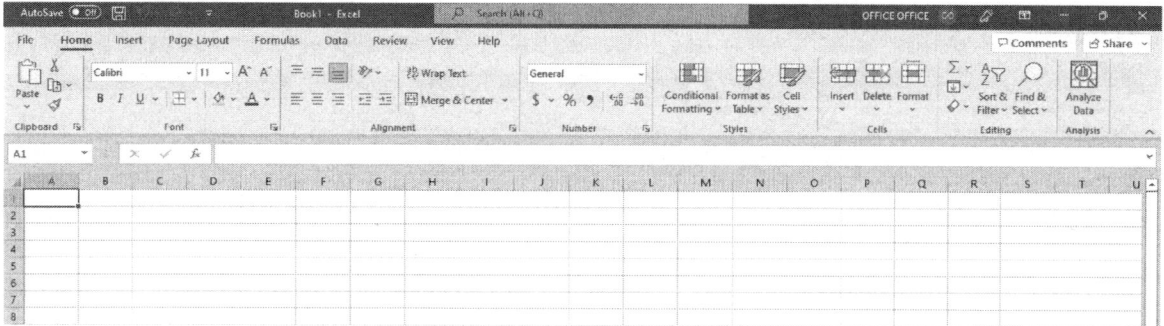

Image 8: Title bar in Windows Platform

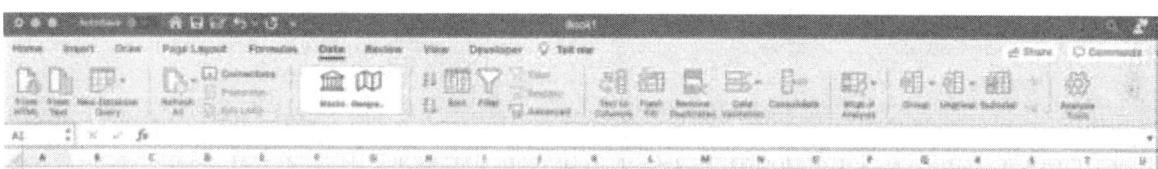

Image 9: Title bar in Mac platform

Book1 is the name of the workbook.

3.3 Ribbon

The ribbon is the primary working element of the Microsoft Excel interface and includes all instructions necessary to do most basic operations. You will realize it is divided into tabs with a set or group of commands.

Image 10: The ribbon

Excel Ribbon Tabs

The Excel ribbon has nine tabs: File, Home, Insert, Page Layout, Formulas, Data, Review, View, and Help. You can add additional tabs with your preferred command buttons like Draw and Developer to create a customized Ribbon.

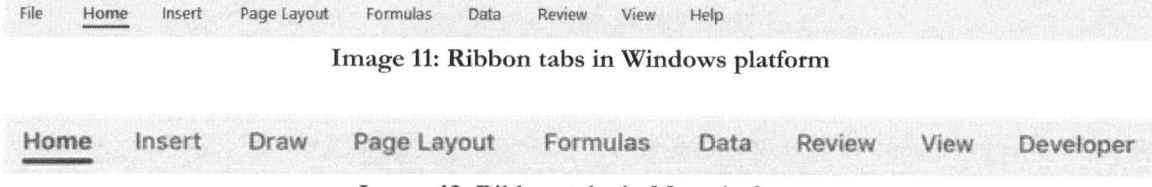

Image 11: Ribbon tabs in Windows platform

Image 12: Ribbon tabs in Mac platform

Home

Contains the most often used commands, such as copy and paste, find and replace, sort, filter, and format data. You can also meet the format painter and other clipboard functions.

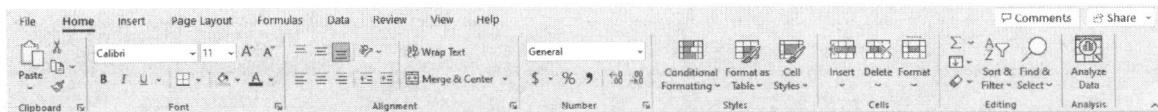

Image 13: Home tab in Windows platform

Image 14: Home tab in Mac platform

With the front ribbon, you can get font tools to tweak your font like font name and size, font color, fill color, alignment, wrap text, merge & center, number ribbon for numerical & non-numerical figures, formatting styles, the cell ribbon, and editing ribbon.

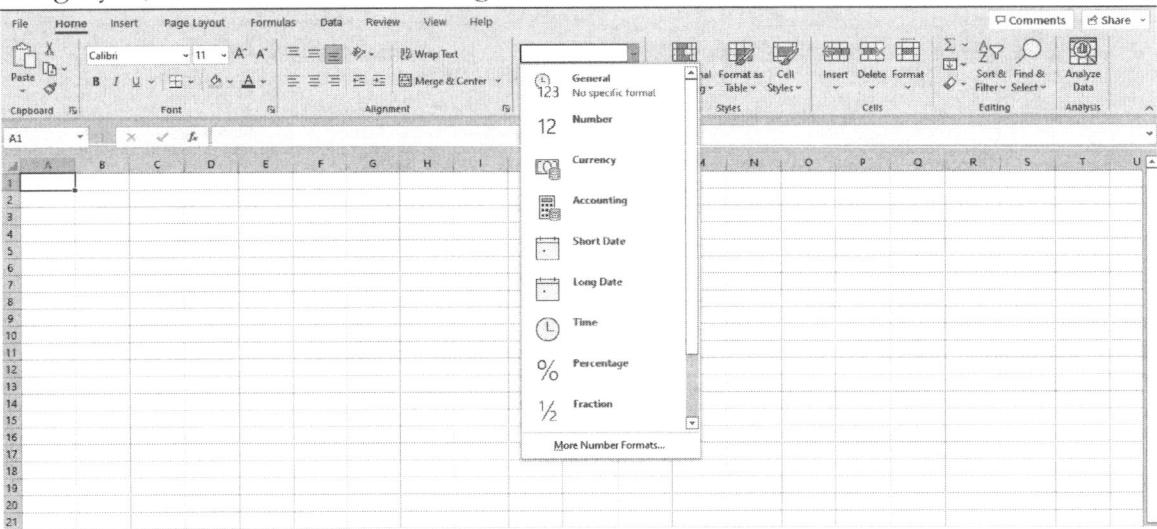

Image 15: Home tab formatting aspects in Windows platform

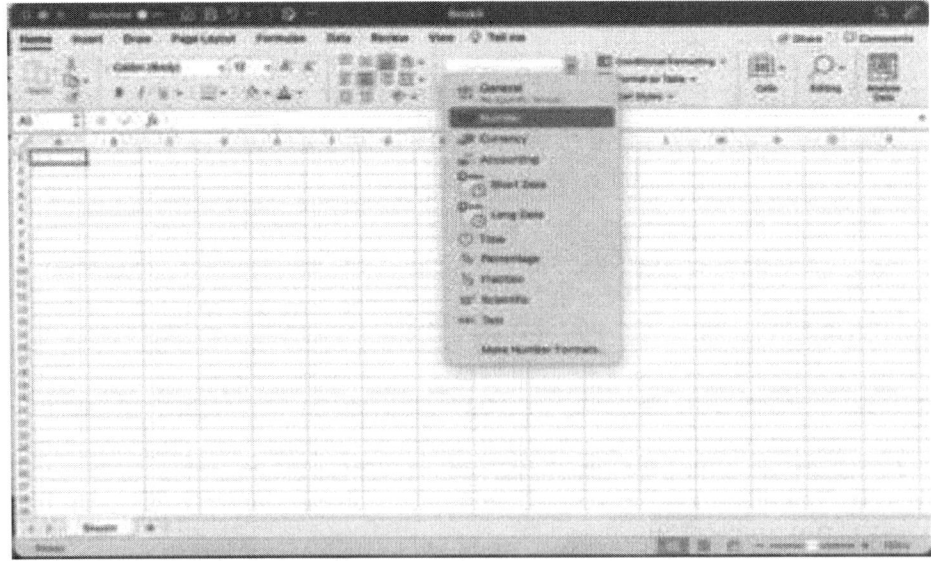

Image 16: Home tab formatting aspects in Mac platform

Commands

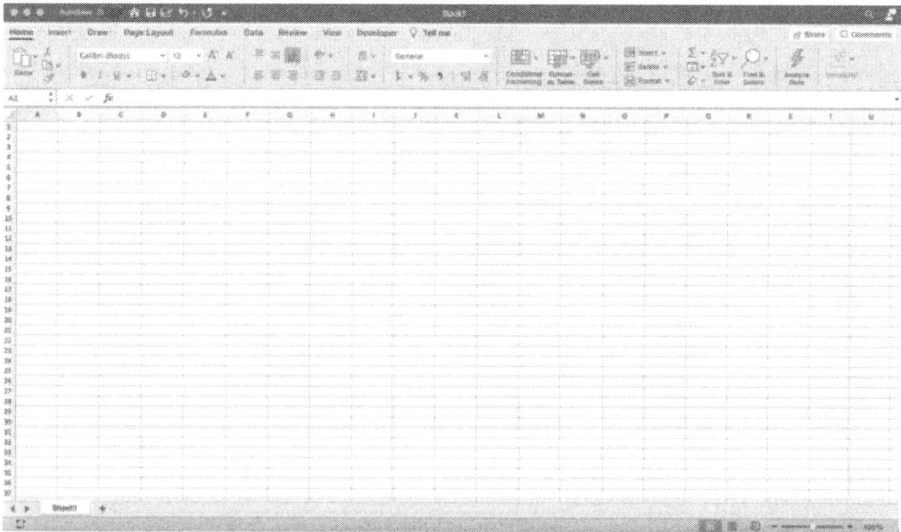

Image 17: Command groups

Commands belong to a group.

Name Box

The Name Box allows you to examine the reference (address) for a single cell or range of cells and set the name for that cell or range of cells.

Functions to Insert

It obtains the desired outcome using a particular function depending on its inputs. It is one of Excel's features.

Formula Bar

You may inspect and alter the function or formula that applies to any cell in the sheet for any calculation in the Formula bar. The resizable bar above the columns of an Excel sheet is known as the formula bar. For better graphics, everything we enter in any cell shows above it. It's excellent for formatting formulae before pressing Enter. The function box on its left is where you pick the kind of functions you wish to perform. For example, let's say you're looking for the average (mean), lowest (MIN), or highest (MAX) numerical values in a batch of data. The name box is located to the left. It shows and informs you of the cell you're in, such as A1.

Image 18: The Formula bar

Row and Column Headings

The column comprises vertical light grey colored lines that carry the letters identifying each column within a spreadsheet. It has a column header at the top (above the first row). Each row in a worksheet is identified by a group of horizontal light grey colored lines with each row identified with a number. Row Heading shows at top of the page (left of first column).

The Vertical/Horizontal Scrollbar

The scrollbar is important for seeing regions of the worksheet by scrolling up, down, left, or right using the Vertical or Horizontal scrollbar.

Page View Options

Page View Options are at the screen's right side, with one on taskbar.

Normal: Default view in the worksheet.

Page Layout: Separates worksheet into many page sizes for print previewing.

Page Break Preview: Displays the worksheet as individual pages with content to examine how a page appears.

Zoom Slider/Toolbar

Zoom slider is at the workbook's bottom right corner. Used for zooming in and out the spreadsheet to appropriate size.

Select all with a single click

To select the full worksheet, click the top left below the Name Box. Ctrl + A is the same thing.

Gridlines

Horizontal and vertical light grey lines in a worksheet.

Cell

We form a cell at the point rows and columns in a worksheet intersect.

Cell Address

The column letter identifies a cell's position, while the row number is the cell address or reference.

Active Cell

A bold cell with a black outline is an Active Cell. An active cell is a distinguishable mark that allows you to input and change data.

Sheet tab/active sheet

The name of sheet tab is bold and shows in the workbook's bottom left corner while a chosen worksheet is presently being utilized.

Cell range

A range of cells is defined as more than two cells chosen horizontally or vertically in the Microsoft Excel Spreadsheet Environment.

Tabs on sheets

Sheet tabs are the sheet names that emerge from the worksheet's bottom left corner in the Microsoft Excel Spreadsheet Environment.

Insert Tab

The Insert tab is mostly used for visualizing data. Using images, charts, and 3D maps entails bringing your data to life.

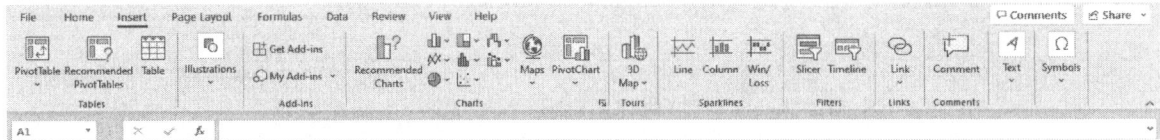

Image 19: The Insert tab in Windows platform

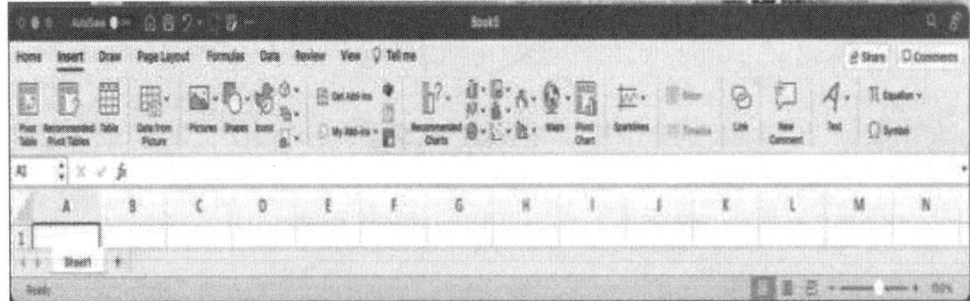

Image 20: The Insert tab in Mac platform

Page Layout

This tab is used to set up pages and print them. It controls the worksheet's layout, margins, alignment, and print area.

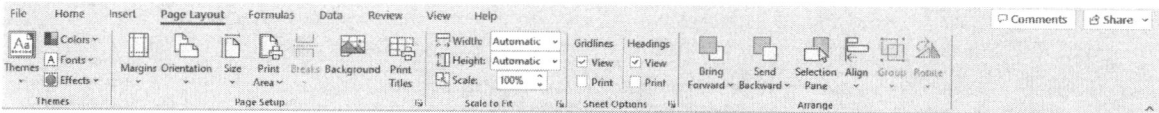

Image 21: Page Layout in Windows

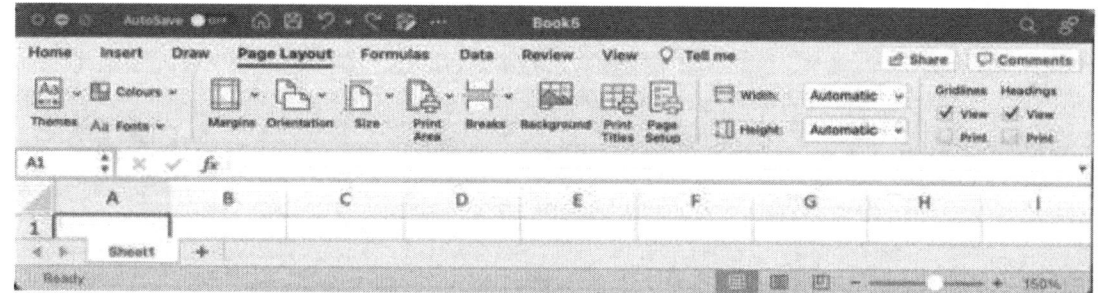

Image 22: Page Layout in Mac

Formulas

This tab allows you to enter functions name variables and change the values of calculation parameters. It is in charge of the computation choices.

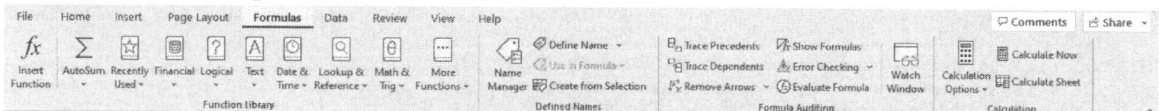

Image 23: Formula bar in Windows

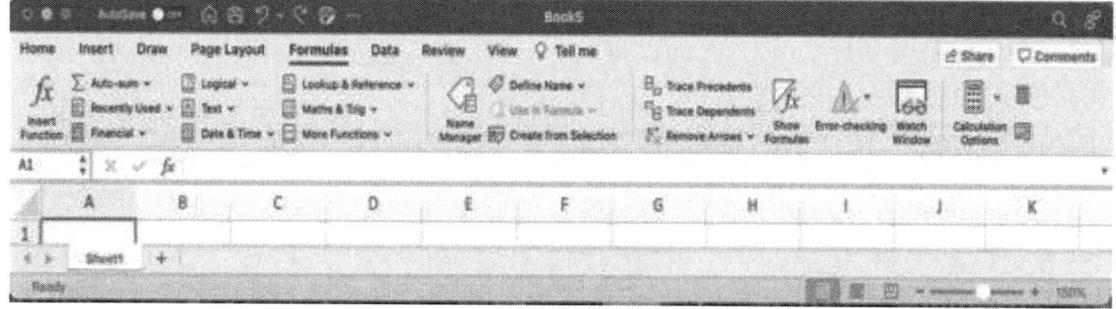

Image 24: Formula bar in Mac

Data

This tab includes controls for manipulating worksheet data and connecting to other data sources. In addition, it has features for sorting, filtering, and modifying data.

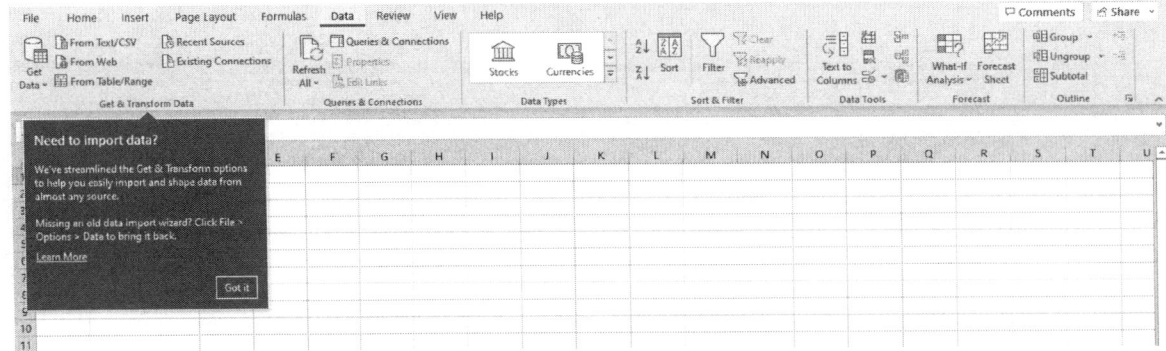

Image 25: Data bar in Windows

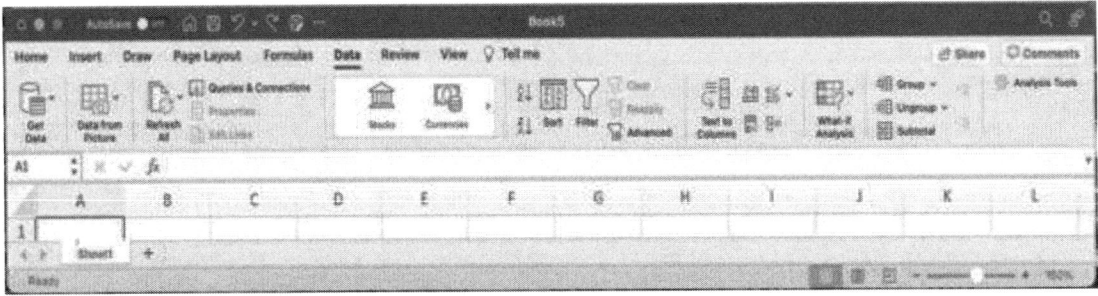

Image 26: Data bar in Mac

Review

This tab mainly provides capabilities for verifying spells, documenting changes, making notes and comments, sharing, and safeguarding worksheets in Excel workbooks.

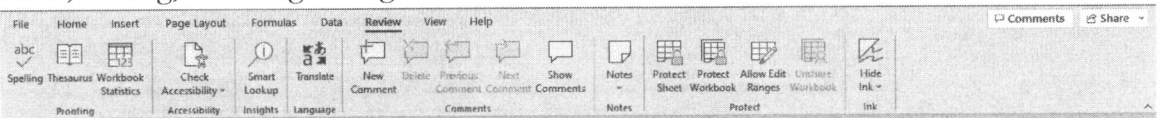

Image 27: Review Tab in Windows

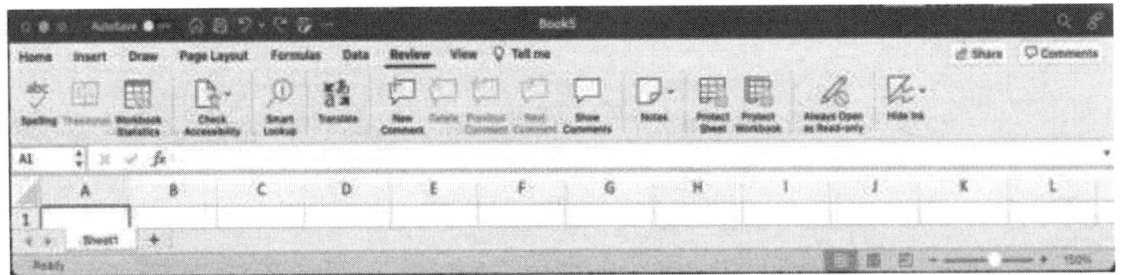

Image 28: Review tab in Mac

View

Switch between worksheets, see excel worksheets, freeze panes, and organize and manage numerous windows are all available from the View tab.

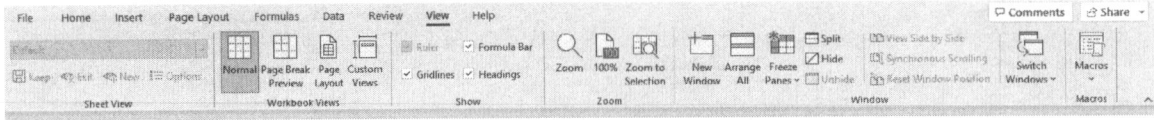

Image 29: View tab in Windows

Image 30: View tab in Mac

Help

The tab opens the Help Task Pane, where you can search any term and learn more.

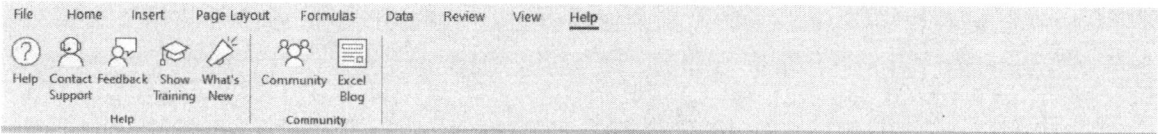

Image 31: The Help tab

The developer is the term for this. The developer tab may be accessed by selecting the File tab, then heading to Options, selecting "Customized Ribbon," selecting the developer option, ticking the box, and clicking OK.

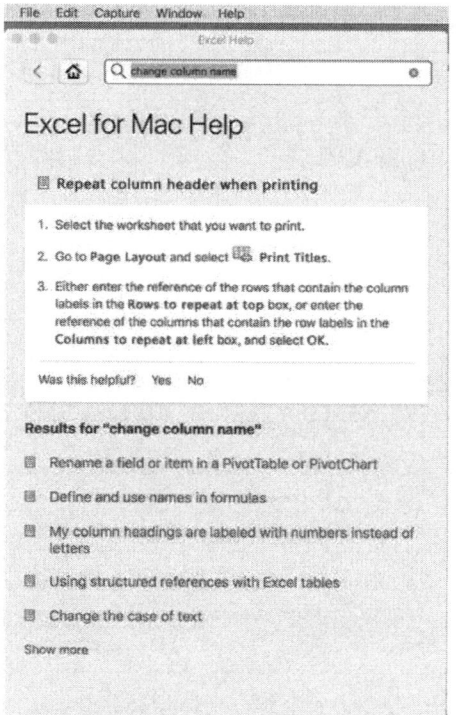

Image 32: Excel for Mac Help

4 The power of sorting and filtering

A spreadsheet is a tool that helps you organize and present data. Microsoft Excel is available for Android, macOS, Windows, and iOS. Its tools include graphing, pivot tables, calculation, and Visual Basic for Applications. It is part of Microsoft Office software suite. First, learn the benefits of filters and sorting. Then you can use them to create useful charts.

The power of sorting and filtering in Excel can assist one organize and subset data to make it easier to analyze. Most users flock to Data tab in the Ribbon and click the Sort and Filter icons. But there's a better way. Learn to use Excel's sort and filter options to create your custom filters. Here's how. But first, let's get familiar with the essential functions of these commands.

First, select the cells you want to sort. In this case, you want to sort by country. To do this, click on the data cell and choose "Cells" as the column name. Select the first column of the data column and click Sort. Now, go to Data tab and click "Filter." You can also choose to filter by date ranges. Make sure you select a date range from which you intend to sort the data.

Sorting and filtering in Microsoft Excel help you understand the data better. By removing unnecessary data, you'll be able to make better decisions. You can easily access the data that you want by using the functions. You'll notice the difference in a matter of seconds! If you're unsure how to sort your data, read the following guide. And remember, there are several ways to sort data in Excel.

Before deciding on your filtering and sorting options, know what each column of data means. Then, you'll need to decide how much information you want to filter. You can sort your data by selecting different criteria. For instance, you might wish to filter all the data corresponding to the cells' color. You can also sort by date. The key is to find out which data you want to filter based on your criteria.

4.1 Sorting data

Before sorting data, you must first decide whether to sort a cell range or the entire worksheet. One column organizes all the data on your worksheet. When you apply Sort, related information from every row is kept together. When working with a sheet with numerous tables, sorting a range sorts the data in a range of cells, which might be helpful. Other texts on the worksheet will not be affected by sorting a range.

To sort data from a Sheet

1. In the example, we alphabetically sort a T-shirt order form using the Last Name.

	A	B	C	D	E
1	**Homeroom**	**First Name**	**Last Name**	**T-Shirt Size**	**Payment Options**
2	115	Susan	Evers	Medium	Pending
3	115	Sharon	Bouvier	Medium	Check bounced
4	115	Andy	Womder	Large	Cash
5	120	George	Bluth	Extra large	Cash
6	120	Dee	Reynolds	Medium	Money Order
7	115	Mario	Bobsey	Large	Check
8	115	Luigi	Boris	Small	Check
9	120	Fred	Cartwright	Small	Cash
10	115	Ronnie	Furlan	Medium	Debit Card
11					

Image 33: Table with T-shirt orders

2. Choose a cell within column C to use for sorting. Use cell C2 as an example.

3. Click A-Z command to sort from A to Z or the Z-A command for sorting Z to A on the Ribbon's Data tab. We'll sort A to Z, for example.

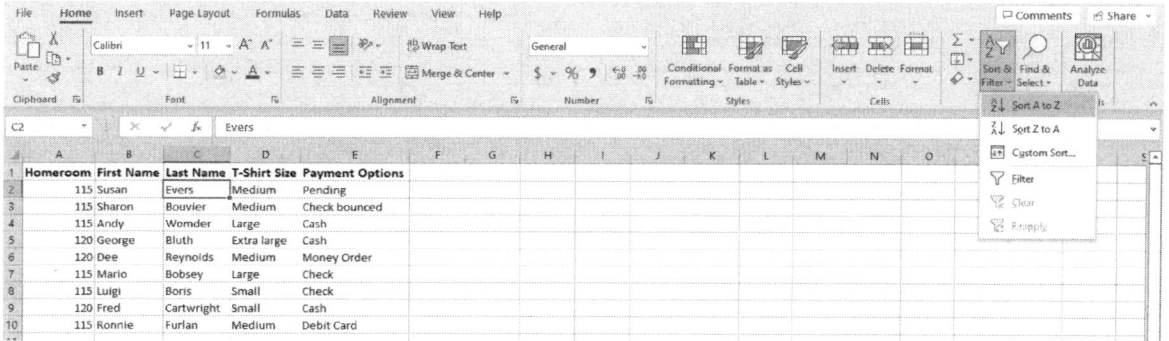

Image 34: Sorting T-shirt orders using last name column

4. The selected column will be used to sort the worksheet. The last name will sort the worksheet in the example.

	A	B	C	D	E
1	Homeroom	First Name	Last Name	T-Shirt Size	Payment Options
2	120	George	Bluth	Extra large	Cash
3	115	Mario	Bobsey	Large	Check
4	115	Luigi	Boris	Small	Check
5	115	Sharon	Bouvier	Medium	Check bounced
6	120	Fred	Cartwright	Small	Cash
7	115	Susan	Evers	Medium	Pending
8	115	Ronnie	Furlan	Medium	Debit Card
9	120	Dee	Reynolds	Medium	Money Order
10	115	Andy	Womder	Large	Cash
11					

Image 35: Sorted data on T-shirt orders

To sort data of Cell Range

1. Choose the cell range that you'd want to sort.

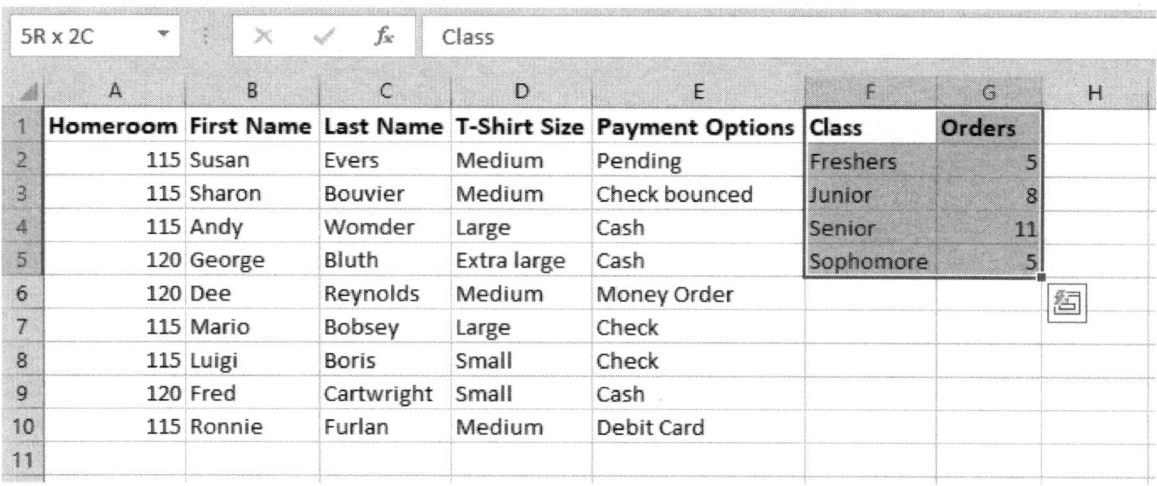

Image 36: Choosing cell range to sort

2. On the Ribbon, pick the Data tab, then Sort command.

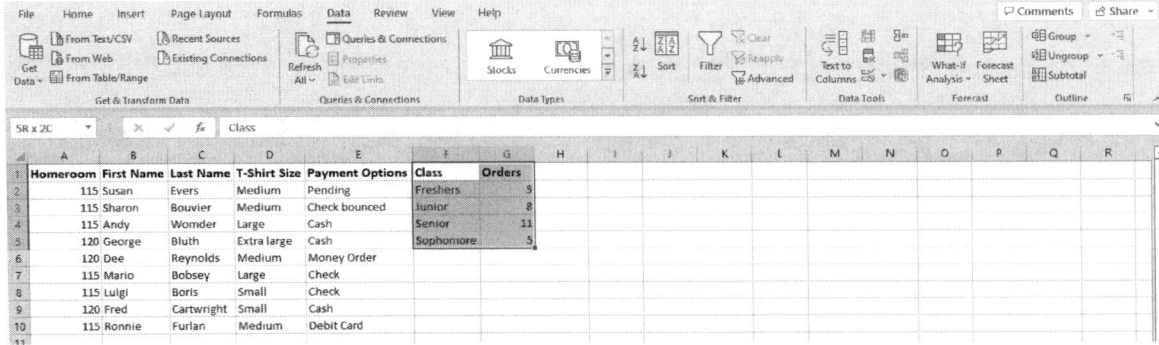

Image 37: Selecting the Data tab in Windows

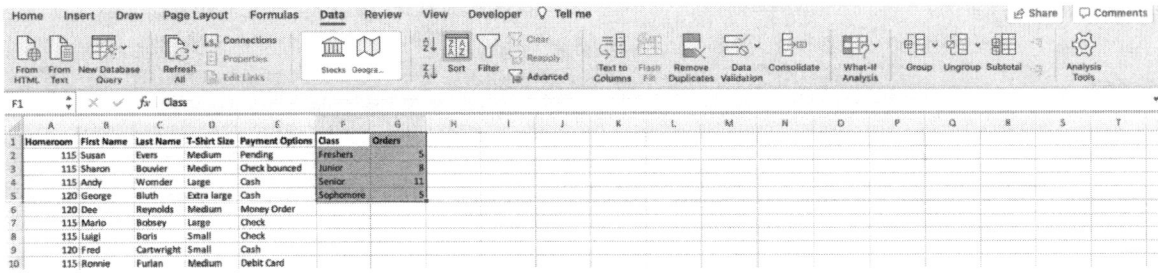

Image 38: Selecting the Data tab in Mac

3. A dialogue box for sorting will display. Select the column that you'd want to sort by.

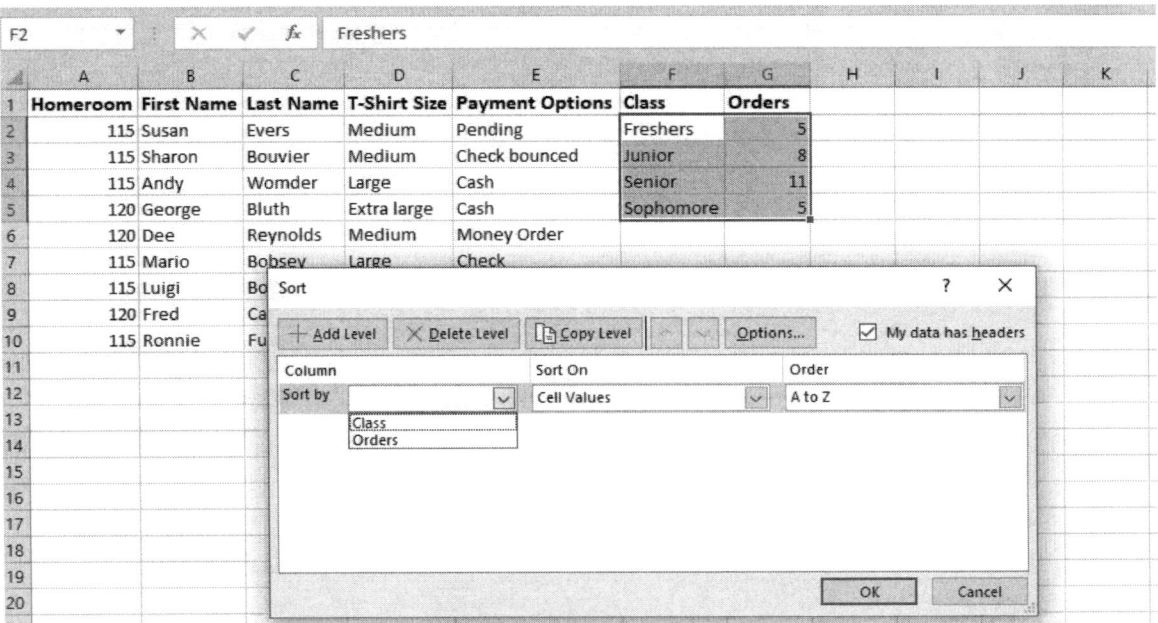

Image 39: The Sort dialogue box in Windows

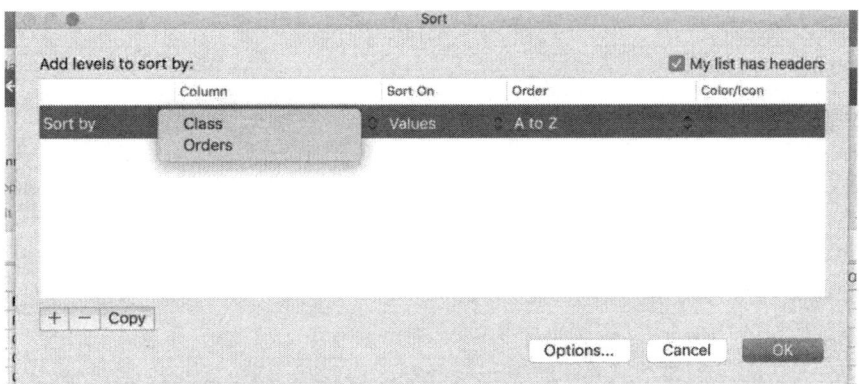

Image 40: The Sort dialogue box in Mac

4. Choose ascending/descending order.

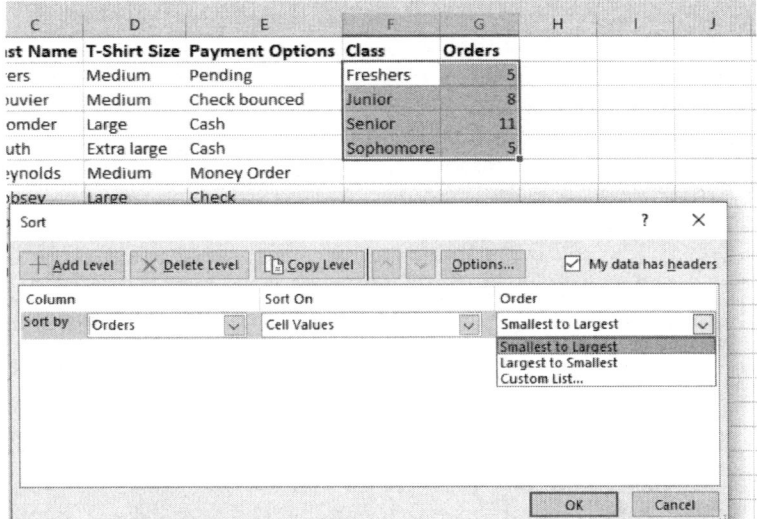

Image 41: Choosing the sorting order in Windows

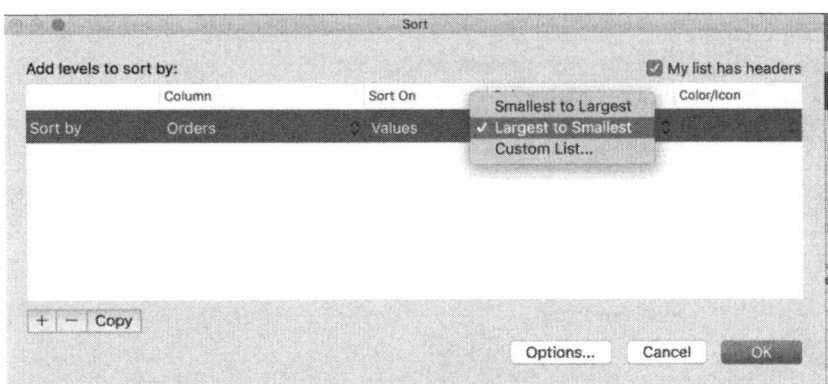

Image 42: Choosing the sorting order in Mac

5. Click OK.

The selected column will be used to sort the cell range. The Orders column will be ordered from highest to lowest, for example. It's worth noting that the Sort did not affect the rest of the worksheet's information.

To Sort Data in one column

Execute the steps below to sort on a single column:

1. Select any cell in the column to sort by clicking on it.

2. Click AZ to sort in ascending order in the Sort & Filter group on the Data tab.

To Sort Data in multiple Columns

Execute the steps below to sort on multiple columns:

1. Select Sort from the Sort & Filter group on the Data tab.

2. The Sort dialogue box is displayed.

3. From the 'Sort by' dropdown menu, choose Last Name.

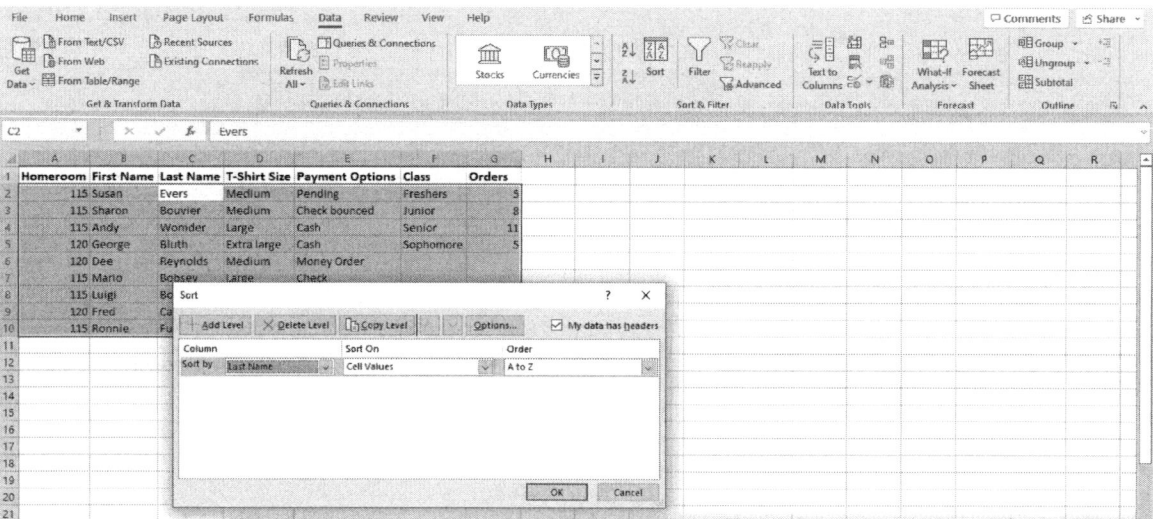

Image 43: Steps for sorting multiple columns

4. Select Add Level from the dropdown menu.

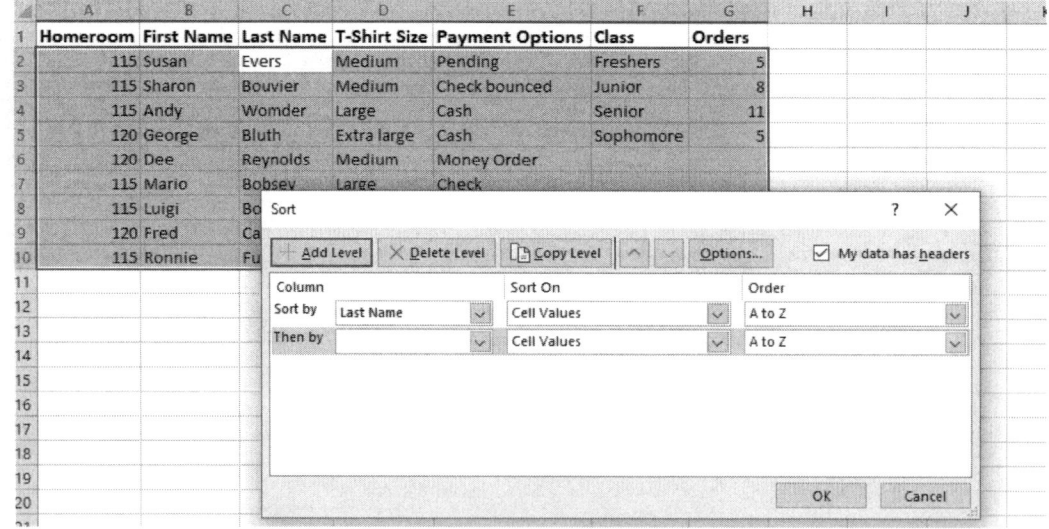

Image 44: Adding level for sorting multiple column

5. From the 'Then by' dropdown list, choose Orders.

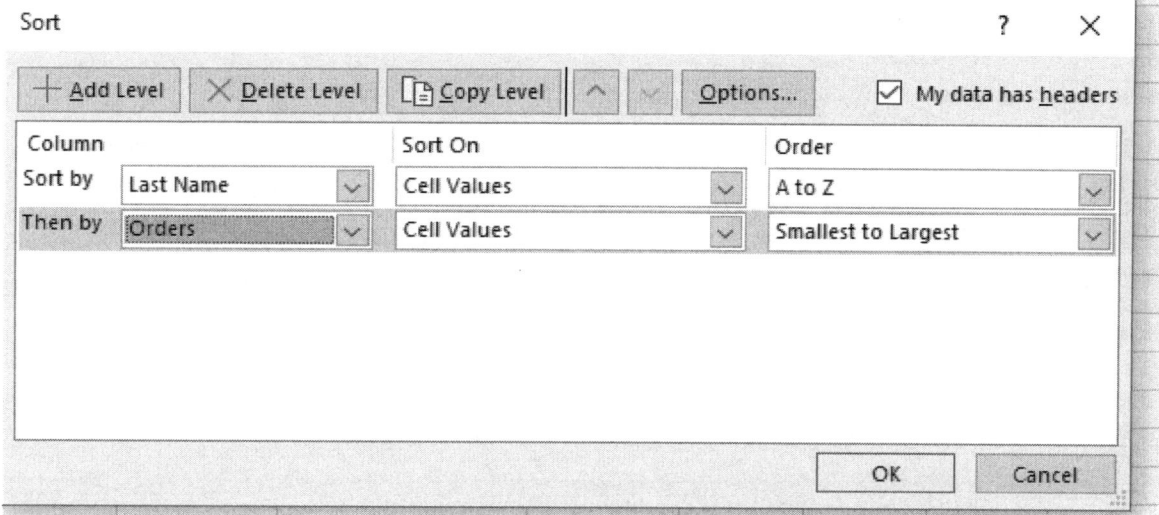

Image 45: The Then by sorting order

6. Select OK.

7. Result. The records are arranged by Last Name first, then by Orders in the example.

	A	B	C	D	E	F	G	H
1	Homeroom	First Name	Last Name	T-Shirt Size	Payment Options	Class	Orders	
2	120	George	Bluth	Extra large	Cash	Sophomore	5	
3	115	Mario	Bobsey	Large	Check			
4	115	Luigi	Boris	Small	Check			
5	115	Sharon	Bouvier	Medium	Check bounced	Junior	8	
6	120	Fred	Cartwright	Small	Cash			
7	115	Susan	Evers	Medium	Pending	Freshers	5	
8	115	Ronnie	Furlan	Medium	Debit Card			
9	120	Dee	Reynolds	Medium	Money Order			
10	115	Andy	Womder	Large	Cash	Senior	11	
11								
12								
13								
14								
15								

Image 46: Results of sorting multiple columns

4.2 Custom Sorting

The default sorting options may not always be able to sort data in the order you require. Fortunately, Excel allows you to establish your sorting order by creating a custom list.

A quick word on Custom Sort: This allows you to choose how the data is sorted within a given column. For instance, rather than sorting information alphabetically, you might wish to arrange it by size. In this scenario, you'll need to make a custom list for the sort order.

1. Select the data to sort by clicking on it.

2. Select Custom Sort from the dropdown menu after clicking the Sort command.

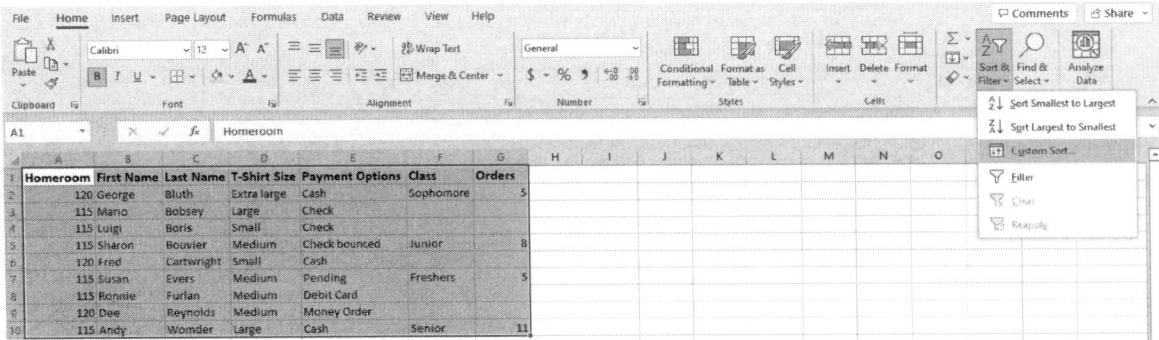

Image 47: Selecting the Custom Sort

3. The Sort window shows up, letting you choose the column and how to sort it.

4. You may use default selections (weekdays or months) or come up with a new list. Select the Custom List option from Order column, then NEW LIST to create a new list.

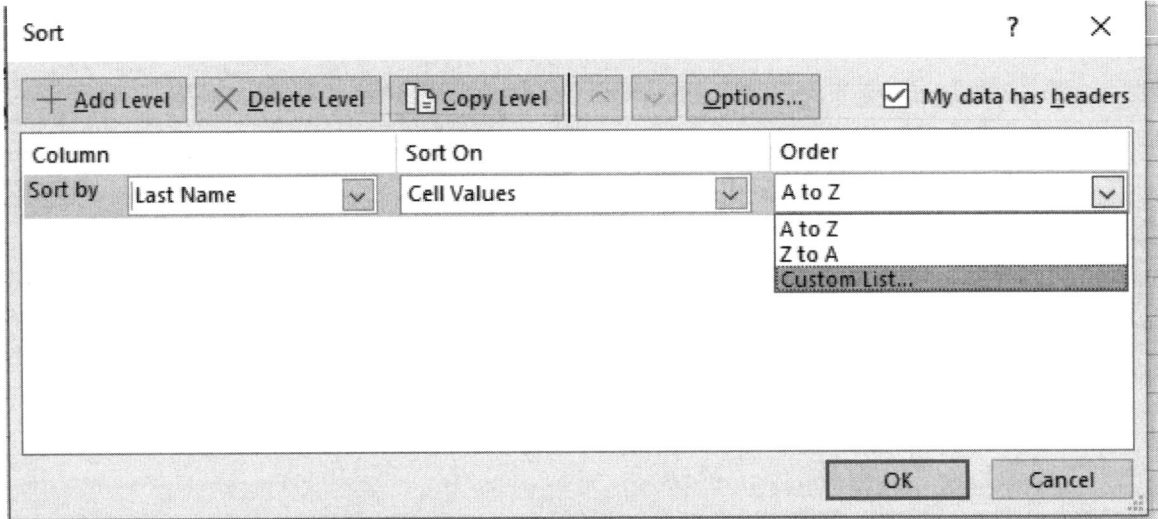

Image 48: Selecting the Custom List option

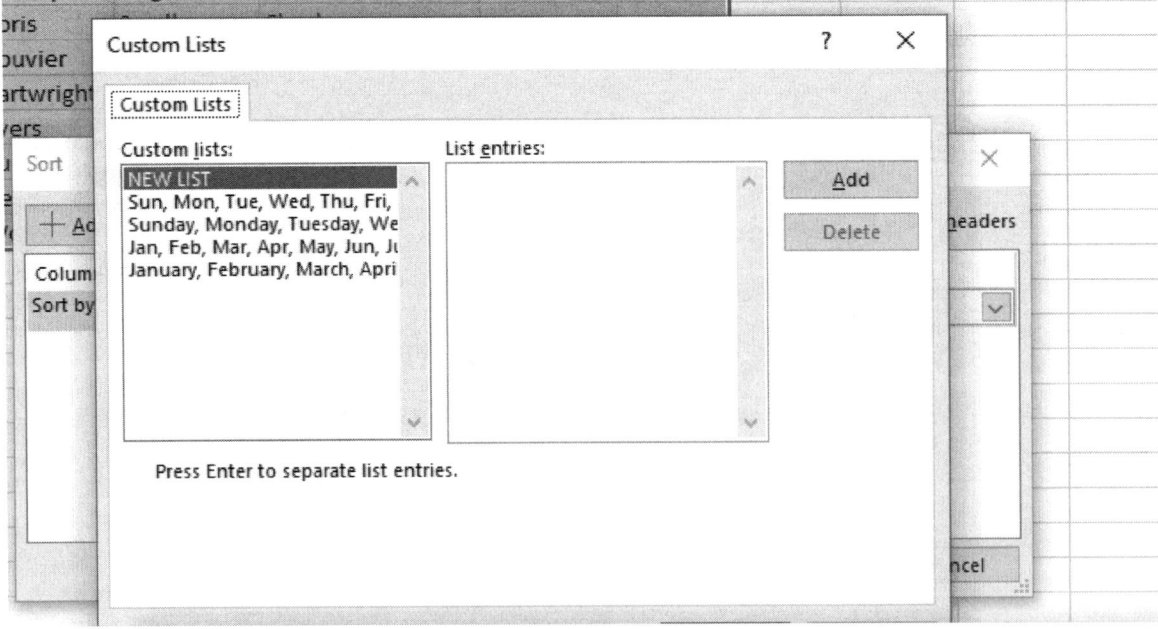

Image 49: Selecting the New List

5. If you're constructing a custom list, type the order you want the data to be sorted. An example is sorting by size from tiny to large.

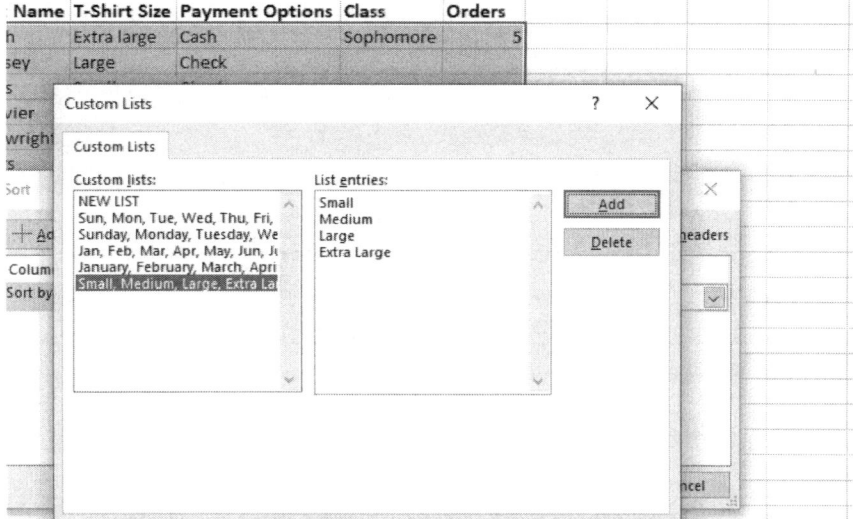

Image 50: Creating your Custom List

6. Your custom ordering list will show in original Order dropdown menu after clicking add.

7. After that, select your personalized list and click OK.

8. It will sort the data.

	A	B	C	D	E	F	G
1	Homeroom	First Name	Last Name	T-Shirt Size	Payment Options	Class	Orders
2	115	Luigi	Boris	Small	Check		
3	120	Fred	Cartwright	Small	Cash		
4	115	Sharon	Bouvier	Medium	Check bounced	Junior	8
5	115	Susan	Evers	Medium	Pending	Freshers	5
6	115	Ronnie	Furlan	Medium	Debit Card		
7	120	Dee	Reynolds	Medium	Money Order		
8	115	Mario	Bobsey	Large	Check		
9	115	Andy	Womder	Large	Cash	Senior	11
10	120	George	Bluth	Extra large	Cash	Sophomore	5

Image 51: Outcome of the Custom List

It's simple to control which column is sorted first in a multilayer sort if you need to change the order. Select the column and alter its priority by clicking the Move Up or Move Down arrow.

Sorting by Conditional formatting

A spreadsheet's most commonly used feature is conditional formatting, which allows users to apply formats to a cell or group. A set of criteria usually determines the formats. It makes it easier to spot differences in cell values at a glance. For instance, you have two entries that are either true or false. For simple identification of circumstances, you might use a custom color scheme.

Implementing Conditional Formatting to more than one cell is the same as adding one or more formulas to each cell. As a result, applying Conditional Formatting to many cells may degrade performance. When working with vast ranges, be cautious. Many datasets contain icons created using Excel's Conditional Formatting. You can sort the data in a specific order depending on these icons. Icon sets replace regular conditional formatting choices focusing on font and cell formatting modifications.

To sort data:

1. Select a range of cells.

2. Select Sort & Filter option, then Custom Sort from the Home tab.

3. Choose the column holding the conditional icons from the Column dropdown arrow.

4. Select Conditional Formatting Icon from the Sort using the dropdown arrow.

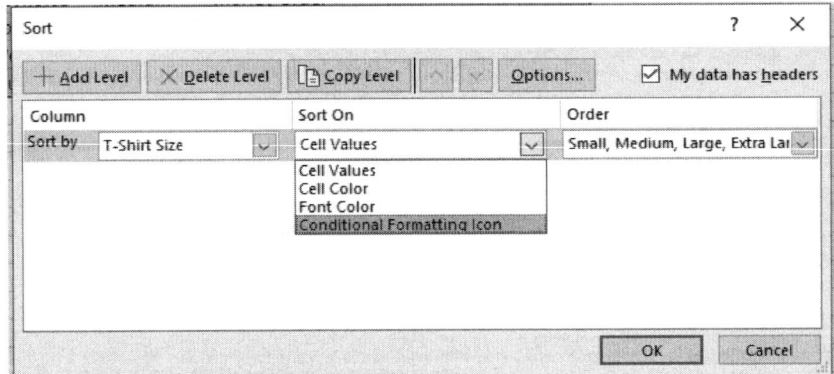

Image 52: Conditional Formatting Icon

5. Choose a color from the dropdown arrow under the order, for example, green.

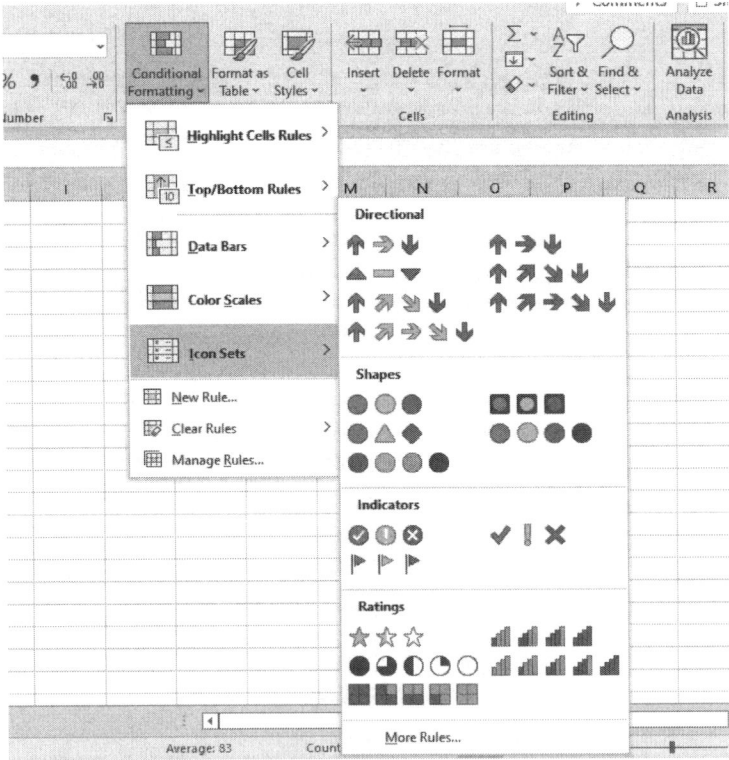

Image 53: Choice of color in Conditional Formatting

6. The color icon items you chose will be at the top of the list if you select on the top from the dropdown list next to the sort order box.

7. To add a second sort level, select Add.

8. Use the same parameters as the previous sort level, but select another color from the Order dropdown arrow. For example, choose yellow.

9. Select Create to add a third sort level, then apply the same parameters as the first two levels, but this time choose a different hue from the Order dropdown arrow, such as Red.

10. It will sort the data and close the dialogue box by selecting OK.

11. At the top of the data range, entries with the green icon are placed together, followed by entries with the yellow icon, and records with the red icon.

4.3 What is a filter?

Filtering data is a common task, but you might wonder how to create a filter in Microsoft Excel. There are several ways to create a filter in Microsoft Excel. Listed below is a sample filter formula. To use the filter, you must enter the desired criteria in the criteria range or a set of cells outside the list. The criteria range must contain the names of the fields in the list and the desired criteria in the rows below. The criteria range may span several rows, so you may want to enter your list of desired criteria in a single row.

The FILTER function takes three arguments: an array of data to filter, a cell reference, and a condition. You can filter by several criteria, including the size or number of rows or columns in the source range. Once you have determined the criteria, use the filter only to display relevant data in the result range. The filter results are dynamic and will automatically update when the data in the source range changes. When a filter is applied to a data range, it spills into more than one cell, so you may need to create a second worksheet to view the results.

A FILTER function is an array filter in Excel that filters a set of data. It belongs to the Dynamic Arrays group of functions. The result of this filter spills into a range of cells, starting from the cell in which the formula is entered. To filter data, you need to supply an array with the included criteria, or you can use text strings. Like a number, you must place text in quotation marks.

4.4 Filtering Data

The filter in Excel aids in the display of pertinent data by temporarily removing unnecessary elements from the screen. Then, the information is filtered according to specified criteria. The goal of sorting is to concentrate on the most important aspects of an information set. For example, an organization's city-level sales data can be filtered by location. Then, the user can see the sales of several cities at any one time. Working with a large database necessitates the use of a filter. The filter, a widely used tool, transforms a complex view into one that is simple to comprehend. The dataset must have a header row that provides the name of each column to apply filters. Working with filters is beneficial because they cater to our specific requirements. To filter data, check the boxes next to the entries you want to see and uncheck the boxes of the ones you don't.

What are the types of filter

In Excel, there are two types of filters: number filters and text filters. You can use a number filter to only display data that matches specific criteria, while a text filter lets you hide the data from any column. The difference between these two types is the way they work. A number filter lets you specify which column or row contains a specific character or word, while a text filter lets you select the range of values it includes. The first type of filter is the basic, or default, filter. The second type is the advanced filter, which lets you specify complex criteria for filtering data. The advanced filter is a more advanced type, allowing you to compare a filtered list to the complete one. You can even copy a list you create with a filter to another worksheet. These are both useful in many situations, and you can find the one that's right for your needs the easiest. The criteria range is a range of Excel cells containing the criteria you'd like to compare. It can be located outside the list itself. In this case, the criteria range must contain the names of the list field and the desired criteria in the cells below. Sometimes, the criteria range spans several rows. It is possible to have multiple criteria in the same row, called compound criteria. It is not necessary to use all three types of criteria. The advanced text filter allows you to exclude certain words or dates from the list. It helps search for specific records, such as the top 5,000 in column B. The advanced date filter allows you to select a particular period. This type of filter lets you specify whether you want the filter to be applied only to records that are higher than $2,200. If you are unsure of the best filter for your data, you can always use the advanced date filter.

How to smartly use Filters

To effectively filter data, you must know how to apply filters. You can apply multiple filters to multiple columns, but this section will focus on using just one. Then, you must sort the results using the options in the top-right corner of the pop-up window. Then, choose the condition, value, or color filter. Once you've selected the filter, select it and click OK. Once your filters are in place, select a data range. In modern versions of Excel, you can define parts of a worksheet as Tables. Although Tables don't look like ordinary cells, they can enable advanced features. You should note that if you sort a range of cells inside a table, the Filter and Sort options will be grayed out. You must first look for the Table option on the Ribbon to identify whether the cells are part of a table. The filter you apply to a column will only show data within the specified range. Therefore, if your workbook has rows and columns that span multiple sheets, it may not work. To avoid this, use the Go To Special feature. You can use the filter to select a range of cells or apply the filter to one cell range and ignore the rest. If unsure, use the arrows to indicate where to apply the filter. In addition to using filters to narrow the range of data, you can also utilize advanced Excel formulas to analyze filtered data. These include pivot tables and pie charts. This will help you analyze and visualize your data, and you can apply and remove filters quickly and easily. You will be amazed by the number of possibilities! The best part is that Excel has so many filters that you're bound to find one that suits your needs.

How to add a filter

To add a filter in Microsoft Excel, click the Advanced tab. You will then see the drop-down arrow in the column header. To clear the filter, click the range's name and OK. The filtered data will be displayed in the sheet. You can click the Clear Filter button if you don't want to see any filtered data in the sheet. To add a filter in Excel, follow the instructions below.

When creating a filter in Microsoft Excel, the first step is to create the desired range of data. If the filter is based on cell value, you can attach the criteria to the cell. For example, if you need to view employees' hours, you can select the employees who work full-time. Click OK to hide other information. Click the Filter icon to apply the filter. You can also use the Advanced Filter option to add a date range filter in Excel. The FILTER function is a formula entered in a spreadsheet cell. This differs from the filter commands on the toolbar or the pop-up menu. The FILTER function filters a range of data and only shows rows/columns that meet the condition. The source range can be a single column or a list of several columns. To use the filter in Excel, type the FILTER function in the appropriate cells, click on "Data" along the top toolbar, and then click on "Filter." Before adding a filter, you must add a header row on the table to indicate column labels. Once this is done, you must click "Filter" in the Sort & Filter group. Then, you can sort the data and choose the boxes you want to display. When you've selected the data, the arrow button will turn into a "Filter" button, and your filter will be applied to all the rows. The following are the three methods for adding filters to Excel:

- Under the Home tab, there is a filter option.

- Under the Data tab, there is a filter option.

- Using a shortcut key

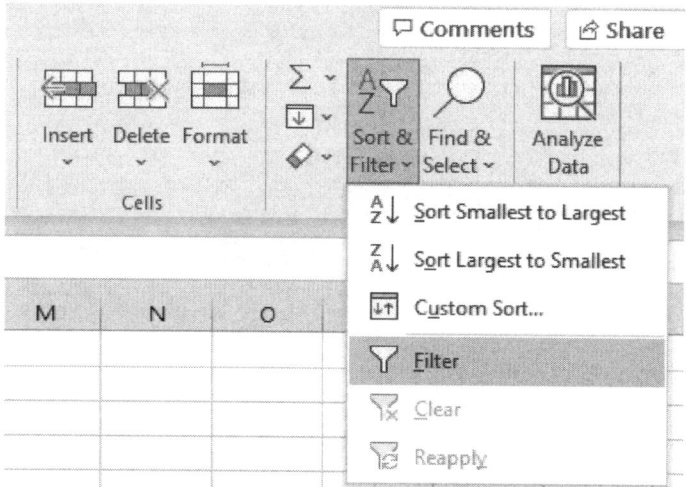

Image 54: The filter option

Method 1:

1. Under the "Sort and Filter" dropdown, select the data and click Filter in Home Tab.

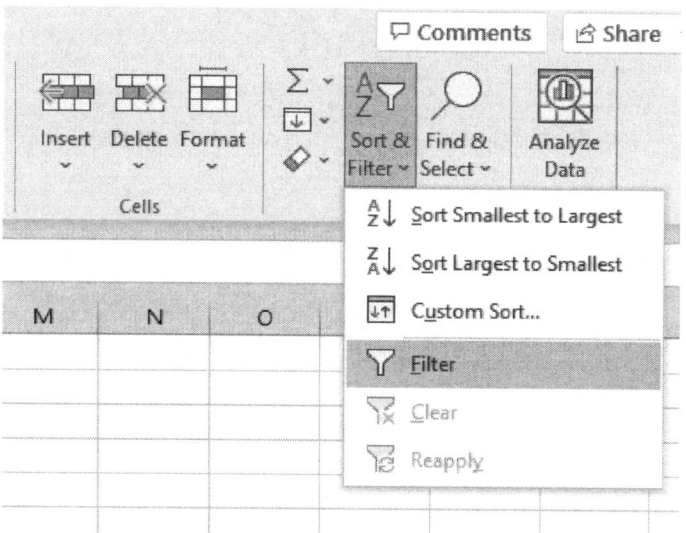

Image 55: Maneuvering to the Filter option in home tab

2. The filters are applied to the data range that has been chosen. Filters are the dropdown arrows within the red boxes.

Image 56: Filter dropdowns columns

3. To see the different names of the cities, click the dropdown arrow in the column "city."

Image 57: Filtering by city

4. Select "Delhi" and uncheck all other boxes to get only the invoice values for "Delhi."

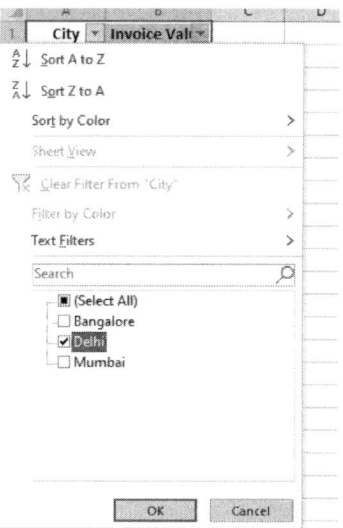

Image 58: Choosing the Delhi option

5. Filtered and showed statistics for the city of "Delhi.

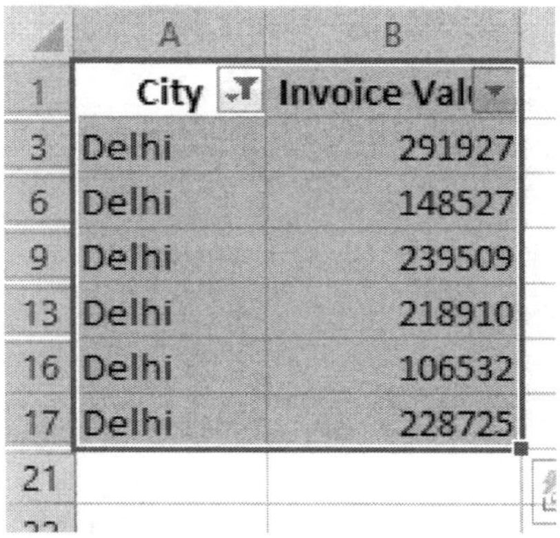

	City	Invoice Val
3	Delhi	291927
6	Delhi	148527
9	Delhi	239509
13	Delhi	218910
16	Delhi	106532
17	Delhi	228725
21		

Image 59: Results of filtering by city

Method 2:

Under the "sort and filter" area of the Data tab, select the "filter" option.

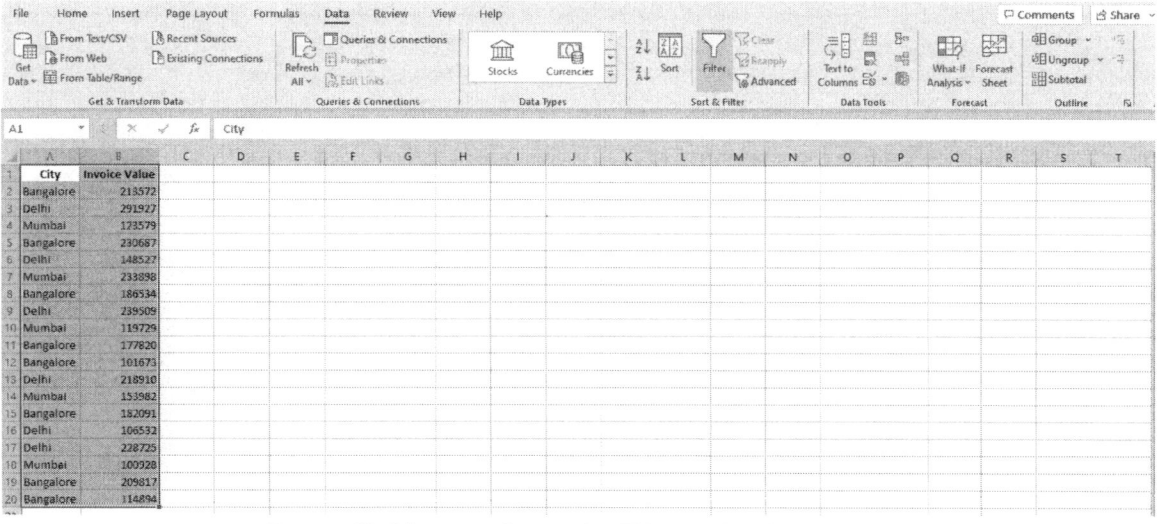

Image 60: Maneuvering to the Filter option in Data tab

Method 3:

Keyboard shortcuts are an excellent method to make everyday tasks go faster. Using one of the shortcuts below, select the data and apply the filter:

Press the keys "Shift+Ctrl+L" at the same time.

How to Add Filters

Advanced strategies are used to filter numbers. Let's look at some examples to grasp better how Excel filters function:

Number Filters Option

Examples:

- To find integers larger than 100000 in column B (invoice value).

- Use the filter to find numbers greater than 100000 but smaller than 200000 in column B.

Use a filter with a number larger than 100000.

Step 1: Click on the filter symbol in column B (invoice value) to open the filter.

Step 2: In the "number filters" section, select "greater than," as seen in the image below.

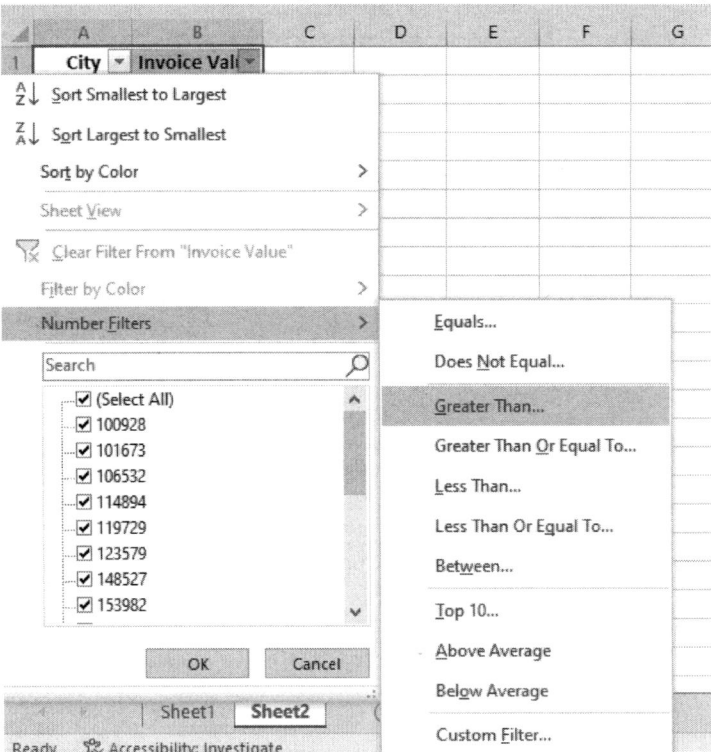

Image 61: Number filtering

Step 3: A box called "custom auto-filter" appears.

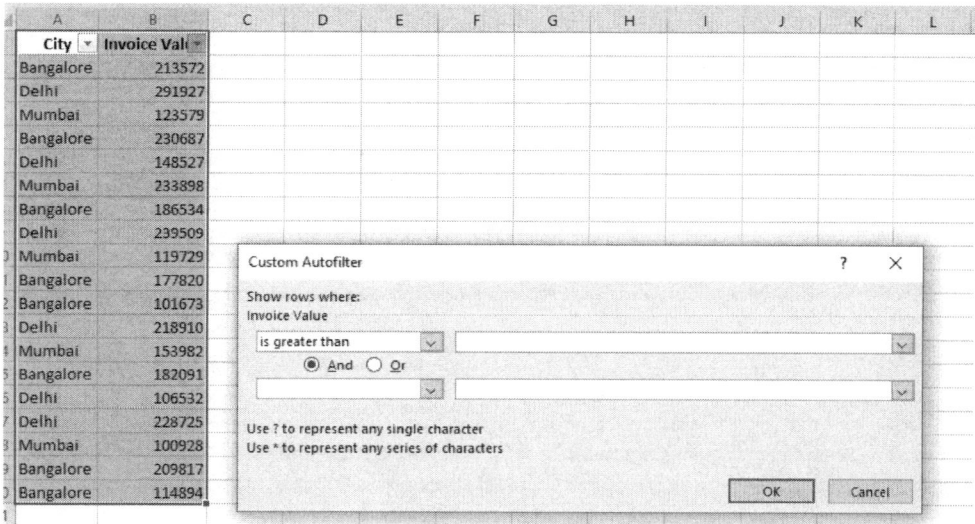

Image 62: Custom auto-filter

Step 4: In the box to the right of "is greater than," type 100000.

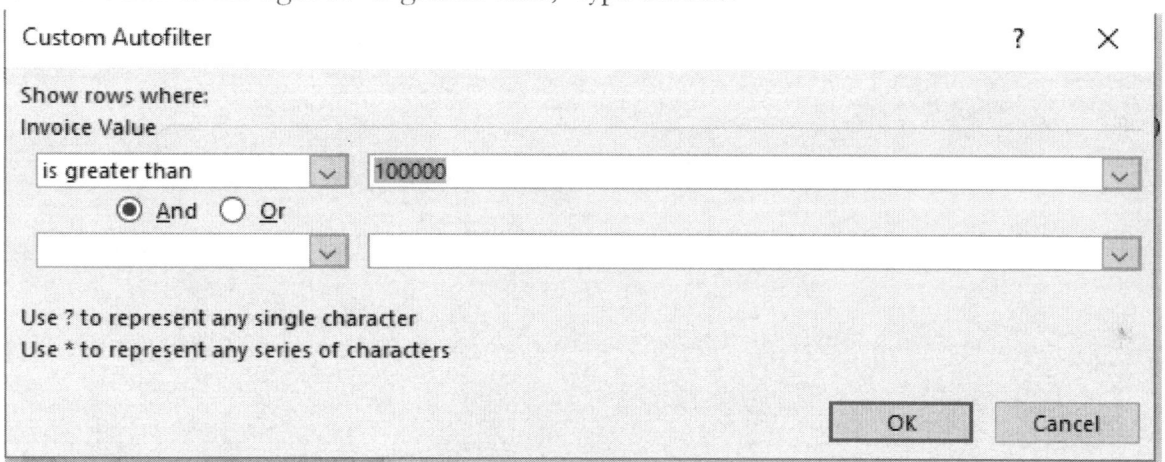

Image 63: Is greater than option

Step 5: The invoice values above 100,000 are displayed in the output. The filter icon is the symbol within the highlighted box.

City	Invoice Value
Bangalore	213572
Delhi	291927
Mumbai	123579
Bangalore	230687
Delhi	148527
Mumbai	233898
Bangalore	186534
Delhi	239509
Mumbai	119729
Bangalore	177820
Bangalore	101673
Delhi	218910
Mumbai	153982
Bangalore	182091
Delhi	106532
Delhi	228725
Mumbai	100928
Bangalore	209817
Bangalore	114894

Image 64: Results of is greater than option

And the filter has been applied to column B, as indicated.

Filter numbers larger than 100000 but fewer than 200000.

Step 1: Select "greater than" from the "number filters" menu.

Step 2: Select "is less than" in the second box on the left-hand side of the "custom auto filter" box.

Step 3: In the box to the right of "is greater than," type 100000. In the box to the right of "is less than," type the number 200000.

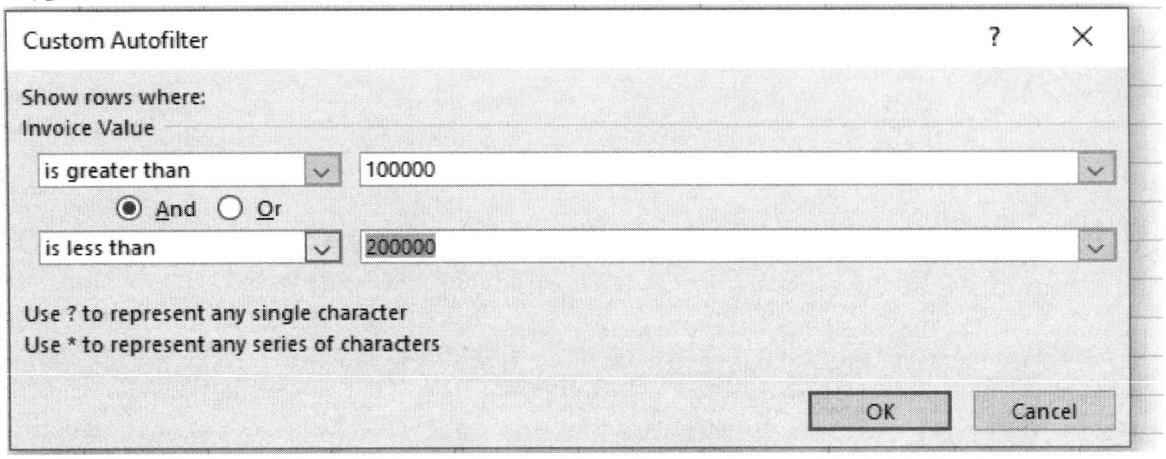

Image 65: Greater than and less than

Step 4: The invoice values larger than 100,000 but less than 200,000 are displayed in the output.

	A	B	C
1	City	Invoice Val	
4	Mumbai	123579	
6	Delhi	148527	
8	Bangalore	186534	
10	Mumbai	119729	
11	Bangalore	177820	
12	Bangalore	101673	
14	Mumbai	153982	
15	Bangalore	182091	
16	Delhi	106532	
18	Mumbai	100928	
20	Bangalore	114894	
21			

Image 66: Results of greater than and less than

"Search Box" Option:

Example:

For example, the first column (city) with product IDs is replaced while working on the data under the preceding item to filter the product ID "prd 1" 's details.

The following are the steps:

Step 1: Filter the "product ID" columns and "invoice value" with filters.

Image 67: Applying filters with search box

Step 2: Type the value to be filtered into the search box. So, type "prd 1" into the box.

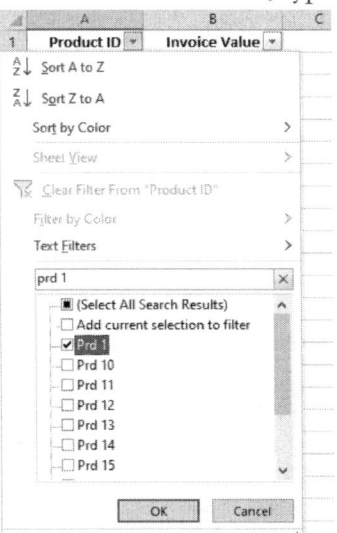

Image 68: Typing in the filter search box

Step 3: As seen in the accompanying image, the output only shows the filtered value from the list. As a result, the billing value of the product ID "prd 1" may be shown.

Image 69: Search box results

Text Filters

Text filters are used when you wish to filter a column by a specific word or number; when filter cells start or end with a particular character or text; when filter cells are based on whether or not they contain a specific character or word in the text.

Text filters are used when cells are identical to or not equivalent to a detailed character.

Example:

Let's say you wish to apply the filter on a single item.

1. Select equals from the text filter by clicking on it.

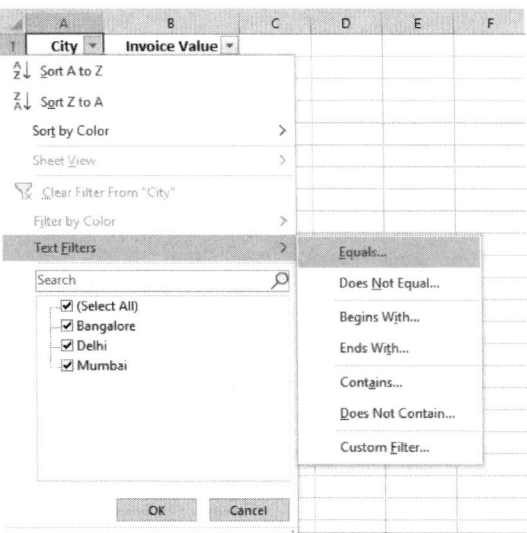

Image 70: Equals text filter

2. It gives you a single dialogue box with a Custom Auto-Filter dialogue box.

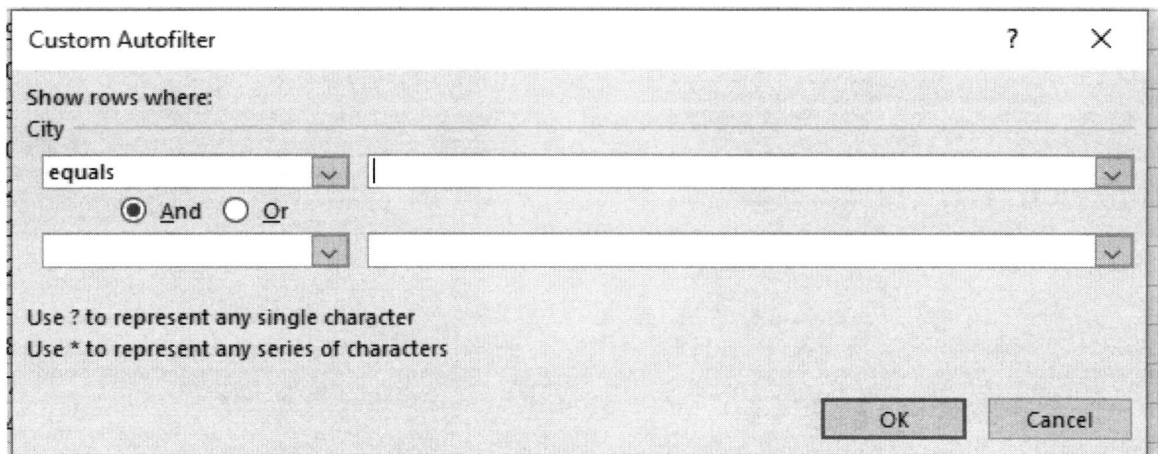

Image 71: Custom Auto-Filter dialogue box for text filter

3. Select Bangalore from the dropdown menu and click OK.

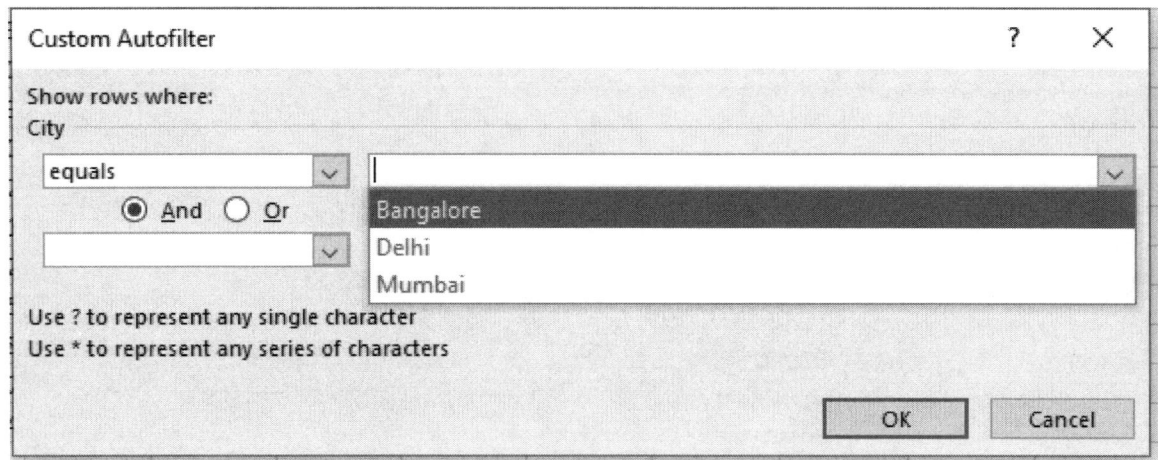

Image 72: Selecting options in Custom Auto-Filter dialogue box

4. Now you'll only see data from the Bangalore category, as seen below.

	A	B
	City	Invoice Value
2	Bangalore	213572
5	Bangalore	230687
8	Bangalore	186534
11	Bangalore	177820
12	Bangalore	101673
15	Bangalore	182091
19	Bangalore	209817
20	Bangalore	114894

Image 73: Data displayed from text filter

Colors can filter data if your data has rows with different colors or cells filled with different colors. Use the "Filter by Color" option.

Grouping and ungrouping lines and columns

You must create a group to create a hierarchy between lines and columns. You can do this by using the Outline class. Then, click on the group, and you'll see an outline around the grouped lines and columns. This outline can have up to eight levels. Once you have created a group, you can use the same method to hide and show individual rows and columns.

To create a group, click the first sheet tab, and all sheets between that tab and the last will be included in that group. You can also ungroup sheets by clicking on one outside the group or right-clicking the grouped tabs and choosing Ungroup Sheets from the pop-up menu. You can also create a group by adding page breaks and formulas. In Excel, the Advanced tab contains more options to create a group, such as page breaks, gridlines, row and column headers, and zeros values.

One way to create a group is by joining rows and columns together. Grouping a sheet is helpful if you want to compare similar content or collapse data areas. For example, group the data by month if you compare monthly sales figures. Or, you can select only the last row and group it by month. To get a clearer picture, you can use a filter.

Another option for grouping and ungrouping lines and columns in MS Excel is to use the Outlines section. Click the "Group" button or the "Subtitle" row to highlight the entries to group rows and columns. You can also click the "Ungroup" button on the data toolbar to remove the grouping. This process is a great way to organize large data sets.

What is conditional formatting in Microsoft Excel?

This formatting function allows you to change how a cell looks based on its values. For example, it can separate dates, hide certain cell contents when printed, and highlight weather descriptions and temperatures. This feature can help you create visually appealing worksheets. You can download example data and practice using it.

The conditional formatting feature in Excel lets you highlight specific text. It is possible to use conditional formatting in highlighting text based on a value greater than ten, a range of values, or a top-bottom rule. You can type in the value field or use cell references if you need to highlight a specific cell. You can apply this style to any cell in an Excel document. To apply it to multiple cells, choose one rule per cell and select another.

One thing to remember when using conditional formatting is that multiple rules can conflict. If multiple rules evaluate true for the same value, the newer rule will always take precedence over the old one. However, you can change the order of the rules by selecting the Manage Rules dialogue box. Also, if you want to apply more than one rule, you can use the 'This Sheet' option to pull up all lists applied to the current sheet.

Conditional formatting helps you identify and highlight important data. Whether you're highlighting budget constraints, tasks, or budget constraints, conditional formatting can help you make the most of your data and boost productivity. Learn how to apply conditional formatting to your spreadsheets and make your work easier and more effective! This guide will walk you through some of the most commonly used conditional formatting options.

Once you've created a conditional rule, click the "Edit" button next to it. The Conditional Formatting Rules Manager window will open. Click Edit Rule in the Formatting Rules Manager to edit or delete the rule. If a condition is false, click the "Stop if true" check box to cancel the conditional formatting. Alternatively, you can click the 'Stop if false' checkbox and OK.

Creating drop-down menus

There are several ways to create drop-down menus in Microsoft Excel. One way is to manually enter the list into the Source box of a cell. To make this work, you must ensure that the cell's column headings are comma-separated and select the option "My table has headers." In addition, to create a drop-down list, you must create a named range.

Once you have selected the cells to include in the drop-down list, go to Data tab. Select Data Validation option from Data tab. This will validate your data and make it more reliable. Once you're done with the Data tab, you can move on to the next step of creating drop-down menus in Excel. Input Message: Type the message you want to display to the user who will be selecting a cell in your drop-down list. The message will appear in a yellow pop-up sticky when the cell is selected. You can also display an error message if the data entered is invalid. However, invalid data will not be displayed. To prevent this from happening, check the Show Error Alert option.

Dynamic Dropdown Menu: You can create dynamic drop-down lists in Microsoft Excel with the use of named ranges. In creating a dynamic list, you must make a cell with a named range containing the items in your drop-down list. Make sure the name of the range contains an equals sign. This will enable a dynamic drop-down menu to update automatically as an item is added or removed.

Removing duplicates

If you have many duplicates, you can remove them from your spreadsheet using the Remove Duplicates feature. This feature will check multiple columns for duplicates. The dialogue box will also tell you how many values are duplicates and how many remain. After removing duplicates, you should recheck your data to ensure that it's accurate. The next time you're working with your spreadsheet, you can use this feature to remove duplicates.

The first step in removing duplicates in Excel is to select the data set you'd like to deduplicate. You'll see a list of duplicate values highlighted in a yellow box. Click "Delete" to remove the duplicate values. The second step involves checking the unique value column to see if it contains a duplicate. If the cell's value is not a duplicate, Excel will highlight it and give you a summary of the values that are removed. Once you have selected the data, you'll have a list of all the columns you'd like to remove. Then, choose the Remove Duplicates tool. This tool will keep the first instance of a column and delete the rest. After removing all duplicates, you can filter, sort, and summarize your data. Selecting the columns to use in the duplicate removal process is a simple process that will save you a lot of time and trouble.

The next step in removing duplicates in Microsoft Excel is to find the column containing the duplicates. To find the duplicates, look for a small square with a downward-pointing triangle. Select the filter icon next to every title to show the list of rows and columns. Then uncheck the checkbox corresponding to the number one. Then, select the rows and columns where the duplicates occur. To remove duplicates from your table, open Power Query editor. Click the left direction arrow button to select the entire dataset. This pop-up menu will hide duplicate data columns. Press CTRL+C to copy the data. Then press CTRL+V to paste it. Then, select the Data tab in the top menu and click Remove Duplicates icon. Once you've selected the column, click OK to close Power Query editor. Once you've finished, you'll be left with a new table free of duplicates.

5 Power of Automatism

What is a formula?

You may be wondering: What is a formula in Microsoft Excel? A formula is an expression that works on the values in a range of cells. If the formula contains an error, it will still return a result, which makes it extremely handy for quick calculations. For example, formulas can be used to calculate addition, subtraction, multiplication, division, and percentages and manipulate date and time values. The most basic type of formula in Excel is a mathematical equation. You can use the standard operators, such as the + and - signs and asterisks (*). You can also use parentheses to surround the part of the equation that you want to calculate first. For example, to change the operation from addition to multiplication, you can replace the (+) sign with parentheses (*).

Another type of formula is a function. We define a function as a predefined formula that performs an action based on specific values. For example, all spreadsheet programs include functions that you can use to find ranges of cells quickly. To use these functions effectively, you need to understand their different parts. Cell references and arguments are essential, as they will guide you through using them correctly. And remember: a formula can only perform certain operations.

How to insert formula

When you're new to Excel, you might wonder how to insert a formula in a cell. You can learn how to do so with the help of the Insert Function wizard, which is located on the formula bar. First, click on the button on the left side of the formula bar and type the function's name in the cell. Then, click on a function in the dialog box, and you'll be presented with a list of related functions. From here, click on the function that you want to insert.

You can also copy the formula by dragging it to another cell. You can copy a formula in Excel using the cell's bottom-right corner. Excel will automatically copy it and adjust the cell references to match the other cells. This is the easiest way to insert a formula in Microsoft Excel. When you copy a formula, Excel will automatically adjust the references, so you'll have no problems with formatting.

To insert a formula in a cell, you need to select it. If you have a range of cells, you can select a cell and insert the formula into that range. The SUM function will calculate the sum of the cells in the range A1-A2 if you select them. If you have more than one cell in the range, you can switch the reference type by pressing F4 or Ctrl+V.

Importance of the language of the formula

The importance of the language of formulas in Microsoft Excel is widely recognized. However, people who are not proficient in computer programming have difficulty creating complex formulas in Excel. One option to deal with this issue is copy-pasting formulas from other programs into cells. But copy-pasting formulas will lead to large formulas, and errors are often undetected. In contrast, the language of formulas in Excel can benefit from the dataflow programming model and the Excel application's IDE capabilities.

The order of calculation is another important factor when it comes to creating an Excel formula. The formula must start with an equal sign (=). On creating a formula using a web browser, the characters following the equal sign are interpreted as a formula. In Excel for the web, the operands, or values to be calculated, are separated by calculation operators. In Excel for the web, it is essential to note that formulas are calculated from left to right.

A formula may be a single cell or a whole column or row. It can refer to multiple values. Typically, a comma or a semicolon is used to separate arguments in a formula. In some countries, the comma acts as a Decimal Symbol. In European countries, semicolon acts as a List Separator.

Importance of the language of the settings

Changing the language of the settings in Microsoft Excel is not as complicated as in earlier versions. Excel used to support only one language for the main interface and multiple languages for proofreading functions. Today, however, it has become much more complex. Fortunately, there are still several options for changing the language of Excel. Most languages are supported automatically, while others may require downloading a language pack. Once you've selected your language, Excel will change its language settings accordingly.

To change the language, go to the Options menu. Click on the Language option. Select the language from the drop-down menu under Choose Editing Language. Left-click on the language, and then click "Set as default." You can also add additional languages to your Excel workspace. This way, you can view your spreadsheets in a language that suits you best. You may want to change your default language to another one, but you should set the correct one for all work with the program.

To change the language of the settings in Microsoft Excel, you need to edit your personal Microsoft account settings. After changing the language in Excel, change the settings in other Office Online products. It is important to note that you can change the language of the settings in Office 365 products, such as Dropbox and SharePoint. Make sure you change the language of all these settings to have the best product experience.

Most common function to use inside the formulas

One of the most common functions in Excel is SUM function. This function adds the values or ranges of cells, returning the sum of the values. To use the sum function, type the =SUM() or =SUM(a1:a10) or +SUM(B3-B13) into the cell and drag the mouse down the column. The AVERAGE function is also very useful for finding the average value.

To sort data, drag the mouse down a column. The MIN function returns the minimum value in a column, and MAX finds the maximum value. Both these functions are helpful when you need to find a high or low value in a data set.

Another useful function to use inside a formula is the lookup function. This function returns a value based on data in a specific cell. The lookup value must be in the table's leftmost column. Usually, it will be in cell B2.

You must specify the cell reference when using the TODAY or NOW function. For example, the NOW or HOME function must be entered in the home cell (A1) or cell A1. In addition, the cell reference must be set to date format if you are using the TODAY function inside a formula. Otherwise, the function will not update when you recalculate the spreadsheet. For example, type =TODAY() into cell A1 to change the format of the TODAY function.

If you want to combine two data records, the most common function to use inside the formulas in Excel is the =CONCATENATE function. It joins two cells or fields with different data types. For example, you can join two records with the same zip code if one is for a city and the other is for a state. The CONCAT function is also useful for combining multiple values.

The order of operations in a formula is also essential. Multiplication is always performed before addition, but you can change this order by using the parentheses symbol. The dollar sign tells Excel to change the cell reference when the formula is moved. The formula itself can be as simple or complex as you want. It's a quick and easy way to calculate numbers. It will not cost you a cent to use Excel's built-in functions.

The TRIM function in Excel is a useful tool for removing extra spaces or padded text. If you need to add numbers to a row, you can use the =TRIM(text) function to get the result without spaces. This function can also remove extra spaces in the middle of words. This is useful when emailing or file-sharing data. Rogue spaces in the formula can mess up the results when a formula is added to multiple rows of numbers.

Remove the formula but keep the result

There are a few ways to remove the formula from an Excel document. The first way is to right-click the cell you want to remove the formula from, then press "Enter." To add a part of the formula to a new cell, press "Return." Then, select the part of the formula you want to add. Note that you can also leave the formula in a partially-formatted state. You can change the calculation settings in your workbook to the manual, such as removing the check mark from the "Recalculate before saving" check box. Changing the behavior of formulas can be useful when you need to hide a formula from someone else.

Another way to remove a formula but keep the result in Microsoft Excel is to select the cells you want to change. Sometimes, you can't see the cell when you're trying to remove the formula, so it's better to highlight the cells containing the formula. You can also click the cells containing the formula and highlight them. A2 is the first cell with data and is the easiest to work with.

Another way to remove the formula in Microsoft Excel is to copy the cells where the formula is and paste it as a value. To do this, you must select the cells containing the formula and paste the values you want to change. Once you've copied the cells, you can use the To Actual utility to remove the formula from those cells. It's a great way to save time and reduce the file size.

Autofill

The Autofill feature in Microsoft Excel allows you to fill cells with data based on the patterns in adjacent cells. You can even use this feature to fill more than one row and column at a time. You simply enter the first day of the week and drag the fill handle to the cell you want to fill. You can also use the Smart Tag to fill formatting only.

The Autofill feature is particularly useful when working with dates and extending a series of numbers, days or months. Excel recognizes dates and times and adds the first two amounts to the range. You can even go back in time by changing the date or year of a date. You can also select an exact number by specifying the initial value in two neighboring cells. This way, you can use Autofill to automatically fill in complex patterns, such as dates, numbers, and more.

Autofill in Microsoft Excel allows you to fill in a range of cells based on a pattern. Select a cell from the list and drag it into another range. This feature also allows you to use the same pattern in multiple cells. For example, if you wanted to fill a cell with a number, you could hold down Ctrl and drag the fill handle to the selected cell. This action will copy the value into the range. Afterward, you can click on the Fill Handle to select additional cells.

Access AutoFill by using Fill handle (the small square to the cell's bottom-right corner that gives the opportunity of filling adjacent cells).

Using AutoFill to Enter a Series of Values

AutoFill command will recognize a given pattern and complete more values. Let's use this to complete days of the week.

- Select cell containing first value for the series (**Monday**)

- Hover your mouse towards the cell's bottom right corner until it forms a black plus symbol.

- Click without releasing and drag either across or down the cell you intend to fill

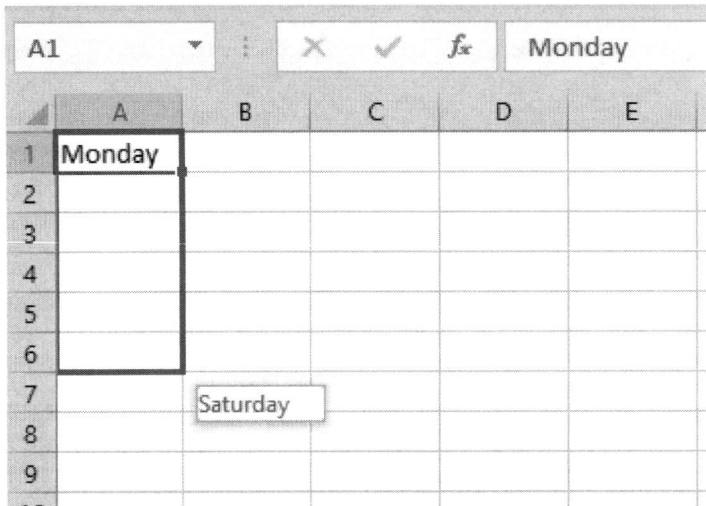

Image 74: Selecting cells to autofill

- The AutoFill will complete days

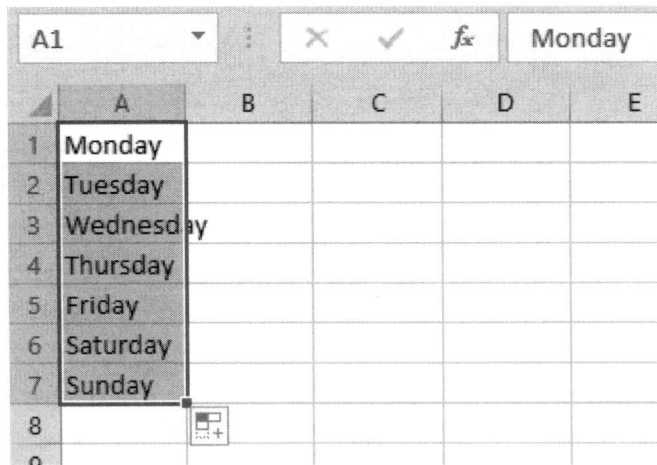

Image 75: Autofilling days

Applying AutoFill in Copying Data

AutoFill Command allows one to copy and paste their data to other cells of the same worksheet. Here are the steps.

- Select cell with the data to copy

- Hover mouse to form the black plus sign

- Click and drag across or down

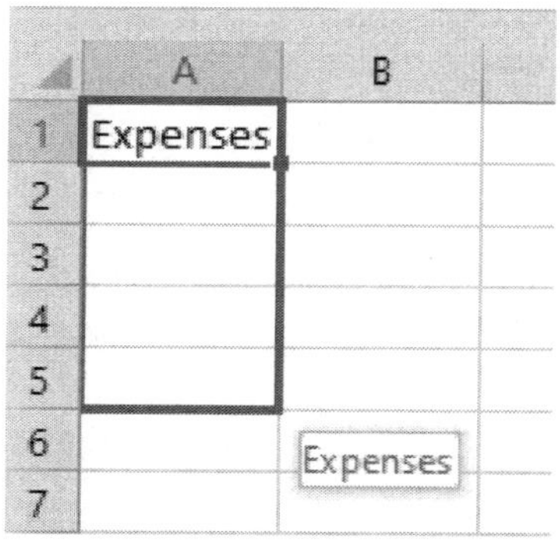

Image 76: Copying through autofill

- AutoFill will copy the data into intended cells.

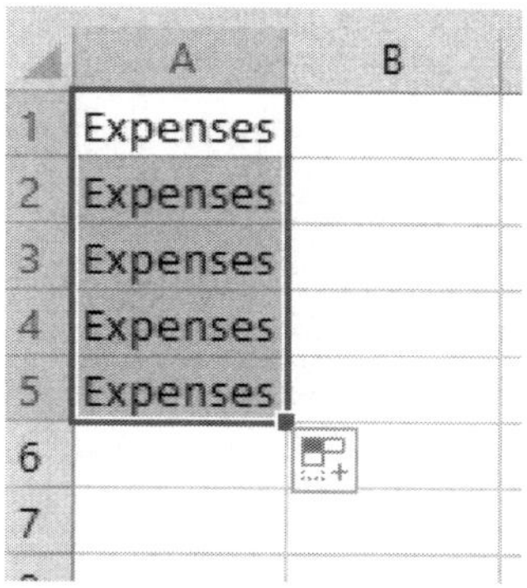

Image 77: Copied data through autofill

What are VBA and MACROs

What are VBA and MACROs? Both are programming languages for Microsoft Excel. Macros allows one automate almost any task within the program, from creating customized charts to performing data-processing functions. Often, these languages are used by programmers to create advanced tools that do not come with the Excel program itself. In addition, VBA is also used to work in non-Microsoft environments, such as in commercial or proprietary applications.

VBA (Visual Basic for Applications) is a programming language that automates tasks in Excel and other Microsoft Office applications. Macros are collections of instructions or code that Excel reads to perform tasks. In addition to automating simple tasks, these programs can create shortcuts for specific functions. Learning the basics of VBA and MACROs in Excel will streamline your work processes.

MACROs allow you to automate repetitive tasks within Microsoft Excel, such as adding values to a list or entering data in a database. You can create custom functions using VBA, but remember to use a unique name for each. Macros are not permitted to share the same name as other macros or Excel functions and properties, so giving them unique names is essential. You can also use a macro to record a specific task that you perform regularly.

To start coding a macro, open the VBA editor by pressing Alt + F11 in Excel. This will show you the code for all open workbooks. You can also view the code by double-clicking an object. Remember, recorded macros always appear in modules. So, before you begin coding, you should define all variables used in the macro. In addition, make sure to save your workbook as a Macro Enabled Workbook.

Where to download excel templates for different needs

A resource library is a great place to start downloading templates. These templates come in various categories, such as business, financial management, planners, and trackers. By selecting a category, you'll be able to see all of the templates that fall under that category. You can then download a template based on its purpose. For example, you might want to create a calendar or a sales report. The resource library will have dozens of calendar templates to choose from.

SpreadsheetZONE is another resource where you can download Excel templates. You can either browse the collection by category or search for specific templates. The templates are alphabetically organized and updated often. Some templates that can be downloaded from the site are Invoice & Inventory Management Tool, Temperature Conversion, Professional Invoice, Global Industry vs. Agriculture Dashboard, and more. This resource is excellent for anyone who needs a spreadsheet for a specific need. It is important to note that SpreadsheetZONE has ads, so you may not immediately see every template you need. Once you get the template you're looking for, you'll need to enter it into the Default personal templates location field in Microsoft Excel. This will allow you to choose the template appearing automatically each time the program opens. Then, you can use it to create a personalized calendar. Another useful resource is Wincalendar, which offers a calendar for different occasions. There's something for everyone: a graph paper template, a fitness chart for a man, and even a weekly meal planner. Other resources include the default Excel Templates Gallery you access when you open the Excel application to create a new workbook, Microsoft Office Resource Library, Spreadsheet123, Vertex42, and Template.net.

What are TRUE and FALSE

What are TRUE and FALSE in MS Excel? TRUE and FALSE are two logical functions that indicate whether or not something is true. In other words, if a cell contains 'True' and 'False,' the cell is TRUE. These functions are needed to make the spreadsheet compatible with other software. While they don't expand the abilities of logical tests, they can be extremely useful for calculating several conditions simultaneously.

This formula compares text values character-by-character in alphabetic order. For example, if cell A1 contains 'ag,' it will return TRUE. On the other hand, if cell A1 contains 'p,' it will return FALSE. In other words, if cell A1 is 'agave,' it will be true, and if cell B1 contains 'p,' it will be FALSE.

To create a logical equation or formula, you must understand how the two functions work. TRUE indicates the logical value, and FALSE indicates the logical opposite of it. So, for example, if you want to create a chart in Excel that contains all the phone numbers of different organizations, you'll need to understand how the two functions work. In addition, you need to understand how these logical operators work in Microsoft Excel to use the formulas effectively.

The formulas in Excel are flexible enough to handle Boolean values. By default, TRUE and FALSE values are numbers, but you can use them in formulas without double quotation marks. If you're wondering how to use these values in Excel, check out the sample file below. You'll learn the basics of using the COUNTIF and COUNTIF functions in Microsoft Excel.

5.1 Cell Referencing

We define a cell reference as an alphanumeric data or value in excel to identify or locate a cell in the worksheet. The cell reference comprises one or more letters for columns and a number for the row, e.g., **A1.** You can locate the data you wish to calculate using the cell reference. The cell reference is also known as the cell address.

Cell Reference Types

Knowing the types of cell references is pertinent to understanding better how to use the cell references together with formulas. So now, let's quickly examine the types of cell references.

Relative References

By default, the cell references in the Excel worksheet are relative. When the cells are copied across multiple cells, the cells change based on the relative position of rows and columns. For instance, when you added **=B3+C3** in cell **D3** and copied it to cell **D4**, the formula will change to **=B4+C4.** The relative references are best used when replicating the same action across multiple rows and columns. To create and copy formula using the relative references, use the following procedures

- Click cell **(D2)** to enter the formula and type in the formula **=(B2*C2)** in the cell to get the anticipated result

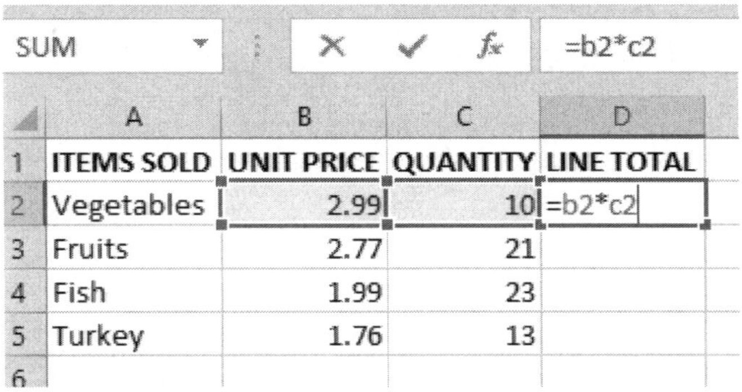

SUM		× ✓ f_x	=b2*c2	
	A	B	C	D
1	ITEMS SOLD	UNIT PRICE	QUANTITY	LINE TOTAL
2	Vegetables	2.99	10	=b2*c2
3	Fruits	2.77	21	
4	Fish	1.99	23	
5	Turkey	1.76	13	
6				

Image 78: Implementing a formula for relative referencing

- Press the **Enter** key, and formula is executed and will show results

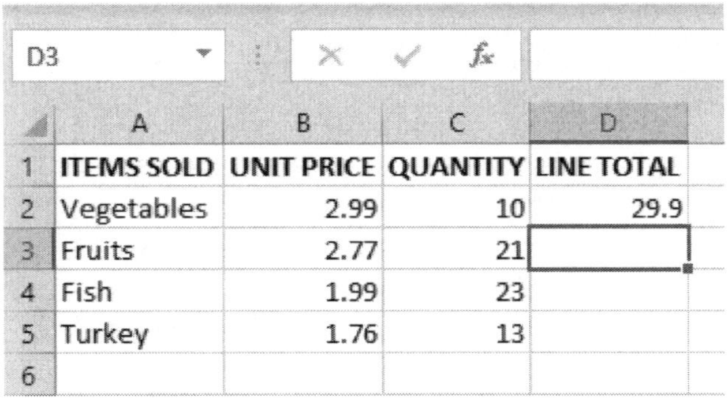

D3		× ✓ f_x		
	A	B	C	D
1	ITEMS SOLD	UNIT PRICE	QUANTITY	LINE TOTAL
2	Vegetables	2.99	10	29.9
3	Fruits	2.77	21	
4	Fish	1.99	23	
5	Turkey	1.76	13	
6				

Image 79: Executed formula for referencing

- Identify the **Fill handle** at lower part of **D2**, click and drag down to **D5**.

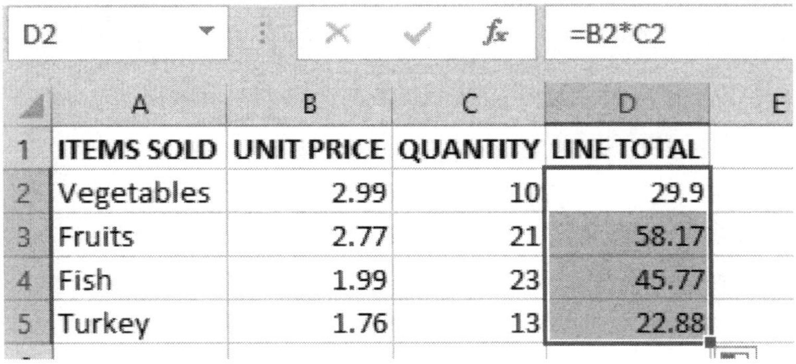

D2		× ✓ f_x	=B2*C2		
	A	B	C	D	E
1	ITEMS SOLD	UNIT PRICE	QUANTITY	LINE TOTAL	
2	Vegetables	2.99	10	29.9	
3	Fruits	2.77	21	58.17	
4	Fish	1.99	23	45.77	
5	Turkey	1.76	13	22.88	

Image 80: Using fill handle to copy formula

- The formula is copied down and the results will show in each cell.

Absolute Cell Reference and Multiple cell Reference

An absolute cell reference stays locked on a specific cell or cell range, even if the formula is changed, making use of the dollar sign ($).

Multiple cells use the dollar sign to keep the row or column constant.

A3	Both column and row won't change on copying data
A$2	**The row remains constant when copied**
$A2	**The column remains constant**

Table 2: Using dollar sign to reference cells

In the example below, we will be using cell D1, which contains the tax rate of 8%, to calculate the sales of each item in column E. However, we must make the D1 constant when we copy the formula to fill other cells. If the D1 is not constant, the following result will be obtained.

SUM	▼	⋮	✕ ✓ f_x	=(b3*c3)*d1		
◢	A	B	C	D	E	F
1			Tax Rate	8%		
2	ITEMS SOLD	UNIT PRICE	QUANTITY	LINE TOTAL	SALES TAX	
3	Vegetables	2.99	10	29.9	=(b3*c3)*d1	
4	Fruits	2.77	21	58.17		
5	Fish	1.99	23	45.77		
6	Turkey	1.76	13	22.88		
7	Chicken	2.49	22	54.78		
8	Beverages	2.76	26	71.76		
9						

Image 81: Tax implementation formula

E3	▼	⋮	✕ ✓ f_x	=(B3*C3)*D1		
◢	A	B	C	D	E	F
1			Tax Rate	8%		
2	ITEMS SOLD	UNIT PRICE	QUANTITY	LINE TOTAL	SALES TAX	
3	Vegetables	2.99	10	29.9	2.392	
4	Fruits	2.77	21	58.17	#VALUE!	
5	Fish	1.99	23	45.77	1368.523	
6	Turkey	1.76	13	22.88	1330.93	
7	Chicken	2.49	22	54.78	2507.281	
8	Beverages	2.76	26	71.76	1641.869	
9						
10						

Image 82: Copied formula for tax implementation

To avoid getting the result shown in the table above, follow these steps using the dollar sign

- Click on the cell **(E3)** where the formula will contain and type in the formula **=(B3*C3)*D1** in the cell to get the anticipated result.

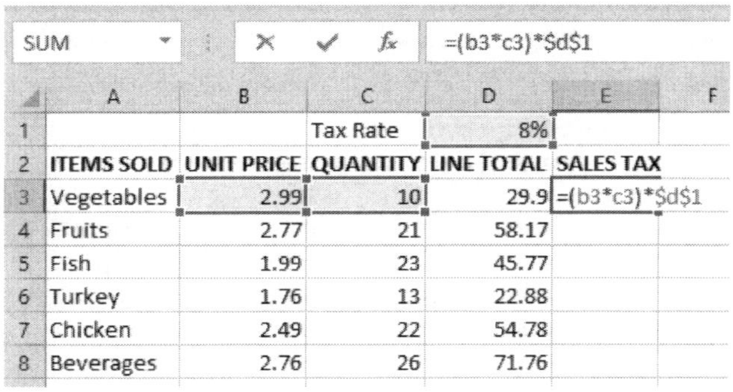

Image 83: Using the dollar sign to avoid errors

- Press the Enter key to execute the formula, showing the outcome in the cell.

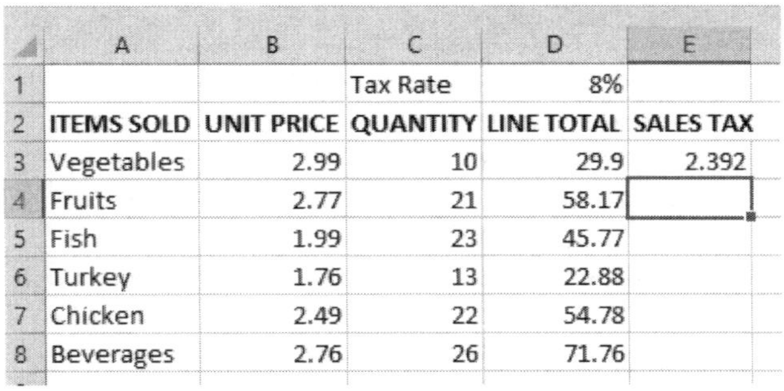

Image 84: Outcome of the formula with the dollar sign

- Use **Fill handle** on cell **E4** and drag upto cell **E8.**

- Release your mouse and you will see the result in each cell

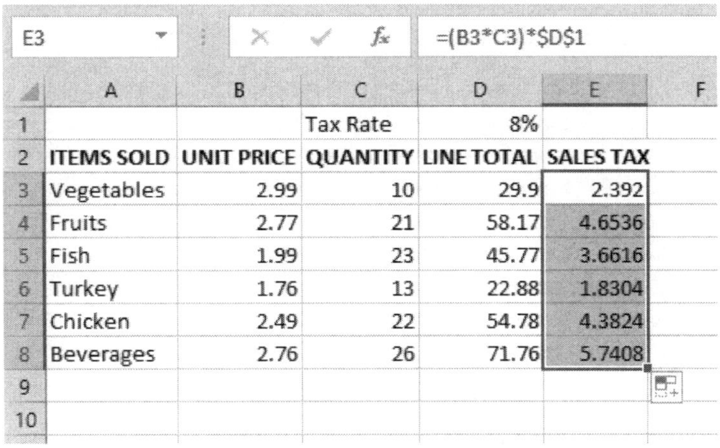

Image 85: Autofill results without errors of the formula

6 Graphs and Charts

6.1 What is a graph?

Using graphs in Excel is simple, quick, and useful for many calculation purposes. The chart feature of Microsoft Excel offers several different graph types. While a chart represents values, a graph represents the relative percentage of data in a set of values. Line graphs are popular with Microsoft Excel users. This type shows changes over time and can be used to compare trends. For example, you can plot an employee's compensation or the number of hours they worked in a week against their annual leave. A graph in Excel is a representation of data in a worksheet. A graph represents a network consisting of a finite set of vertices and edges. Graphs have many real-life applications and represent various networks, including telephone networks, circuit networks, and city paths. Graphs are also used in social networks such as Facebook, representing each person as a vertex, with a corresponding node containing their name, gender, and location. It allows users to analyze data more efficiently. Graphs in Excel are easy to create and can represent a variety of metrics. The first step is to know your data. Then, you can sort the data before making a graph and add a border to separate the data points. In a presentation, a graph can be a huge impact. You can choose from many different graph types to make your presentation look good. Make sure to understand all the different graph types and find the one that fits your needs.

What are the types of graphs?

A line graph is one of the simplest and easiest to read. It is also helpful in displaying changes over time. Line graphs also have the benefit of displaying multiple results with different lines. For example, if you compare three different types of smartphones, you could use a line graph with different colors for each. As you can see, there are many graphs in MS Excel. However, choosing the right one for your project depends on your data and the argument you're trying to make. So the first step is deciding what you want to display, then arranging and formatting the data.

Line Graphs

The line graph is the most common, straightforward, and fundamental type of chart graph. This is the most effective way of displaying many closely related data series. In addition, because line graphs are incredibly lightweight (they are made up of mere lines, as opposed to more sophisticated chart types, as seen below), they are great for achieving a minimalistic style.

Tips:

- Eliminate all gridlines

- Eliminate all shading and borders

- Each series should be highlighted with a different color.

Column Graphs

Observers may also use column graphs to see if parameters shift over time. If only one data parameter is included, they are called "graphs." When several parameters are active, users cannot gain much input into how every parameter has improved. When the avg. No. Of hours worked /week and the avg. No annual leaves are plotted side by side. As seen in the Column graph below, the avg number of hours worked/ week, and the avg number of Annual leaves do not have the same consistency as the Line graph.

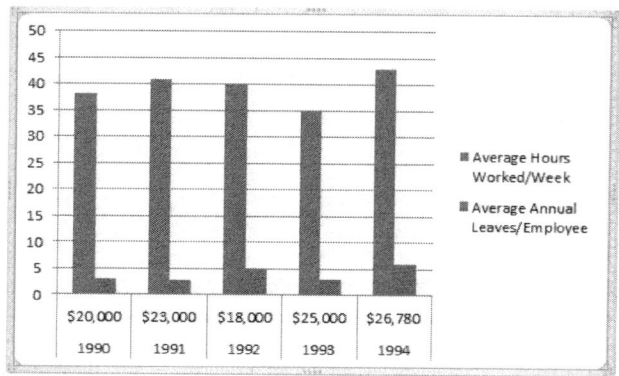

Image 86: Column graph

Bar Graphs

These are identical to column graphs in that the constant variable is allocated to Y-axis, and the parameters are measured against the X-axis. When displaying a single data series, bar graphs (or columns) are the most effective representation method. Because bar charts are heavier than line graphs, they are more successful at emphasizing a point and standing out on a page than the other two.

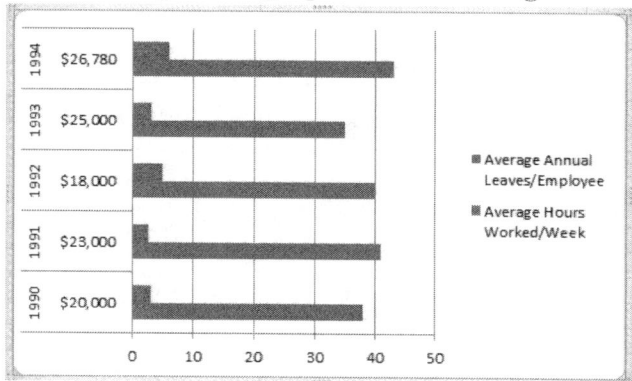

Image 87: Bar graph

Tips

- Eliminate all gridlines
- Reduce the width of the space between bars

Combinations graphs

Combining the two graphs above results in a combo chart containing bars and lines of different lengths. In the case of two data series that are on entirely different scales and may be expressed in completely different units, this is incredibly useful. For example, the most frequently used illustration is a bar graph with money on one axis and percentages on the other.

Tips

- Eliminate all borders and gridlines.
- Include a legend
- Reduce the breadth of the bars' gaps.
- Axis adjustment

How do you create graphs?

For example, if you are a movie theater owner, you may want to keep track of ticket sales of older movies. You can choose the names of the movies to show in column A, the number of tickets sold each month in column B, and so on. You can also add bold headings to make the chart more readable. The type of graph you choose depends on your data, including how many parameters you wish to include. Another popular type of graph is a line graph. This graph can show data in a specific period, from one day to five years. The line graph is the most basic type and is available in all versions of MS Excel. It is possible to make a variety of different types of line graphs, depending on your needs.

To create a graph in Excel, you first must import data into the spreadsheet. Then, you can either type in the data manually or copy and paste it. Then, you need to assign the correct data type to each column. If the data isn't formatted properly, your graph will not show up.

Another method of creating a graph in MS Excel is to save it as a picture or insert it into a visual template. To do this, you can right-click on the chart and click on "Save As Picture." You can give the picture a name and select the file type from there. The file type is JPEG. Click on "Save" when finished. Microsoft Excel is still the favored tool among finance and accounting professionals for many activities, and data visualization is no different. MS Excel provides the ability to create a wide range of charts and graphs. In addition, the templates are easily modifiable, allowing you to improve the financial models. Finally, graphs and charts created in Excel can be exported to other applications to be included in your report or presentation.

How to Create a Graph in Excel: A Step-by-Step Guide

The following section explains how to create any type of chart in Microsoft Excel:

- When entering the data, Microsoft Excel should be utilized. Another feature of Microsoft Excel is importing data from other apps.

- Check that the data is organized in a table format and that all variables are labeled accurately.

- Select the data that will be used to construct the graph. Make sure to include the labels, as well.

- Select the appropriate data and select Insert -> Charts from the menu bar. Using one of the templates will save time if you are definite about the type of graph that would be most useful for your project. If you're unsure which graph type to use, you can look at the Recommended Charts section. Excel will then give you a plethora of appropriate graph options for your data.

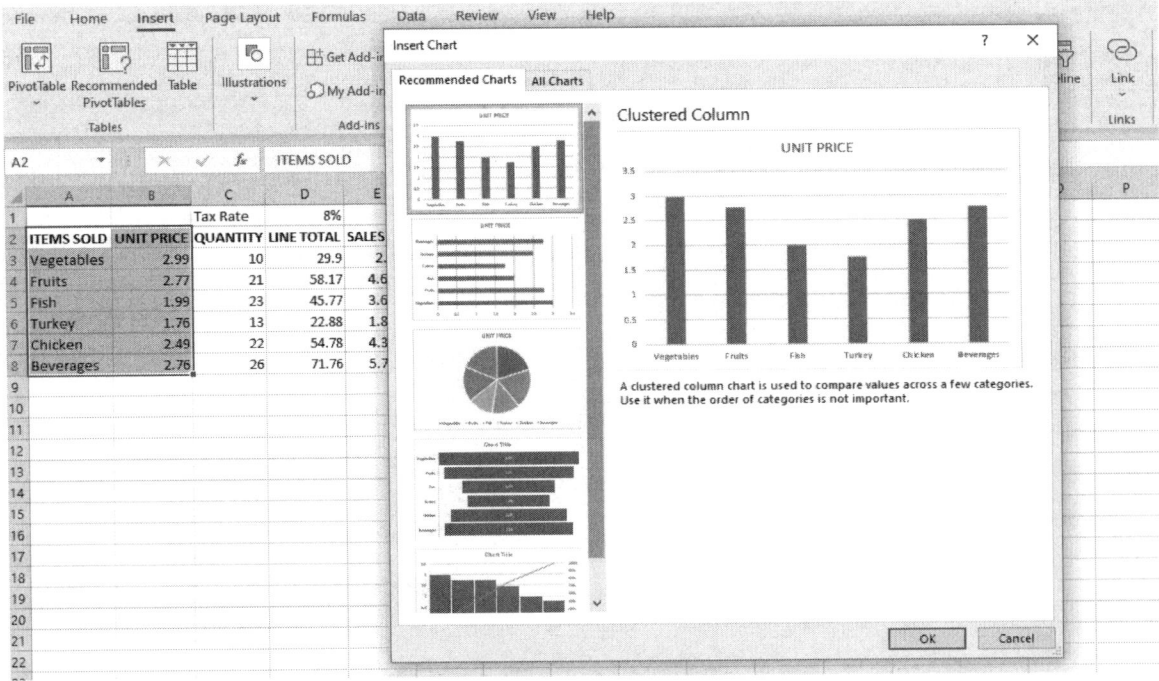

Image 88: Inserting a graph

6.2 What is a chart?

The first step to creating your chart is giving it a name. This is a simple process and can be fun. The default title of the chart will probably be "Chart Title," but you can change it to something more meaningful to you. You can also change the size and color of labels. A chart is an excellent way to represent data visually. In Excel, data can be challenging to interpret, so a chart can help make it easier to make sense of the information. In addition, using Excel's built-in charts makes the data analysis process easier and faster. There are many charts, each with different functionality and presentation styles. In business presentations, most presentations feature charts to help audiences remember information. Charts can help businesspeople visualize key data and take action based on the findings. As companies become more data-driven, they're becoming more essential. For example, department heads use charts to assess the effectiveness of new marketing campaigns or strategies. For example, a chart can help show how many orders are fulfilled at a warehouse per hour. When used in business presentations, charts can help executives visualize data more easily and make their presentations more memorable. Charts help people understand complex data. They allow people to easily see trends and patterns, and they can tell stories. For example, a column chart may show the number of unique visitors to Computer Hope over time. As sales increase, the bar lengths increase, indicating an increase. There are many types of charts available to display data. Listed below are some of the most popular ones supported by various programs. You can find one that suits your needs and will help you explain complicated data in an easy-to-understand way. There are various types of charts in Excel one can create depending on the data you're working with. You can create pie charts, scatter plot charts, and bar charts. Once you've decided on the chart type, you can use the Chart Design tab. Column charts are one of the most common charts used in presentations. These types of charts compare multiple values in a single column. They are best used when there are several data sets and you want to compare multiple variables simultaneously. You can also create combo charts by combining a series with multiple values. A column chart can use pictures or numbers. For example, a pictograph can show how many calories a cheese and bacon hamburger has. A pictograph showing the number of calories in beet greens is another example. A chart that shows stock market data is another type of chart. Stock market charts can display information about stocks or the volume of shares traded over time. Excel has several different types of charts, and each shows different information.

6.3 Types of charts

Several different charts are available in MS Excel, including line charts, column charts, and pie charts. Each of these types of chart can be used for different purposes. A line chart, for example, may show the number of times a value occurs. A column chart, on the other hand, may show information about two discrete objects, such as stocks, prices, or profits. A pie chart is a basic chart, but more advanced versions are available for more complex applications. For example, a university might use a pie chart to show the racial makeup of its students. A doughnut chart lets you visualize a single data series in a pie chart format. It also enables you to add additional data sets in layers to the chart. The best use for this type of chart is to compare two different sets of information. Another chart type in Excel is the area chart. This has the same pattern as the line chart and is a better choice for indicating the change between different data sets. Similarly, the pie chart and doughnut chart help show percentages, while the surface chart represents an optimum combination of two data sets. Again, excel makes these charts and graphs very easy to create once you've mastered a few basic steps.

Column Charts

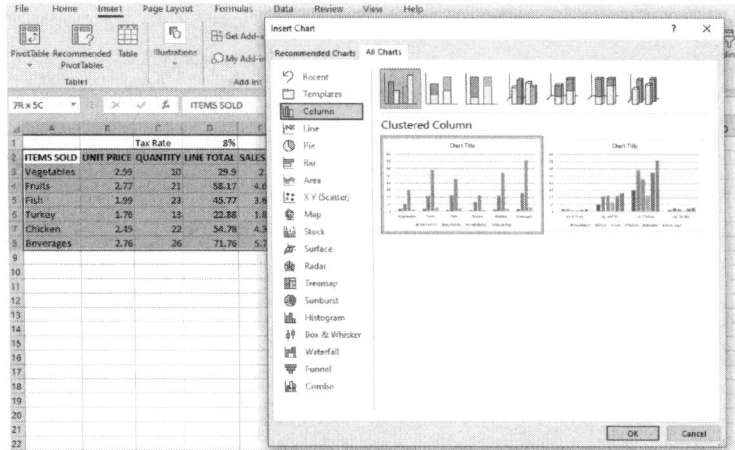

Image 89: Column chart selection

These charts represent data with vertical bars. They are important when comparing groups of data. To use the column charts:

- Highlight your data

- Select the option for **Columns** and then **Clustered Columns** in the chart menu.

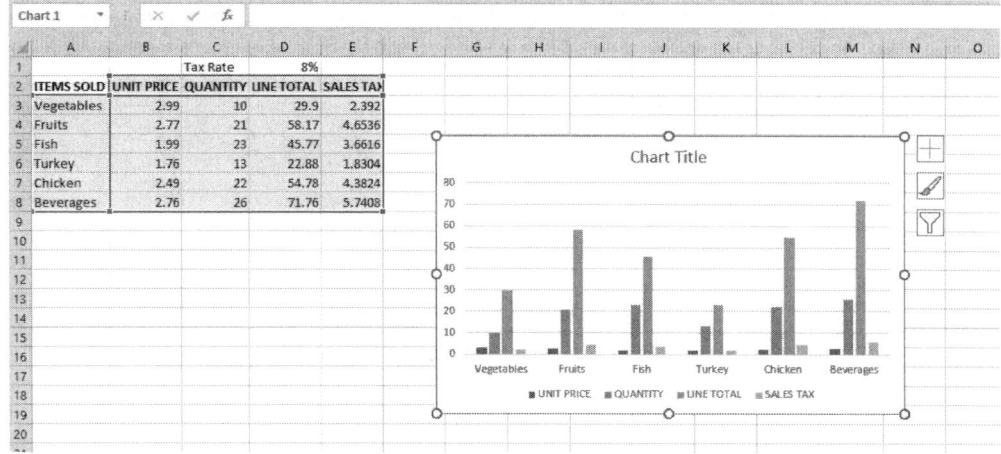

Image 90: Inserting column chart

Bar Charts

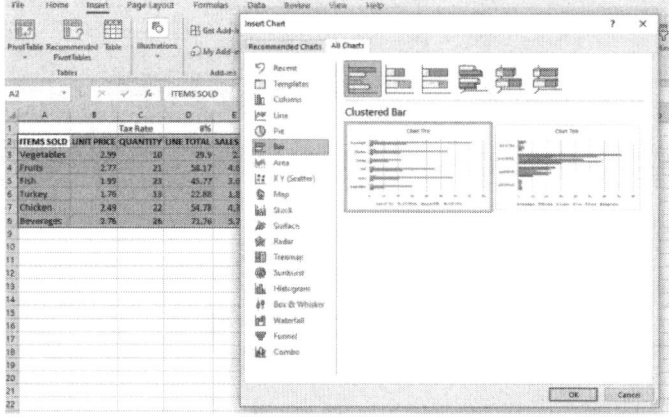

Image 91: Bar chart options

You can also use them for comparing a group of data. They differ from column charts because they represent data with horizontal bars. To use column charts:

- Highlight your data set

- Select the option for **Columns** and then **Clustered Bars** in the chart menu.

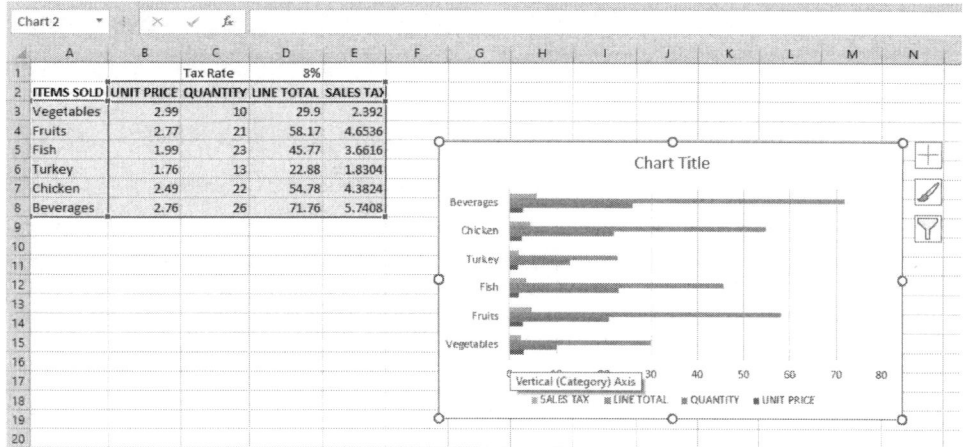

Image 92: Inserting the bar chart

Line Charts

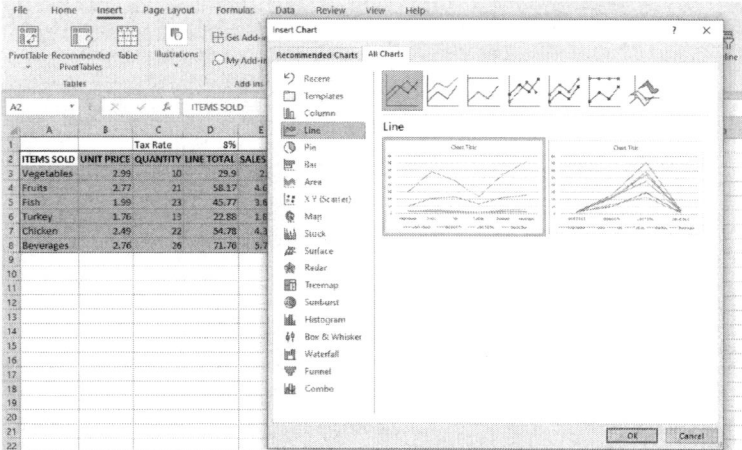

Image 93: Line chart options

These are used for showing data progression or trends. To use line charts:

- Highlight your data

- Select the option for **Lines** and then select any style for the chart.

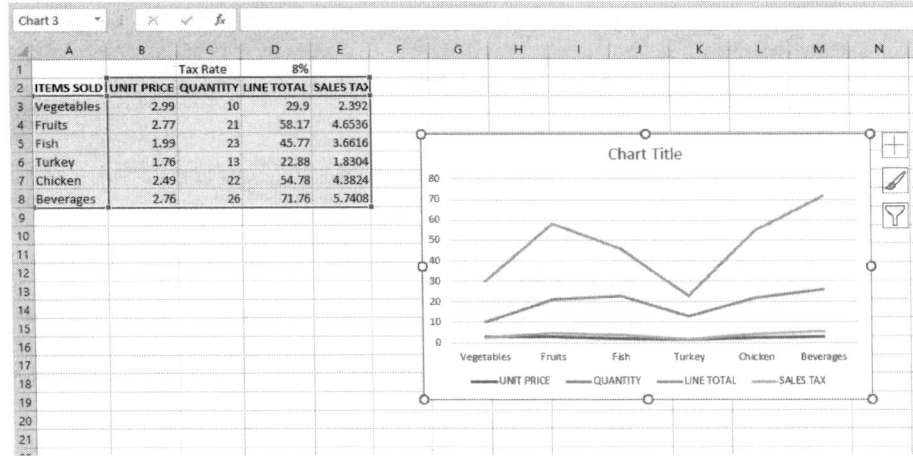

Image 94: Inserting a line chart

Pie Charts

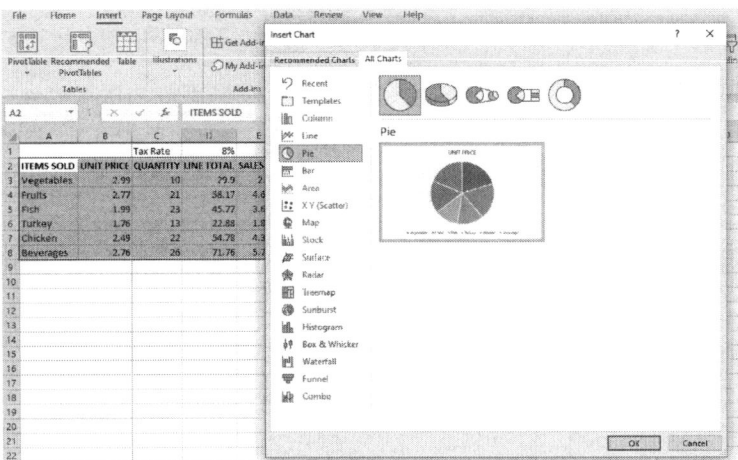

Image 95: Pie chart options

These are used for showing data in sections. To use pie charts, highlight your data and then select the option for **Pie Charts.**

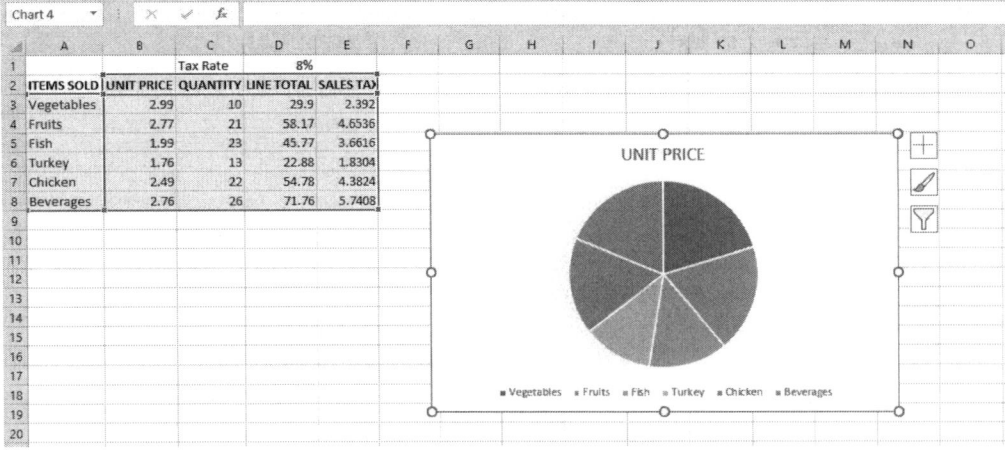

Image 96: Inserting a pie chart

Scatter Plots or XY Charts

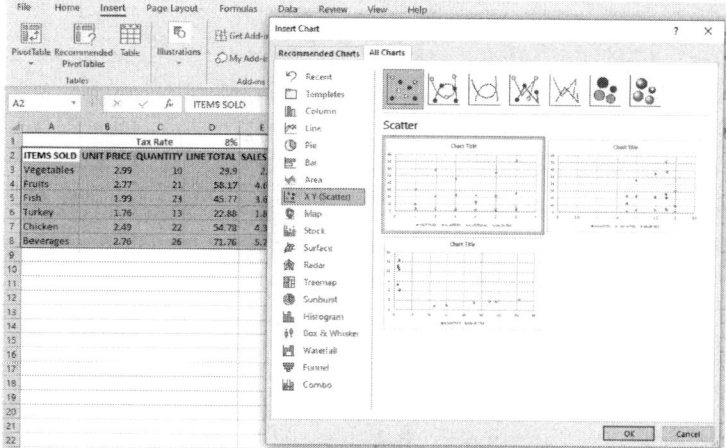

Image 97: Scatter plot options

These are used when finding how X affects Y in a data series. To use scatterplots, highlight your data and select the option for **Scatter.**

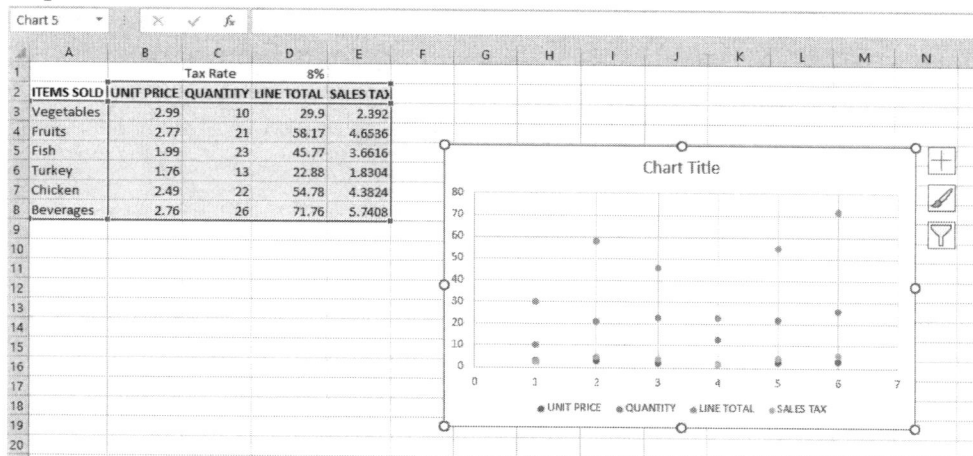

Image 98: Inserting a scatter plot

Area Charts

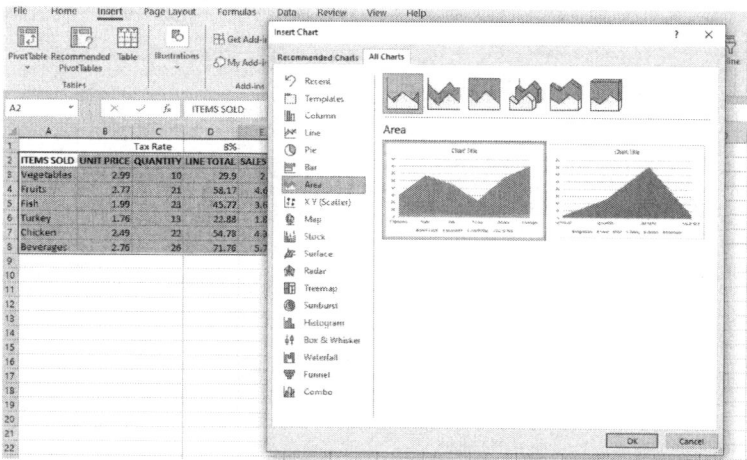

Image 99: Options for area charts

These represent data in filled colored areas. They can be inserted by selecting the **Line** chart option and then choosing **Area** under area for 2-D options.

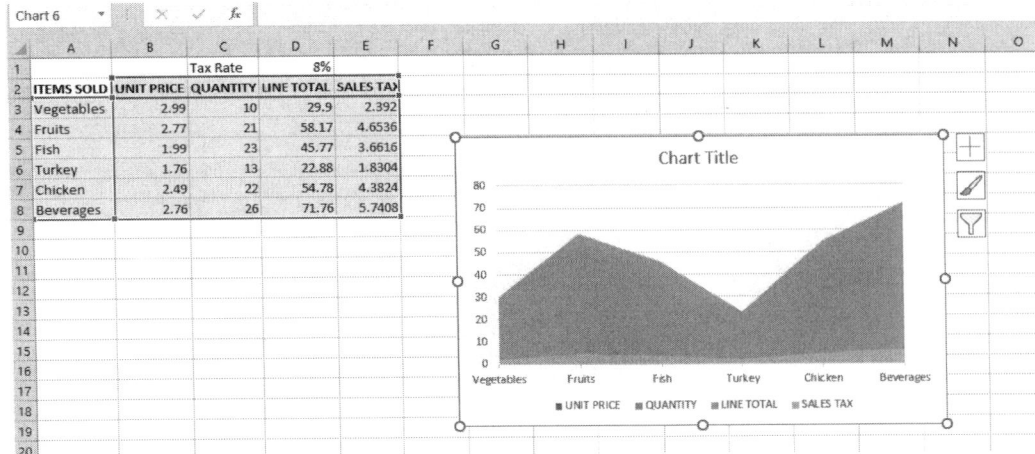

Image 100: Inserting area chart

Radar Charts

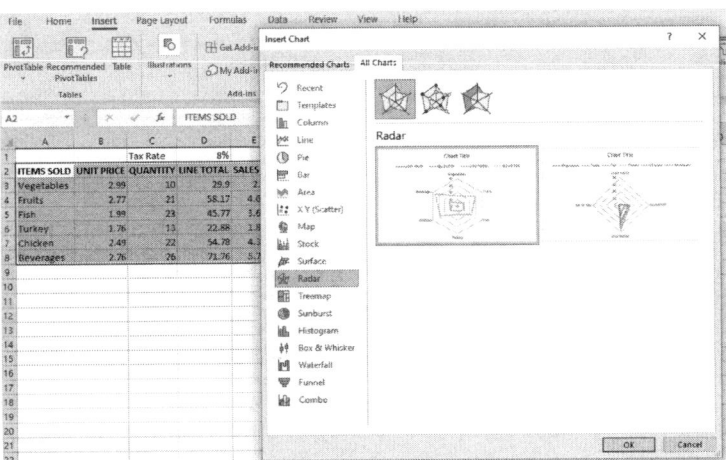

Image 101: Radar chart options

These charts compare multiple items in 2-D representation in a data set. They are otherwise known as Spider Charts. Radar charts can be added to your worksheet by selecting the option for additional charts in the **Insert** menu and choosing appropriately after highlighting your data.

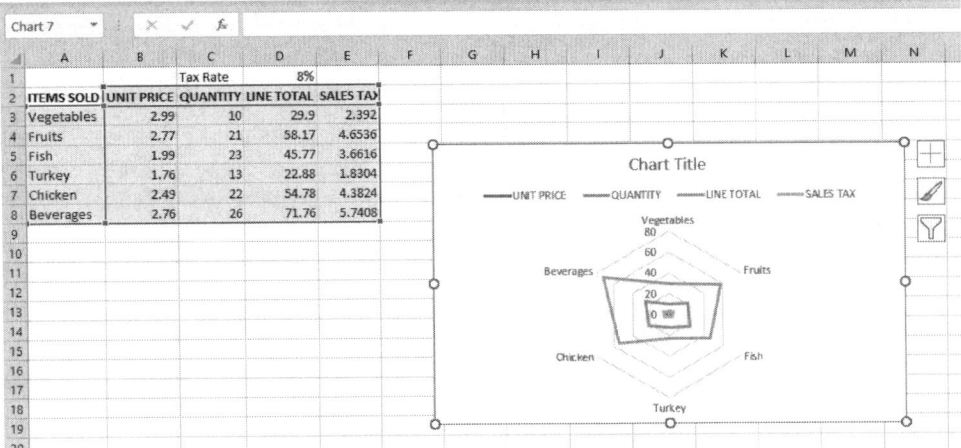

Image 102: Inserting the radar chart

Surface Charts

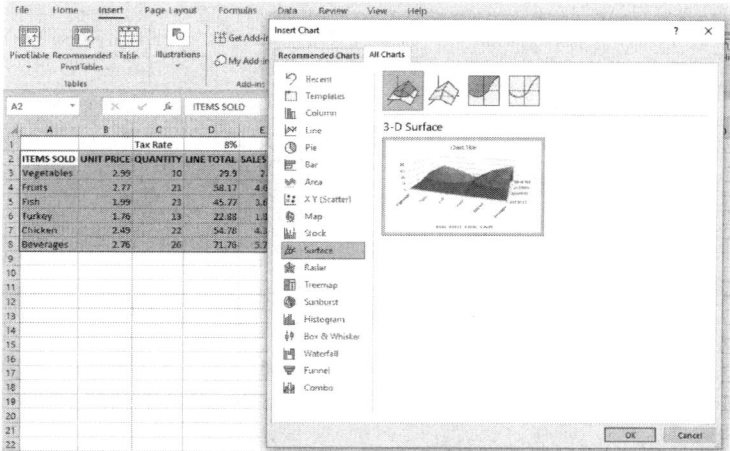

Image 103: Surface chart options

These represent your data in clear 3-D formats. They can be inserted by selecting the option for additional charts in the **Insert** menu and choosing appropriately after highlighting your data.

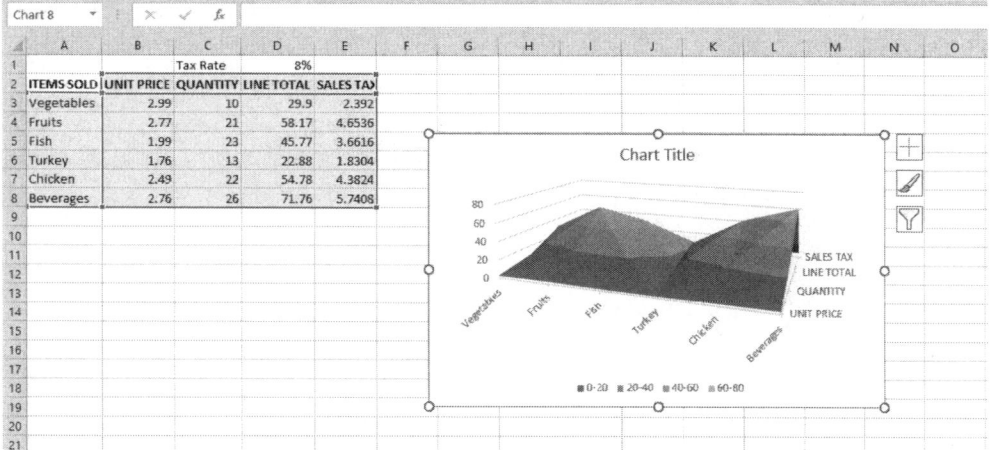

Image 104: Inserting the surface chart

Stock Charts

Just as the name implies, they are best used for representing stocks in a data set. They can be inserted into your worksheet following the same procedure as Surface charts.

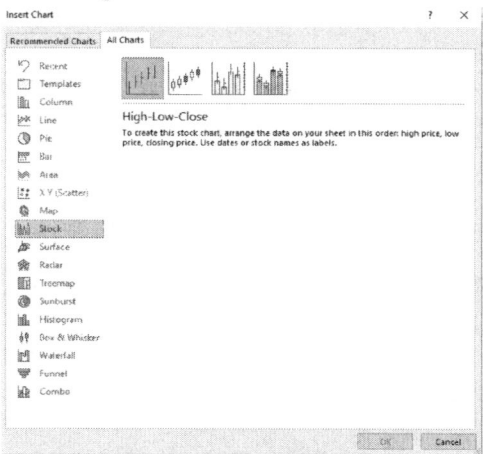

Image 105: Stock charts

Bubble Charts

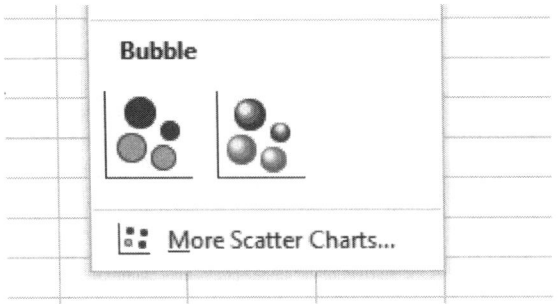

Image 106: Bubble charts

Highlight your data, select the option for additional charts, and select **Bubble** charts.

OTHER TYPES OF CHARTS IN EXCEL

Histogram

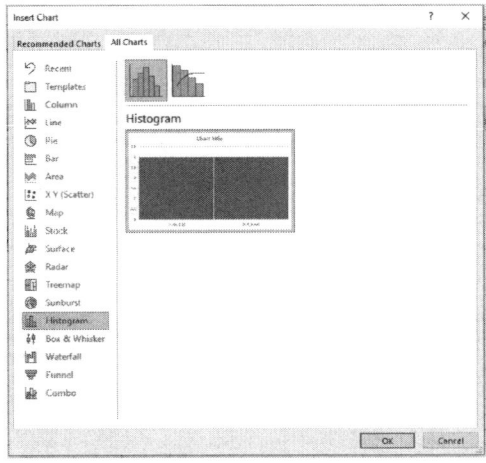

Image 107: Histogram element

This chart shows how often an event or item occurs in a data set. Insert histograms by selecting the option for **Static Charts** on the **Insert** menu and then choose the **Histogram** option. Do not forget to highlight your data. You can format the bars by right-clicking on the chart and selecting the format option.

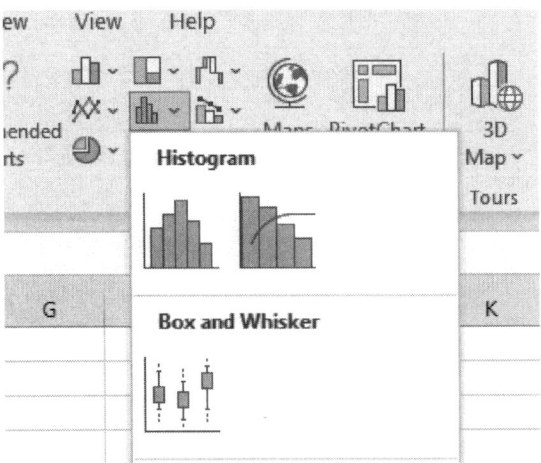

Image 108: Inserting the histogram

Waterfall Charts

- Highlight your data

- Select the option for **Stacked Columns** in the **Insert** menu

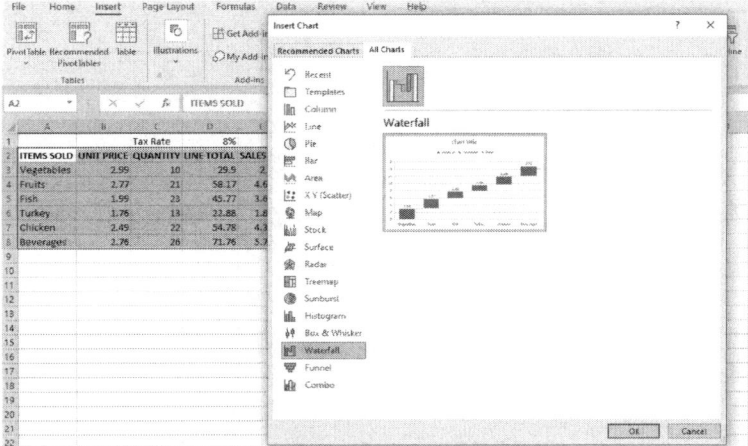

Image 109: Waterfall charts

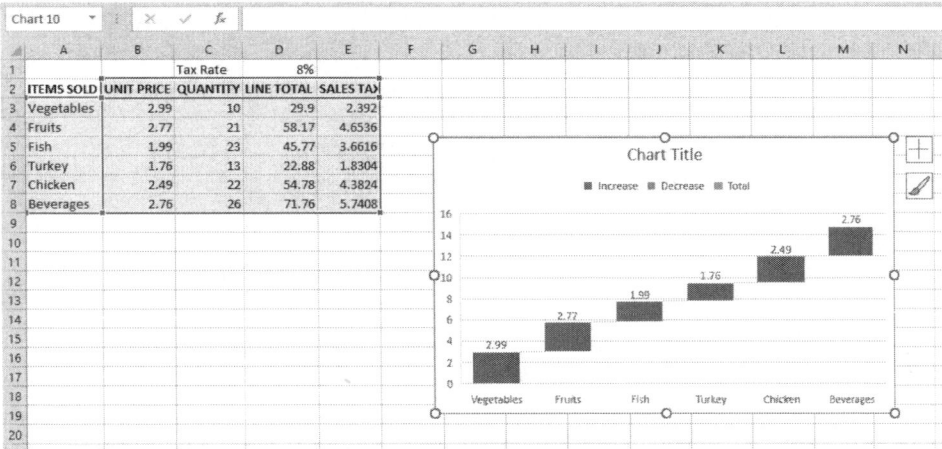

Image 110: Inserting the waterfall chart

- Right-click the inserted chart and choose the format option

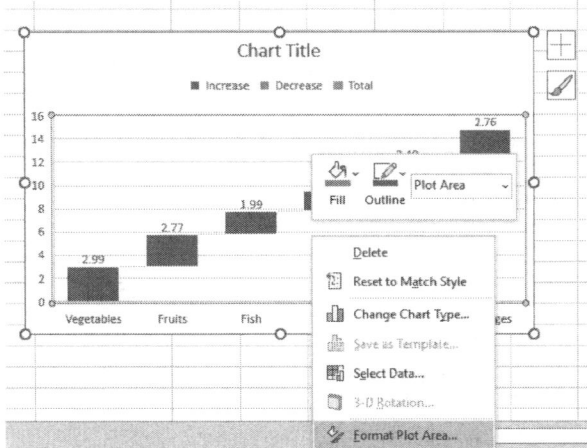

Image 111: Formatting the waterfall chart

- Select the options to remove fill and borders in the **Format** window

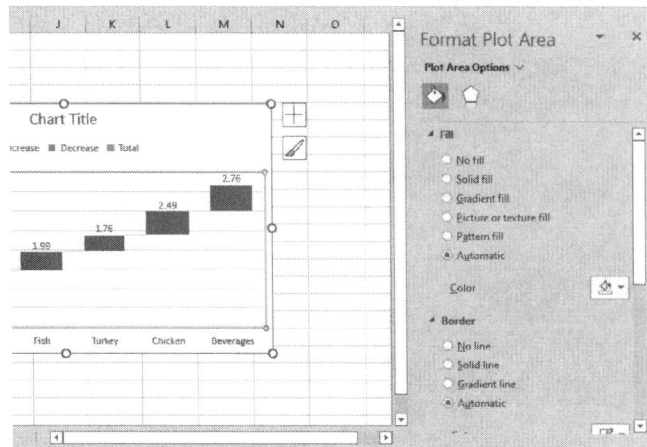

Image 112: The Format Plot Area

Waterfall charts show graphically how data flows in a data set.

Box and Whisker Charts

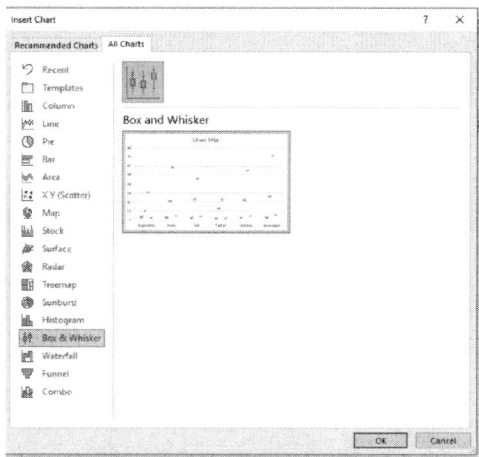

Image 113: Box and whisker charts

These show specific values of your data. Insert box and whisker charts by first highlighting your data, selecting the option for **Static Charts** on the **Insert** menu, and then choosing the appropriate option.

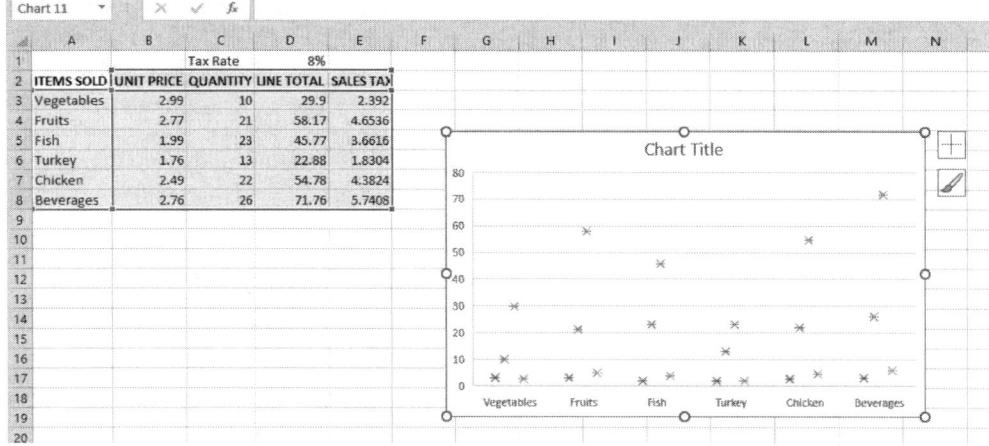

Image 114: Inserting the box and whisker chart

Sunburst Charts

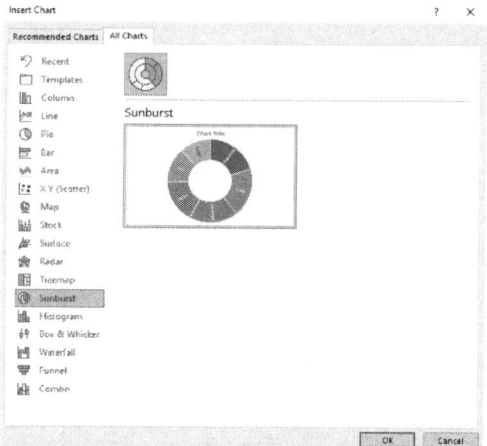

Image 115: Sunburst chart

- Highlight your data

- Navigate to the option for Hierarchical charts

- Select **Sunburst** charts

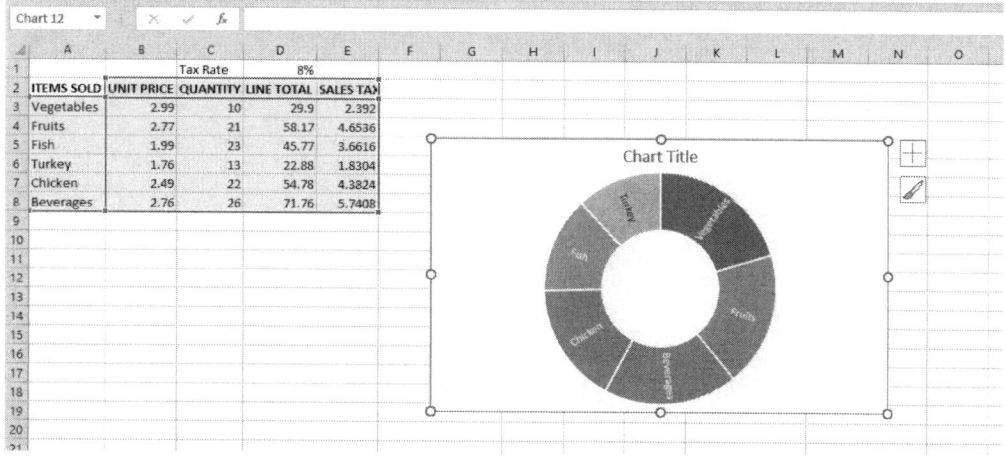

Image 116: Inserting the sunburst chart

Treemap Charts

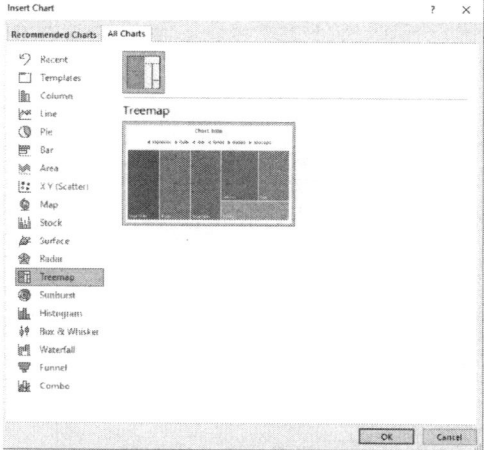

Image 117: Treemap chart

- Highlight your data

- Navigate to the option for Hierarchical charts

- Select **Treemap** charts

Funnel Charts

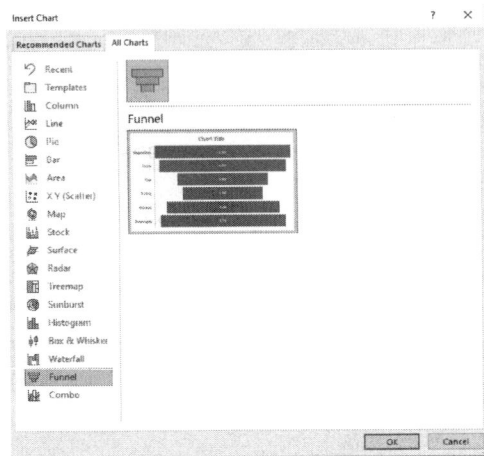

Image 118: Funnel chart

- Highlight your data

- Navigate to the icon for **Waterfall** charts

- Select **Funnel** charts

Map Charts

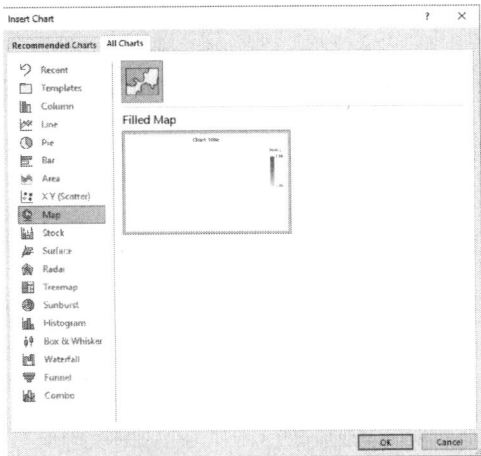

Image 119: Map chart

- Select your data

- Navigate to the **Maps** option and select **Filled Maps**

How do you create charts?

Charts in MS Excel can be formatted to look just the way you want them to. To change the look of a chart, you can change the style and colors of each element. You can also change the data that you are plotting. The chart can look as complex as you want it to be or as simple as you want it to be. The next step in creating a chart is choosing which cells you would like to include in the chart. You can highlight cells and then drag the cursor from the top left cell to the bottom right cell. You can also choose what kind of chart you want to create from the charts group on the ribbon. You can also click on a specific cell to display its description. There are several ways to create charts and graphs in MS Excel. Column charts display categorized data, while bar charts show data arranged horizontally. A column chart is more suitable for showing data about a single category, while a bar chart is better for a group of categories. Another option is to format individual data as a table. This makes it easier to update the data range. When you add more data, Excel automatically updates the table and chart.

7 Microsoft Excel Data Analysis

If you are a business person, you are probably familiar with Microsoft Excel Data analysis. But if you have never performed any analysis in Excel, you may be wondering what it is all about. This chapter will explain this type of analysis, how to do it, and which functions to use to create your analysis. First, learn why it's important to perform Excel data analysis. You can begin by exploring the Data Analysis ToolPak in the Tools menu.

What is Excel Data analysis?

When analyzing data, using Excel is an excellent choice. You can get data from many sources, including financial records, sales figures, and customer reviews. Excel has many features that make it easier to analyze the data and find patterns.

Histogram: Use the Histogram function on the Data Analysis menu to create a histogram. If you have three adjacent cells with data, enter the numbers in these cells. If the values are missing, Excel will accept blank cells. For other missing values, enter 0,1,2 or the range of three adjacent cells. This function will not label the output based on column and row numbers, which can be confusing when working with many variables.

=FIND: The =FIND function helps find the values that meet a condition. The COUNTIFS function can determine the number of cells that satisfy certain conditions. It also does not require a sum range. The COUNTA function is a useful data analysis function because it can identify if a cell is empty. You can use this to analyze gaps. This function can also help you identify patterns and anomalies.

Spikelines: MS Excel offers a visualization feature called sparklines. Sparklines are mini-graphs that can be inserted within cells. Sparklines are excellent for visualizing trends. You can add one or multiple sparklines to a data range, so you can easily see which ones are trending the most. You can even use Excel to create graphs that look like a stacked area chart. And the possibilities are endless.

Sorting: Sorting and filtering data in Excel allows you to visualize the important values. For example, in conditional formatting, you can color-code cells and place symbols next to values. Conditional formatting allows you to exclude duplicate rows and sort them by color. You can also sort data by a specific rule or a color scale. You can also use the "Subtotal" function to ignore hidden rows. It can even create heat maps.

How to do Excel Data analysis

Whether you're looking to analyze your data for a business presentation or just interested in making your spreadsheets look nice, you'll find that the tools in Excel can help you perform various functions.

For example, you can sort data in descending or ascending order, filter, highlight records that meet criteria and create charts. In this book, we'll go over some of the more important Excel tools and how to use them for data analysis. Sparklines are little line charts that display data from a range of values. They are a great way to identify trends and highlight high and low values. Moreover, you can use these charts to perform a what-if analysis, which lets you create different scenarios and compare the results. The Excel Goal Seeker can be another useful tool for analyzing data in Excel. You can find a great example of this in the following video. What-If Analysis involves exploring different scenarios by changing formula values. Solver, an add-in program for Excel, can help you perform this type of analysis by locating the optimal formula value for an objective cell, subject to other constraints and limitations placed on other formula cells. This function is particularly useful for data analysis. These tools can help you visualize huge data sets. They are an indispensable tool in any business's arsenal. But it's only the beginning of what Excel can do for you. Sorting is another way to analyze data in Excel. For example, if you have a dataset that includes people with allergies, you can either manually count them or use an Excel formula to calculate them. Then, you can choose the specific cells you want to analyze and use the Quick Analysis feature or CRTL + Q. This feature helps you create charts that show trends and analyze smaller data sets.

Pivot tables are one of the most powerful features in Excel when it comes to data analysis. Pivot tables, also called cross-tabulation, help you summarize and slice data so that you can focus on specific aspects of your data. Pivot tables are easy to create, and you don't need to learn complex formulas to build one. You can also blend the information, such as the percentages of different factors in an industry. Pivot tables can also help you identify trends.

Functions to use in Excel Data analysis

You can use various functions to manipulate data in a Microsoft Excel Data analysis. The LOOKUP function, for example, returns a value from a column to a row. The SELECT function combines two functions, allowing you to combine and summarize data from several ranges. In addition to these functions, Excel also provides lookup functions, such as Vlookup and Hlookup, which you can use to find the values in a column. The Median function is a useful formula for finding an array's middle number. To use this function, sort your data into ascending order. The formula performs this automatically. You can use the standard deviation function if you need to find the most common value in a data group. Finally, the SUM() function returns the sum of the numbers that have passed. However, make sure that you sort your data first. One of the most useful Excel functions is =RANK, which allows you to show values in either ascending or descending order. This function is often used in data analysis to determine which clients order the most of a certain product. You can also use =RANK to display the values in order of popularity. For instance, if you sell coffee, you can use =RANK to see which client orders the most.

There are more than 20 types of charts in Microsoft Excel. Although most people get by with a Line chart, Bar chart, and Pie chart, you can also try a Scatter chart, which requires two sets of corresponding data. Regardless of your business, you should consider using Excel for data analysis. The benefits are endless! Just learn the correct way to use these functions in Microsoft Excel.

If you need to calculate how many values of a certain type are in a cell, you can use the COUNTIFS function to perform the calculation. This powerful function allows you to count the number of values that match the criteria. The result is a set of values for which you can calculate an average. This is a powerful function that can help you analyze large data sets with ease. When used correctly, this function will help you find the most relevant information in the data.

Importance of Excel Data Analysis

The Importance of Excel data analysis for businesses can't be underestimated. Its advanced features help analyze large volumes of data with ease. It also lets you sort data, both in ascending and descending order. In addition, you can apply various filters to data, including a 'What-If' analysis to determine the effect of changing formula values. The Solver add-in uses operations research methods to find optimal solutions to decision-making problems. It even comes with its analysis tool, Analysis ToolPak, an add-in to Excel.

If you're new to data analysis, you may be wondering how you can begin with this method. While many programs can analyze large amounts of data, Excel is a powerful tool for creating reports and data analysis. It doesn't require previous experience and doesn't require you to download any software or install any programs. To use the Excel data analysis ToolPak, search the Help for "Data Analysis Tools." One thing you should know about Excel is that it only accepts data in blank cells if there are no missing values. Often, the same data arrangement won't work for different types of analysis.

The Importance of Excel data analysis continues to grow. Despite the recent advancements in data analysis software, many Excel users still use old versions of the program. Using the Quick Analysis feature in Excel can help you analyze data quickly, with minimal work. The ability to add beauty to a report is also crucial. Before you start editing your workbook, you should turn off Auto Refresh. This will prevent your table from refreshing whenever you make changes.

A pivot table in Excel can make analyzing data easier. For example, the What-If analysis feature lets you highlight specific cells based on their values. You can also use the "what-if" function to find duplicate rows. This feature enables you to shade a row if it has a duplicate value. Another useful feature in Excel is the Conditional Formatting feature, which allows you to ignore rows with no data. You can even use the Conditional Formatting feature to generate Heat Maps.

8 Common Problems and Mistakes with Microsoft Excel

A few of the most common mistakes and problems people encounter with Microsoft Excel are listed below. Each problem and mistake has a solution. For example, learn how to unlock an excel with a password or where to locate temporary Excel files. If you have ever encountered this error, this book is here to help you! It will show you how to quickly fix them and ensure you don't make any more mistakes. So read on to discover the most

What are the common problems and mistakes

While Excel is one of the most widely used data processing and spreadsheet applications, it rarely develops severe errors. But even when it does, it can still cause problems with its performance and usability. There are many reasons why users experience these problems, such as missing DLL files, corrupt workbooks, or macros. In addition, there are also instances where users encounter malware or infection. To understand why this happens, you should first know how to identify the root cause of the error. The #NUM error occurs when a formula or function contains invalid numbers. Excel can't display the values if the formula doesn't specify the right width. Check if the number contains text, blank cells, or special characters. If you find such errors, you can fix them by replacing the values. Remember that the types of inputs that cause Excel errors can save you from having to redo your work. Another common mistake is circular references. Circular references can occur for various reasons, but the spreadsheet's creator easily fixes most. To avoid this problem, you should ensure that the name of the cell is correctly spelled. Also, ensure that you use quotation marks around any text in the formula. Keeping the names of formulas short and simple will help you avoid these problems. Moreover, it will save you time when solving errors in your work.

A list with problems and solutions for each one

A list of common problems and solutions for Microsoft Office applications is a must-have for any Excel user. It's an excellent tool for simple lists, but it can become a complex project if you're using it for macro programming or automating data processing. Listed below are some of the most common problems you may encounter when using Excel to create a project. These problems can affect performance, stability, and development. You should first check your software if you're experiencing freezing issues when using Microsoft Excel. This could result from failing to install the latest update, an add-in conflicting with Excel, or another process using it. You can usually fix this problem by uninstalling the add-in or reinstalling the program. Also, you should make sure to install the latest update for Microsoft Office so it can fix any loopholes and replace outdated files. There are many reasons that Microsoft Excel can freeze, including outdated antivirus software, an erroneous add-in, or a faulty program. The most common solution is to start Excel in safe mode. Otherwise, you may need to install the latest update to resolve the issue. However, it may be necessary to uninstall the add-in first. If the issue persists, you might need to restart Excel using the safe mode.

How to unlock an excel with a password

If you've ever been caught trying to unlock an Excel spreadsheet, you probably know how frustrating it can be. Fortunately, you're not the only one who has encountered this problem. Here are a few common mistakes when unlocking Excel documents with passwords. Using a simple password cracking application can significantly speed up the process. But remember to always re-save your spreadsheet after cracking a password, and you can re-use it with a password.

You may have made a mistake when you set up the password, causing the file to become unusable. Therefore, you should always write down the password and store it in a safe place, so you don't forget it. Alternatively, a password-protected file may be impossible to open. However, fortunately, there are solutions available. Excel File Repair Tool (EFRT) is one such program. It can help you fix corrupt Excel files, preview them, and save them. The first mistake is to open the workbook with the worksheet that has been password protected. If you don't have this permission, you can still use the method by saving it in an older version. To do so, open the workbook and select "Excel 97-2003" (*.xls) when you save it. After saving the workbook, you should follow the prompts to edit or download the protected sheet.

Where excel saves temporary files

Where does Excel save its temporary files? In most cases, Excel stores all its files in C:UserscyAppDataLocalMicrosoftOfficeUnsavedFiles. But if you accidentally delete a recent Excel file, you won't know where to find it. If you're a Mac user, you can find your unsaved Excel file in the temporary files folder. Then, you can copy it to another location and open it in Excel. Alternatively, you can save it through the app instead of Excel. Regardless of where the Excel temporary file is stored, you can still open it as an actual workbook. This way, you can recover unsaved workbooks. But there are a few tips you can follow to ensure that you don't delete the files by accident. First, open Microsoft Excel and change the file extension to xls or xlsx. Secondly, you can choose to hide these files by checking the "Hide" option when you right-click on them. In addition, you can recover unsaved Excel files by reopening the program. After reopening Excel, you should see a sidebar with your available files. Select the AutoSave Excel version from the list. Next, navigate to the Temp folder. This folder will store the temp files of your work, so it's important to note that these files don't contain all your work.

The Document Auto Recovery Command

This feature allows one to recover documents when incase there is a computer failure, crash or power failure leading to data loss. Auto Recovery is automatically saves changes you make to your workbook. Enable Auto Recovery command

- Click **File** tab and choose **Options**

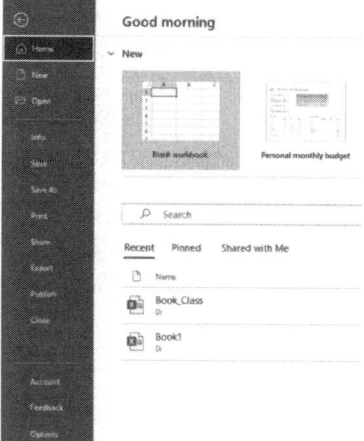

Image 120: First step to setting Auto Recovery

- Click on **Save** in the **Options** dialog box that pops up.

- Key in minutes for the interval within **Save AutoRecovery Information Every** box. Could be 1 or 2 minutes

- click **Ok**

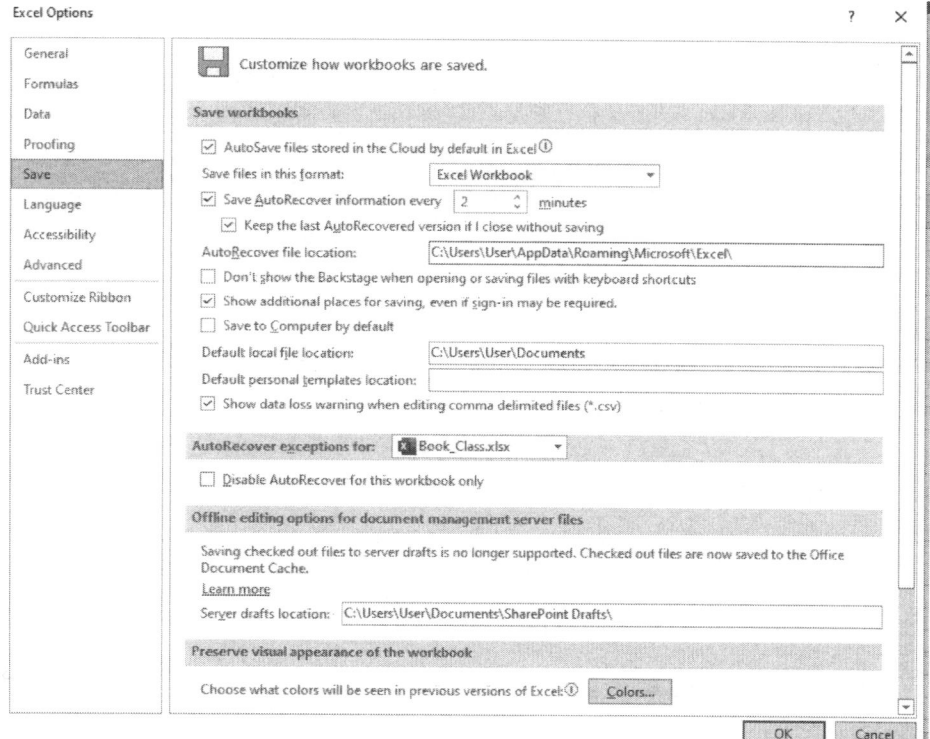

Image 121: Setting number of minutes

How to recover corrupted files

You're not alone if you're unsure how to recover corrupted Excel files. This corruption can be caused by viruses, system errors, or even unidentified reasons. If you've ever encountered this problem, you may wonder how to recover corrupted Excel files and restore lost data. The good news is that recovering corrupted files is not as difficult as it seems. Below are some techniques to use to recover corrupted Excel files.

The first step in fixing a corrupted Excel file is to open it. To do so, open the file in Microsoft Office Excel, or use the repair tool. If this method fails, save the file in another format. It's important to remember that this process is a bit risky and will lose formatting and formulas. The best method to fix corrupted Excel files is to use an alternative file format that the operating system can open.

To open a corrupted.xls file, you must first install a Microsoft Office Excel converter. Otherwise, you won't be able to open it in Word. Then, to fix a corrupted.xls file, you need to change the format to a newer, more compatible format. For example, if you've saved the file in the XLSX format, you need to change it back to the older XLS file format to use the same file.

How to set autosave

To avoid losing data, you must set AutoSave in Microsoft Excel to save your work in the right place. By default, the program saves your work in a temporary file with an arbitrary name and then gives it a more meaningful name when it saves it. However, this feature can be hindered by various obstructions, including accidentally deleted files in the Recycle Bin. It also generates various errors when it tries to access the file.

To enable AutoSave, go to File tab, then select Options. Click Save tab. In Save tab, click AutoSave files and set AutoRecover information every X minutes. Enter a time that you want the program to save your changes. You can also select the file location and specify exceptions. If you accidentally delete an important document, you can restore it by choosing the AutoRecovery option.

In addition to misplacing the autosave option, you can accidentally delete the temporary file that Excel creates. This may occur if you are using an external hard drive. Sometimes, the error is caused by deleting or renaming a temporary file. In such cases, Excel will try to save the file without autosave, resulting in an error message that says, "Cannot access the document because it is read-only."

Which Excel has lookup

VLOOKUP is one of the many features of Microsoft Excel. This function searches data in a column for an identifier similar to the lookup value. This function searches in columns that are listed vertically. It also searches to the right of the old data to find new data to the right of the old. In addition, VLOOKUP requires that the data be listed in ascending order.

However, sometimes the lookup function returns incorrect results. In such cases, you should first sort the lookup ranges to contain the data you're looking for. Otherwise, the function will return results that are not relevant. In such cases, you can combine the IF() and EXACT() functions to get the desired results. While these functions may seem the simplest way to search for data, they're not. When using a lookup function in a cell, you need to specify which type of match you want. You can use an exact or non-exact match, but you'll need to remember to enter the values in ascending order. Also, remember that an array formula requires multiple cells. If you're a beginner, this method might be too complex for you to try. You can also use an INDEX. This function helps search an array.

9 Personal Finance Use

How to Use Microsoft Excel for Personal Finance

If you want to use Microsoft Excel for personal finance, here are some tips to get you started. You will learn how to efficiently keep track of your earnings and expenses, create a budget, and analyze your financial situation. You'll also learn how to synchronize your financial accounts with other apps. And since Microsoft isn't responsible for your personal financial information, you can trust that your information will remain private. You can even use it for tax purposes.

Keeping track of earnings and expenses Efficiently

Keeping track of your earnings and expenses is essential for planning cash flow, maximizing the use of loans and credit, and ensuring that you pay the right amount of tax. Detailed records can also help plan your cash flow and help you prepare accurate financial statements. In addition, tracking your earnings and expenses can help you find ways to save money and make more informed business decisions. Even though you can keep track of all transactions manually, it's best to consider an accounting software solution that automates this process. Using Microsoft Excel to track expenses is easy to keep tabs on your spending. A dedicated income and expense worksheet will make it easier to enter transaction data. It also has a tab for common expenses, such as rent and mortgage. An expense tab can be tailored to your specific needs. Keeping track of personal expenses is crucial during college, when time and distractions may cause you to spend more than you intended. If you'd like to create a spreadsheet to keep track of bills and income, you can download the free Monthly college budget workbook. You can upload it to OneDrive to access it online or print it for manual tracking. There are many free spreadsheet alternatives available, including Google Docs and OpenOffice. While Excel is not free, it's easy to use, and you can make it work for your needs. In addition to using the Microsoft Excel software, you can also download a free Excel budget template. Excel templates are available online and can be customized to suit your specific needs. With a little effort, you can create and maintain a budget spreadsheet that can track your earnings and expenses in a way that is convenient for you. While tracking your income is essential, it's not enough to have it tracked. You should review your expenses regularly and look for inconsistencies or inefficiencies. Doing so can ensure that your finances are under control and help you set goals. For example, suppose you have an irregular income. In that case, you may be able to identify any cash flow shortfalls before they happen and use your extra money for debt repayment or savings.

Creating a budget

If you're looking to create a budget, you'll find that a spreadsheet is your best bet. Microsoft Excel has several features to customize and create a budget workbook that suits your needs. For instance, you can create columns to track income and expenses by category and totals and labels. Once you've established your monthly budget, you can make it more visually appealing by using border colors, fonts, and formatting options. Microsoft Excel is a great way to start if you're just budgeting. There are many budget templates available on the Microsoft Office Template website. You can search for the template that best suits your budget needs, downloads it, and use it. This can save you time by calculating your finances without spending hours each month on the project. Moreover, these budget templates are free, so you don't have to worry about investing large amounts of money to get started. Even though budgeting is tedious, it is vital to track your income and expenses and set aside a portion of your salary for designated savings. This way, you increase your chances of meeting current needs while planning for future goals. Creating a budget is an excellent idea, even if you're on a modest income. It can also improve your financial position. So, how do you create a budget using Microsoft Excel? Creating a budget spreadsheet with Microsoft Excel is easier than you might think. You can simply input estimated amounts into columns, drag them to the desired location and enter the totals. This way, the spreadsheet will look more attractive. You can also use formatting functions to make the spreadsheet more visually appealing. If you're not a computer geek, you can also download and install a free trial of Microsoft Excel.

To create a budget spreadsheet, use a template to track your income and expenses. In Excel, you can label each row with a different color. You can also use the Fill tool on the menu bar. It looks like a paint can tipping over and pouring out. Click the Fill button and select the color you want to add to each row. Avoid dark or bright colors, and be sure not to use too many.

Debt Management

Money in Excel is a financial management tool that works within Microsoft Excel. You can link your various financial accounts into your spreadsheet and view all their information in one convenient location. The tool also gives you insights into your spending habits, including monthly expenses. This feature was designed to replace Microsoft Money but was recently upgraded. Using Microsoft Money, you'll probably want to upgrade to the new version. For more information about Money in Excel, visit the Microsoft website. Money in Excel has some notable benefits. It's extremely secure, backed by Plaid, which all the major financial institutions use. It delivers a ton of information. The Recurring Expenses template shows recurring charges across various credit cards. While some credit card companies offer similar features, many people do not have one comprehensive view of all their cards. The Money in Excel software lets you easily sort your expenses, categorize them, and set priorities for spending.

Financial Analysis

If you are interested in personal finance analysis, you may want to try using Microsoft Excel. There are numerous benefits to using Microsoft Excel for personal finance analysis. It is highly secure and a solution used by many financial institutions, including banks and credit unions. You can view a wealth of information about your finances, including recurring expenses on different credit cards. This template is beneficial because many credit card companies have similar features, but most people don't have one comprehensive view of all their credit card usage. To begin using Excel for personal finance analysis, download a free template. This template works with both Excel online and desktop software. You'll find two separate worksheets: the Expense tab and the Summary tab. Once you've logged in, you can compare your monthly income and expenses to see how they compare. The Summary worksheet automatically displays your cash flow status. The spreadsheet contains standard expense categories and subcategories for each category. There are also tabs for filtering and sorting to get a quick overview of your finances. Another great way to use Excel for personal finance analysis is to subscribe to a service like Tiller, which automatically populates spreadsheets with automated data feeds. This service was developed for Google Sheets but recently made its way to Microsoft Excel. Microsoft recently recommended Tiller to subscribers of its Microsoft 365 service. You can try it for free for 60 days and pay $79/year afterward. There are also many other features to choose from. Money in Excel is an Excel add-in that connects your financial accounts to your spreadsheet. With this tool, you can track your spending habits and generate a budget based on your spending habits. Money in Excel will also let you view your monthly expenditures by category. And it's compatible with over 10,000 financial institutions. If you don't want to use Money in Excel, you can use another personal finance analysis software, like MSN Money.

10 Engineer and Statistician Use of Microsoft Excel

Engineers and statisticians extensively use Microsoft Excel and other statistical tools to improve the accuracy of repetitive calculations. These programs also help engineers collect data and create statistical charts that display their findings. Learn how to use Microsoft Excel for your next engineering or statistical project. This section will explore Essential formulas to learn, functions that connect numbers and search for data in a specific column, and how to perform Engineering Analysis with Numerical Solutions.

Essential formulas to know

You need to know some essential formulas in Excel for engineers and statisticians, but not everyone knows what they are. There are many formulas in Excel for engineers, including basic arithmetic and calculus. This book is for you if you want to learn to use these in your work. The book will take you through the basics of Excel and then teach you how to use these formulas to solve engineering problems. For example, the MROUND function lets one to round a number to a specific multiple. It is also possible to use the FLOOR or CEILING functions in rounding a number to the nearest integer. Lastly, the COUNTIF function counts the number of cells meeting the given criteria. You can use this formula to compute a group's average number of shareholders. However, you should use quotation marks when using the COUNTIF function. When using Microsoft Excel, you will want to know what functions you can use to solve technical problems. Using these functions will help you calculate numbers more quickly. In addition to basic math operations, you can also use Excel to manipulate date and time values. You can even create tables, graphs, and other types of data to visualize the results of your calculations. The more you know about formulas, the more confident you will be with the program. Using the CONVERT function to convert between complex units is also a helpful skill. It is also valuable for converting complex units like decimals and kiloliters. Data Validation is located under the Data tab of the ribbon. You can also use Named Ranges to eliminate the pain of referencing Excel cells. You can also use the LOOKUP and HLOOKUP functions to look up data by column or table. Suppose functions are helpful for logical tests. They test more than one condition and return a value if it's true or false. The IF functions are essential for data analysts because they automate decision-making. However, they are difficult to use, and if you're not sure what to use, try searching online. A basic understanding of Excel formulas is essential for many careers in today's world.

Functions connected to numbers for approximation

The Excel formula COUNTIFS is a way to calculate the number of places in a fraction, decimal, or percentage. The exponent "E" stands for the number of decimal places. This method is sometimes less accurate, but generally, it is the same. The difference is the way the calculator treats numbers over 15 significant figures. It treats a number differently if it is more than 15 significant figures, and this difference can sometimes be beneficial. The second type of function, TCROUND, can display arbitrary sums and 3-D references to other sheets or files. The TCROUND function can also display arbitrary numbers, although it cannot integrate results from a think-cell round. Integrating a formula with multiple decimal digits is also impossible using TCROUND statements. The results of TCROUND statements are treated as separate problems and can be used as input for other formulas. VLOOKUP function is another function used for data extraction. It locates content in Excel table cells by searching for cells with the specified range. This search method determines if a particular value appears more than once. In addition, it helps parse data into similar categories. The XLOOKUP function is similar to VLOOKUP but has more flexibility. It allows the user to perform advanced operations and search across many columns. Rounding is another common function used for approximation. It can be used to reduce long decimal numbers to smaller fractional numbers. It can also be used to round currency values. Microsoft Excel offers different rounding functions, including ROUNDDOWN. The functions are explained with examples. You may want to use these functions as they are often helpful in specific applications. Learning about Excel functions is essential before implementing them into your spreadsheet.

Functions to search data in a specific column

The VLOOKUP function in Microsoft Excel is a powerful tool for finding information in a table's cells. The search range and syntax determine whether a particular cell contains an exact or approximate match. Statisticians and engineers use these functions to draw insights from spreadsheet data. XLOOKUP is similar to VLOOKUP but offers greater flexibility. Here's how to search data in a specific column using the two functions. VLOOKUP searches data in a specific column by performing a vertical lookup in the leftmost column. For instance, if you are working with a budget for home supplies, you can use VLOOKUP to find the serial number for any item in the same row. This function allows it to manipulate data using Excel's functions rather than the usual formulas. Functions are more accurate and productive than formulas and will allow you to analyze data more quickly. EXACT (text1, text2) will compare two text strings and then return TRUE if the values are identical. Otherwise, it returns FALSE if they are not identical. The EXACT function is often used to perform complex tasks but isn't used alone. For example, the EXACT function can search for data in a specific column. However, a similar search in a different column requires using the EQ function. VLOOKUP is the most commonly used function in Microsoft Excel. It searches one or more columns for data, while IFNA searches only one. The VLOOKUP function is a powerful tool that can also return #N/A. The IFERROR function, which searches multiple columns, will be used when the function fails. However, the VLOOKUP function is still more powerful than INDEX, but it can sometimes return an error message.

Engineering Analysis with Numerical Solutions

A literature review of the application of spreadsheets in engineering fields reveals several examples. The spreadsheets were used for different individual applicants but are equally effective in implementing numerical solutions for physical problems. This paper demonstrates how to use Excel as an engineering tool to solve problems. It uses its facilities to calculate integrals and derivatives, which are mathematical operations commonly used in engineering software. Students can perform central differences, calculus, and other analysis procedures using an Excel spreadsheet. This textbook is filled with examples and includes over 100 end-of-chapter problems. It is ideal for graduate and undergraduate courses and does not require programming knowledge. It also allows practitioners to conduct most calculations using their familiar spreadsheet package. The corresponding textbook is a helpful resource for students and researchers in engineering and science fields. This text demonstrates using Microsoft Excel to solve complex engineering problems and create parametric reports. Although Excel provides several functions for analysis, these tools do not always meet the requirements of scientific applications. However, some features are essential for engineers. For instance, DIAdem provides hundreds of calculations for engineering and scientific analysis. Furthermore, these functions can be customized and used without programming, providing full previews. In addition, there is a framework for developing domain-specific calculations, which is extremely useful for engineers.

In addition to its many capabilities, Excel includes the CONVERT function that allows users to convert complex units from one type to another. This feature is especially useful in engineering, where the units are often converted to another. Named Ranges, meanwhile, eliminate the pain of working with Excel cell references. The Excel spreadsheet can also be customized to meet your specific engineering needs. So, start analyzing and creating numerical solutions with Excel today!

11 How Can Business and Management Use Microsoft Excel?

Advanced Excel training can increase employee productivity. Highly-trained employees will finish their tasks faster, offer better customer service, and produce more work in less time. Moreover, advanced Excel training can save up to half an hour per employee, which translates to many extra staff hours a week. And when it comes to the business world, this amount is no joke. So how does advanced Excel training benefit you? Read on to learn more.

People management

One of the most actual applications of Excel in the company is managing people. Employees, clients, sponsors, or training participants may all be organized in MS Excel. Personal data may be saved and accessed effectively with Excel. For example, a spreadsheet row or column may include an individual's name, email address, employee start date, purchases, subscription status, and last contact. In business and management, Microsoft Excel can help you manage huge amounts of data, including human resources functions. With a human resources tool such as Excel, you can record employee data, including their work hours, vacation time, and even their subscription status. The human resources tool also helps you stay on top of your day-to-day tasks and keep track of turnover. In addition, you can use the program to track employee information, such as birthdays and other important dates. When it comes to the day-to-day operations of any business, nothing is more important than people. And the most challenging thing to manage is people. You can't afford to be mediocre in this area. That's why you need to know how to handle people well and keep them happy. You can create pivot tables, understand customer and sales data, and analyze employee costs and productivity.

Office administration project management

You may not realize it, but Microsoft Excel is an excellent tool for office administration. Not only is it useful for project management, but it also supports invoicing, paying bills, and contacting clients and suppliers. It is the all-purpose tool you need to manage all office aspects. You can use Excel to manage your office activities, whether you are an administrative assistant, administrator officer, or supervisor. Here are some tips if you want to use them for project management. Excel is a powerful tool for complicated things but can also be prone to errors. While several tools manage projects, Excel remains a popular choice in most industries. While it may have some limitations, it is universally accessible in organizations using Microsoft Office. You might need to import or export data from other tools depending on your needs. Be sure to know the compatibility of Excel with other tools before you start working. In addition to combining Microsoft Office apps with Excel, MS Project is an excellent tool for contract administrators. Contract management templates are easily customizable and allow you to record contract details in a simple, no-fuss manner. You can even customize the templates to suit a particular contract lifecycle stage. Account managers, in particular, should be skilled in Excel since they deal with customers' records. A simple template for this can save you a lot of time and effort.

Accounts management

You may have heard about its capabilities if you're interested in using Microsoft Excel for business management and accounting. This tool allows you to create charts of accounts and manage your financial data. You can add any number of accounts to your chart of accounts and create them in one convenient location. Accounts management in Microsoft Excel is an essential part of any business. However, it can be challenging to manage your accounts correctly without the right tools.

The software comes with various pre-built templates for financial records, including balance sheets, accounts payable, and accounts receivable. There are also specialized templates available for purchase and download from third-party vendors. In addition to pre-filled spreadsheets, you can also create your accounting templates. To get started, download free accounting templates and create the financial reports you need. Whether you need a simple balance sheet, a detailed balance sheet, or a detailed accounting report, Excel can make the process a breeze. With the help of an Excel add-on, you can create graphs of historical data. In addition, you can perform complex mathematical calculations. You can also use the data in Excel to make business decisions. This tool is the preferred choice for many business owners. Microsoft Excel also offers several features that make it ideal for business accounting. This includes graphs and pre-made templates for the most common accounting functions. Excel is an efficient tool for handling people's information. You can create spreadsheets with personal details such as name, email, start date, last contact, and more. Using Excel, you can manage people by keeping track of their transactions. A column can include information about individual employees, clients, and suppliers. Excel can even track critical dates and schedules. So, you'll never have to worry about not getting the data you need for strategic analysis.

Projections and forecasting

A financial business forecast relies on a method known as forecasting, which involves predicting future sales based on historical data. This allows business owners to calculate other factors such as overhead expenses and staffing. The first step in using a forecast is to choose the appropriate historical data. Most businesses will select three to five years' worth of sales data. After choosing the necessary data, adjust the variables that drive the forecast calculation. The forecast sheet will then appear in a new worksheet. Financial projections can be prepared in Microsoft Excel using the Exl-Plan template. These templates can be customized to include the name of the business, starting date, minimum monthly amount, and other factors. In addition to preparing financial forecasts, these templates can also be used for budgeting and business planning. These tools also contribute substantial spreadsheet know-how. You can download the free trial versions of these programs for a limited period to see how they work.

Financial projections are often inaccurate and must be adjusted based on actual information. However, good planning begins with realistic expectations, and Microsoft Excel is an essential tool for this purpose. Excel's powerful data visualization capabilities and useful insights guide management. Excel-based forecasting tools can help you see the road ahead and avoid pitfalls. And with the right data, the Excel tool can be used to model financial scenarios, making it easier to manage your business. While small business owners might not be in the market to secure bank loans or attract investors, they can still use financial projections to chart their growth potential and create budgets. Financial projections help a business survive and thrive. No matter your business type, Excel can help you with your financial management. And whether you are in the beginning stages or have been in business for years, financial projections are an essential part of any business plan.

12 Most Helpful Formulas

FIND

The FIND function is used to locate where a given text substring occurs within another string or range of text strings. The answer is returned as a number signifying the position at which the first character of the string occurs. That sounds a bit complicated in theory, so let's look at a practical example.

If the string of text "Microsoft Excel" is in cell A1, and we wish to know how far into that string the word "Excel" begins, we can use the function:

=FIND("Excel", A1)

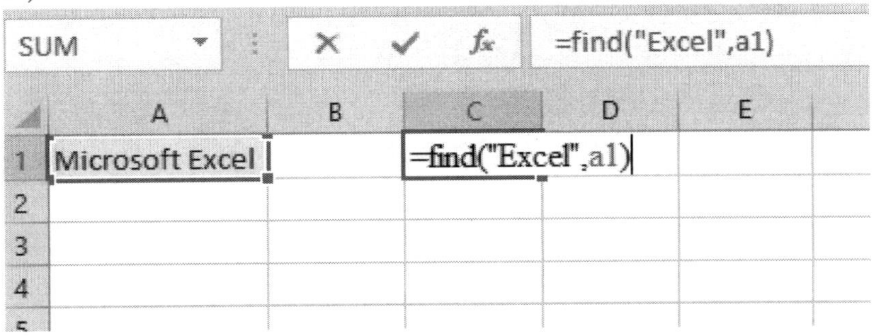

Image 122: The FIND formula in action

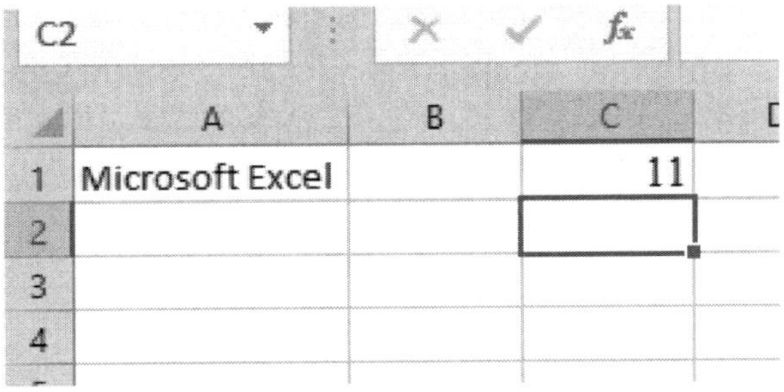

Image 123: The FIND Formula results

This will return an answer of 11. This means that the "E" at the beginning of "Excel" is the 11th character in the string of text "Microsoft Excel."

The FIND has a general structure during its use as shown below:

=FIND(find_text, within_text, starting_position)

The first argument, find_text, is the substring we are searching for. The within_text argument denotes the larger string of text throughout which we are searching. The final argument, starting_position, is optional, hence its omission from the earlier example. This argument allows you to choose where in the string you would like to search from. For example:

=FIND("o", A1, 6)

This function would skip the first "o" present in the string "Microsoft Excel" by beginning its search at the 6th character and would return a value of 7, signifying the position of the next "o" as the 7th character.

It is important to note that the FIND function is also the case- and punctuation-sensitive. Therefore, not only must your search criteria be appropriately capitalized and punctuated, but you must also remain mindful that spaces will be included in the character count.

HYPERLINK

As expected, the HYPERLINK function enables you to embed clickable links in your Excel worksheet. This can be useful if you are referencing external data and must declare your source. The structure for the use of this function is:

=HYPERLINK(link_location, link_name)

The link_location argument should contain the URL for the website that you wish to include. The link_name is an optional argument, but I recommend its use as it enables you to include a shorter clickable title on the embedded hyperlink.

For instance,

"http://www.websitename.com/a_really_long_link_with_lots_of_numbers123456789_and_symbols%#:~:%.pdf" is a long and unwieldy title to include in a single cell. We can instead include this link and call it "Click Here For More Info" using:

=HYPERLINK("http://www.websitename.com/a_really_long_link_with_lots_of_numbers123456789_and_symbols%#:~:%.pdf", "Click Here For More Info")

This will present the link much more tidily and explain to external readers why the link has been included.

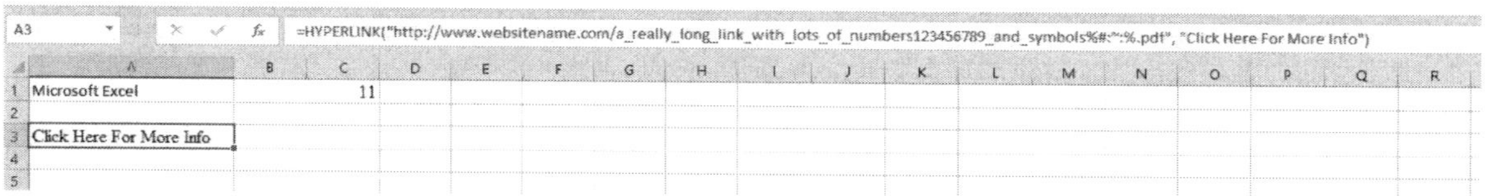

Image 124: HYPERLINK formula

IF()

It is common to use this function when it is essential to sort data following a specified logic setup. This is the most beneficial aspect of the IF formula since it enables you to include formulas and functions inside the formula itself.

- =IF (C2<D3, 'TRUE,' 'FALSE') is an example.

Comparing the two numbers can determine if the value at C2 is less than the value at D3. Ideally, the cell value should be TRUE if the logic is accurate; otherwise, the cell value should be FALSE.

IF functions have two potential outcomes: the value assigned if the test returns as true and the value assigned if the test returns as false. Therefore, their general structure is:

=IF(logical_test, value_if_true, value_if_false)

These kinds of functions can be applied to many situations. For instance, if you are tracking your diet and exercise in an Excel worksheet, you may wish to allow yourself 10% more calories on the days you exercise for an hour or more. The function of your daily caloric allowance might look like this:

=IF(Exercise>59, AvgAllowance*1.1, AvgAllowance)

Suppose functions can also be combined to create more complex logical tests. For example, we may wish to increase your daily caloric allowance by 15% if you exercised for an hour or more at the gym, wish to increase it by 10% if you exercised for an hour or more at home, or increase it by 5% if you completed any form of exercise for less than an hour. These more complex functions will be covered in a later chapter.

LOOKUP

The LOOKUP function searches a row or a column for a value that matches its search criteria. Before using this function, it is advised that you sort your data into ascending order, as described later in this chapter. For now, let us look at the LOOKUP function's structure:

=LOOKUP(lookup_value, lookup_vector, result_vector)

The lookup_value gives the information for which we are searching. This can be a number, a string of text, a cell reference, etc. The lookup_vector argument should contain the data that we wish to search. This data can only be one-dimensional, i.e., spread across a single row or column and composed entirely of neighboring cells. The result_vector is an optional argument and denotes the list of data from which we would like to pull our return value. For instance, if we are looking up Seán's monthly sales, we would search the employee column for Seán's name but would wish to return a value from the monthly sales column. It is important to note that the result vector should be the same length as the lookup vector for the function to operate.

This is possible if you wish to search a two-dimensional range of cells using the LOOKUP function, but the arguments are slightly different.

=LOOKUP(lookup_value, array)

When searching a range of cells across a selection of rows and columns, it is impossible to specify a separate return array. Therefore, the resulting value will be present in the last cell of the same row or column as the discovered lookup value.

HOOKUP

HLOOKUP is for Horizontal Query, and you can use it in obtaining data from a given database by scanning a row to identify any matching data and then print the results coming from relevant column. HLOOKUP checks for a certain value within a row, while VLOOKUP checks for a certain value within a column.

Formula: **=HLOOKUP(value to look up, table area, row number)**

LOWER

The LOWER function converts a given text string to its strictly lowercase version. This can be useful for data commonly presented all in lowercase, such as email addresses. The structure for using this function is quite simple as it only has one argument, the string of text in question.

=LOWER(text)

Since the LOWER function deals exclusively with text, numerical characters and punctuation will remain unaffected by its application. Therefore, you need not fear receiving an error code if your text argument includes numbers and punctuation; the function will simply ignore them.

MATCH

The MATCH function is similar to FIND function in that it searches for a given value and returns its position. However, unlike the FIND function, MATCH does not search a single cell or string of text. Instead, it searches a range of cells, or "array." The structure for the use of the MATCH function is:

=MATCH(lookup_value, lookup_array, match_type)

The lookup_value argument is, of course, the criteria that we are searching for. In a list of groceries, this might be "bananas." The lookup_array is the range of cells we wish to search for our lookup_value, e.g., A: A, which denotes all of column A. The match_type argument is optional and has three potential values. This is another area in which the MATCH function operates differently to FIND. When the match type is set to equal one, if the function cannot locate an exact match to lookup value, it returns the position of the closest match below the lookup value. When you use this option, please ensure that the range of cells being searched is sorted in ascending order, as this will impact what is decided to be the closest match. This is the match type that the function will default to when the argument is omitted, so it is best to sort your list anyway. How to do this is covered later in this chapter.

If the match type argument is set to equal zero, an error will be returned if an exact match cannot be found. This is the only match type in which the search array's order is irrelevant. If the match type is set to equal -1, the function will return the closest match above the lookup value. Therefore, the array of cells being searched should be in descending order.

PROPER

The PROPER function is used to capitalize the first letter in each word in a string of text. Businesses often use this to ensure that their customer names are appropriately capitalized before any communications are sent. For example:

=PROPER("john a. smith")

This function will return "John A. Smith." More commonly, the argument for the PROPER function is a cell reference. This will allow the function to be dragged and copied along entire sections of the worksheet.

PROPER also converts all other letters in the text string to lowercase, so the common internet-joke typing style of capitalizing every second alphabetic character, such as in "aRe YoU oKaY?" can be easily converted to "Are You Okay?"

However, one issue to keep in mind is that Excel reads any letter occurring after an apostrophe (') as the start of a new word. This is great if you are trying to capitalize Irish and Scottish last names like O'Hara, but not so ideal if the text in question reads, "Mike'S Butchers." So, when using the PROPER function, tread carefully where apostrophes are concerned.

SUBSTITUTE

The SUBSTITUTE function replaces text string(s). This is regularly useful if the data imported from an external source is in an incompatible format for the operations we have in mind. The structure for using this function is:

=SUBSTITUTE(text, old_text, new_text, instance_num)

The text argument refers to the cell or range of cells in question. The old_text argument is obviously the text string we wish to replace. As with all text strings used as part of a function, ensure that you surround this argument with quotation marks during use. The new_text is the replacement text that we wish to substitute in place of the old text. The instance_num is the only optional argument in this function. It can specify a specific occurrence of the old_text argument we wish to replace, e.g., "1" would cause the function only to replace the first instance in which the old text occurs. If this argument is omitted, it is assumed that we wish to replace *all* instances of the old text.

Remember that the SUBSTITUTE function *is* case-sensitive, so replacements will only be implemented where the old text is the same as the old_text argument.

UPPER

Like its LOWER counterpart, UPPER converts a string of text to contain capital or uppercase letters entirely. For instance:

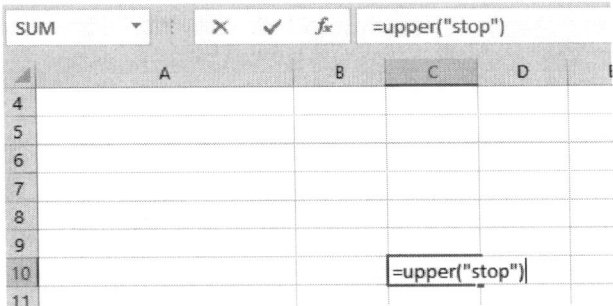

Image 125: UPPER formula in action

=UPPER("stop")

This function will return the word "STOP" entirely in capital letters. More commonly, the function's argument references a cell in which a text string is contained rather than the text itself.

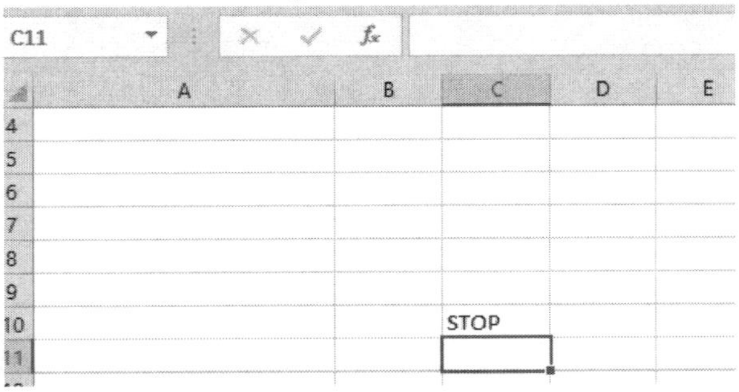

Image 126: UPPER formula results

Remember that the UPPER function deals solely with text and, therefore, will ignore numbers and punctuation present within the text argument in question.

EXACT

The EXACT function compares two or more strings of text. Imagine, for instance, that a business wants to compare the address of a customer entered into a mailing list with that pulled from a database. The EXACT function might be used. The name of this function is not an exaggeration; it will only match text strings that are the same, meaning that it is sensitive to case, punctuation, and spacing. Therefore, "101 S. Blank St." will return a FALSE response when compared against "101 s blank st," "101 s. Blank St.," or "101 S Blank St." using the EXACT function.

For this reason, EXACT is more commonly used to compare case-sensitive data, such as passwords, or unpunctuated data, such as product or item codes. The structure for the use of this function is a simple one.

=EXACT(text1, text2, text3…)

Each argument can be either a string of text contained by quotation marks or a reference to a given cell.

12.1 Upgraded Function in Excel 2023

Average

The AVERAGE function calculates the average of the cell values in a specified range. For example, to obtain the average total sales, just enter "AVERAGE(C3, C4, C5)," as shown in the sample below.

SUM	▼	:	×	✓	fx	=average(c3,c4,c5)

◢	A	B	C	D	E	F
1			Tax Rate	8%		
2	ITEMS SOLD	UNIT PRICE	QUANTITY	LINE TOTAL	SALES TAX	
3	Vegetables	2.99	10	29.9	2.392	
4	Fruits	2.77	21	58.17	4.6536	
5	Fish	1.99	23	45.77	3.6616	
6	Turkey	1.76	13	22.88	1.8304	
7	Chicken	2.49	22	54.78	4.3824	
8	Beverages	2.76	26	71.76	5.7408	
9						
10						
11						
12			=average(c3,c4,c5)			

Image 127: Average formula in action

It calculates the average automatically, and you may save the result anywhere you choose.

◢	A	B	C	D	E
1			Tax Rate	8%	
2	ITEMS SOLD	UNIT PRICE	QUANTITY	LINE TOTAL	SALES TAX
3	Vegetables	2.99	10	29.9	2.392
4	Fruits	2.77	21	58.17	4.6536
5	Fish	1.99	23	45.77	3.6616
6	Turkey	1.76	13	22.88	1.8304
7	Chicken	2.49	22	54.78	4.3824
8	Beverages	2.76	26	71.76	5.7408
9					
10					
11					
12			18		
13					

Image 128: Average formula results

Sum

As the title suggests, this function returns the total value in the supplied cell range. It does addition as if it were a mathematical operation. Here's a sample of what I'm referring to:

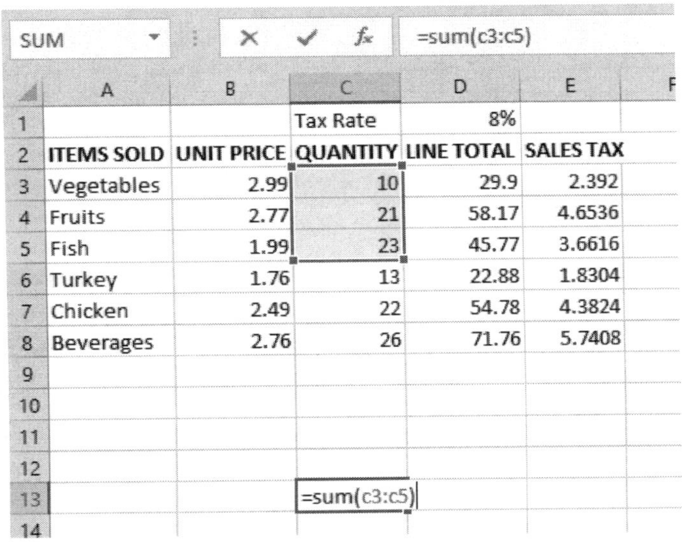

Image 129: SUM formula in action

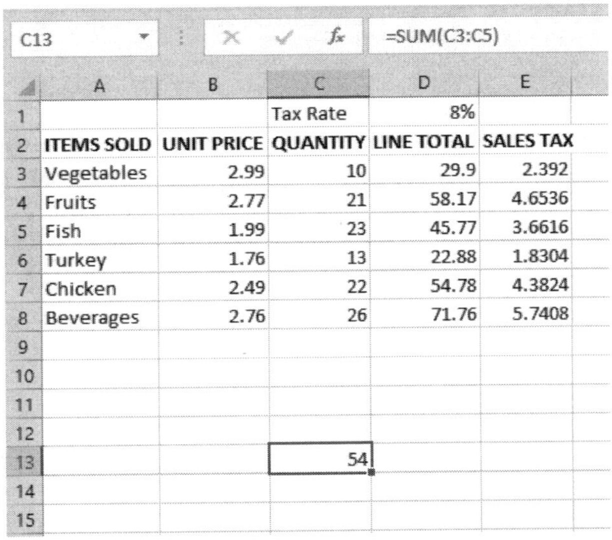

Image 130: SUM formula results

We just wrote in the method "=SUM(C3:C5)" to get the total quantity, as you can see. C13 is where the result is stored.

Subtotal

Let's have a look at how the subtotal method works now. The SUBTOTAL() method returns a database's subtotal. Depending on your needs, you may choose between average, count, total, minimum, maximum, secs, and others. Let's focus on two instances of this.

| SUM | ▼ | : | × | ✓ | fx | =subtotal(1,c3:c8) |

▲	A	B	C	D	E
1			Tax Rate	8%	
2	ITEMS SOLD	UNIT PRICE	QUANTITY	LINE TOTAL	SALES TAX
3	Vegetables	2.99	10	29.9	2.392
4	Fruits	2.77	21	58.17	4.6536
5	Fish	1.99	23	45.77	3.6616
6	Turkey	1.76	13	22.88	1.8304
7	Chicken	2.49	22	54.78	4.3824
8	Beverages	2.76	26	71.76	5.7408
9					
10			=subtotal(1,c3:c8)		

Image 131: Subtotal formula in action

▲	A	B	C	D	E
1			Tax Rate	8%	
2	ITEMS SOLD	UNIT PRICE	QUANTITY	LINE TOTAL	SALES TAX
3	Vegetables	2.99	10	29.9	2.392
4	Fruits	2.77	21	58.17	4.6536
5	Fish	1.99	23	45.77	3.6616
6	Turkey	1.76	13	22.88	1.8304
7	Chicken	2.49	22	54.78	4.3824
8	Beverages	2.76	26	71.76	5.7408
9					
10			19.166667		

Image 132: Subtotal formula results

In the preceding example, we calculated the subtotal on cells spanning from C2 – C8. As you'll see, the method used is "=SUBTOTAL(1, C2: C8)," where "1" refers to the average in the subtotal list. As a result, the method mentioned above will return the mean of C2: C8, with response 19.166667 being put in C10.

"=SUBTOTAL(4, C2: C8)" picks the cell with the highest value between C2 and C8, which is 26. The maximum result is obtained by including "4" in the function.

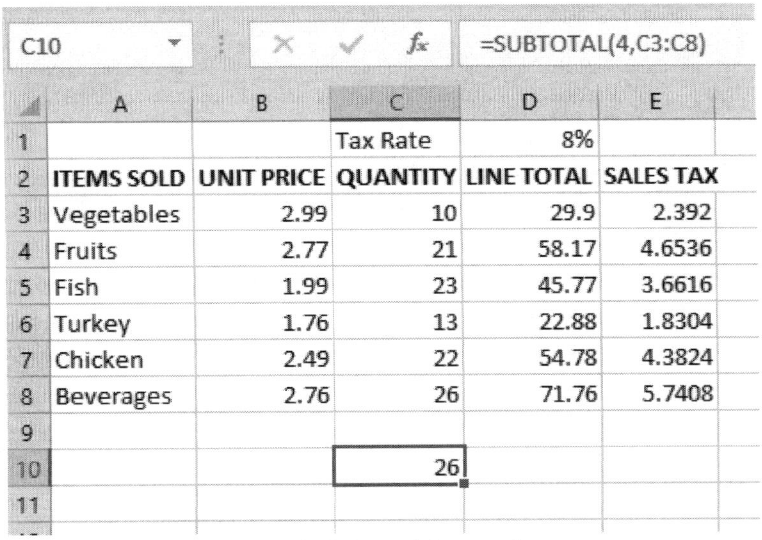

C10		fx	=SUBTOTAL(4,C3:C8)	

	A	B	C	D	E
1			Tax Rate	8%	
2	ITEMS SOLD	UNIT PRICE	QUANTITY	LINE TOTAL	SALES TAX
3	Vegetables	2.99	10	29.9	2.392
4	Fruits	2.77	21	58.17	4.6536
5	Fish	1.99	23	45.77	3.6616
6	Turkey	1.76	13	22.88	1.8304
7	Chicken	2.49	22	54.78	4.3824
8	Beverages	2.76	26	71.76	5.7408
9					
10			26		
11					

Image 133: Subtotal for maximum

Count

This calculates the number of viable cells in a region containing a number. It excludes the empty cells and those that contain data in some other format than numeric.

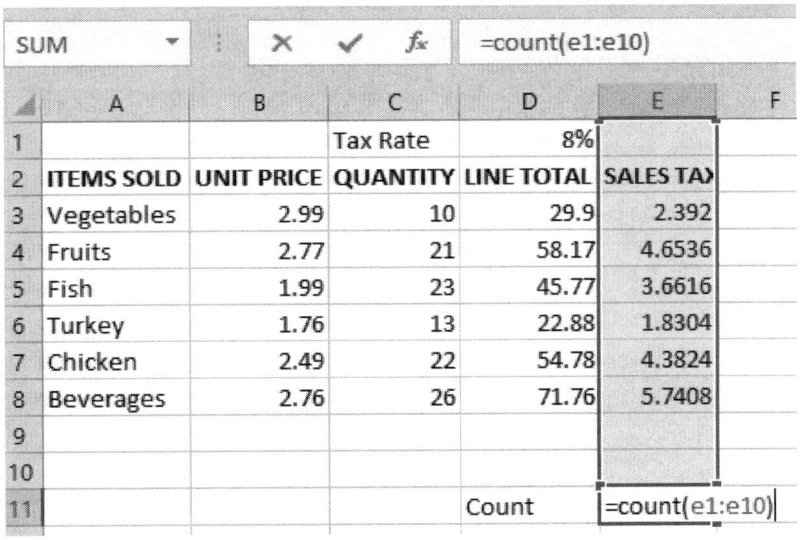

SUM		fx	=count(e1:e10)	

	A	B	C	D	E	F
1			Tax Rate	8%		
2	ITEMS SOLD	UNIT PRICE	QUANTITY	LINE TOTAL	SALES TAX	
3	Vegetables	2.99	10	29.9	2.392	
4	Fruits	2.77	21	58.17	4.6536	
5	Fish	1.99	23	45.77	3.6616	
6	Turkey	1.76	13	22.88	1.8304	
7	Chicken	2.49	22	54.78	4.3824	
8	Beverages	2.76	26	71.76	5.7408	
9						
10						
11				Count	=count(e1:e10)	

Image 134: Count function in action

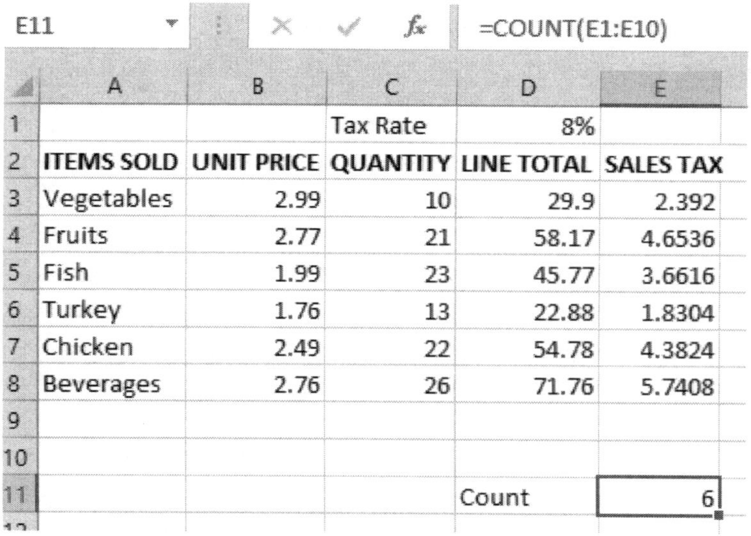

Image 135: Count function results

As you've seen, we're counting from E1 to E10, a total of 10 cells. The result is 6 since the Counts method only examines cells with quantitative data, and the cell with "Sales Tax" is ignored. If you ever need to collect all the cells with numeric values, text, or other data types, use the method 'COUNTA.' COUNTA, but on the other side, it does not include any blank cells in its calculations. COUNTBLANK is a function that counts the number of blank cells in a given cell.

MODULUS

When a divisor subdivides a given integer, the MOD() function returns the residual. Now, for a better understanding, consider the instances below. We divided 10 by 3 in the first case. The remainder is computed using the "=MOD(A2,3)" function. The outcome is saved in B2. We may also use the shortcut "=MOD(10,3)" to get the same result.

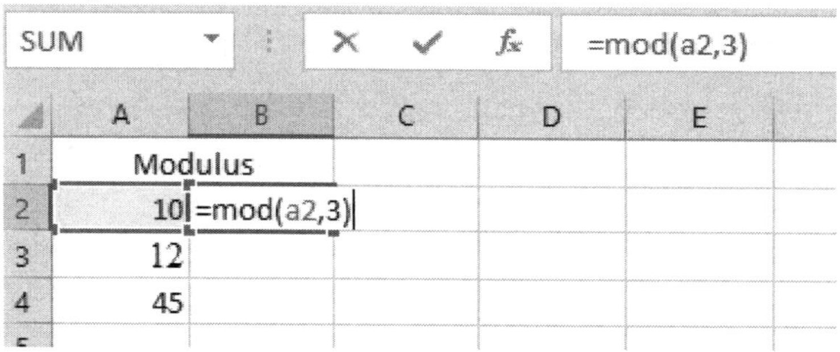

Image 136: Modulus function in action

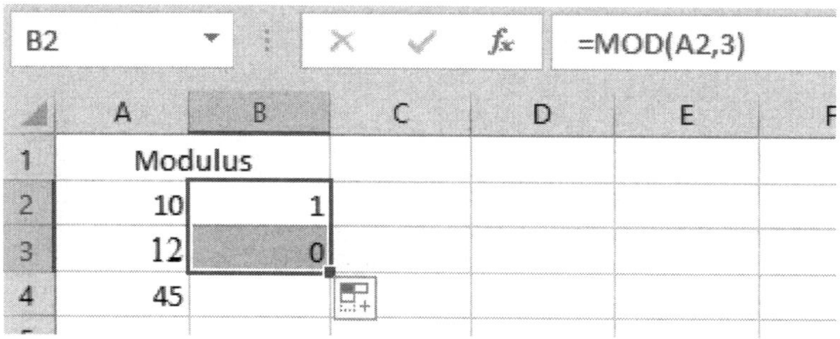

Image 137: Modulus function results

Likewise, we've split 12 by 4 in this case. 0 is remaining, which is saved in B3.

CEILING

Then there's the ceiling function. The CEILING() function takes an integer and rounds it up to the next significant multiple.

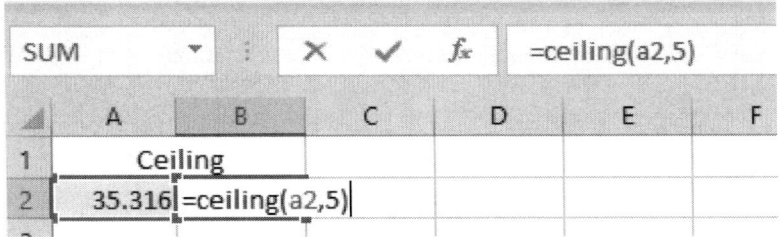

Image 138: Ceiling formula in action

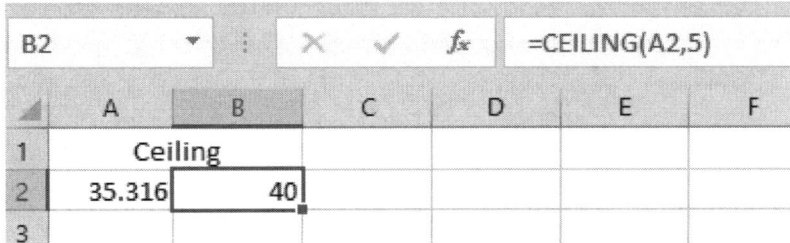

Image 139: Ceiling formula results

For 35.316, the biggest multiple of 5 is 40.

POWER

The "Power()" method produces an output of raising an integer to a given power. Take a look at some of the examples below:

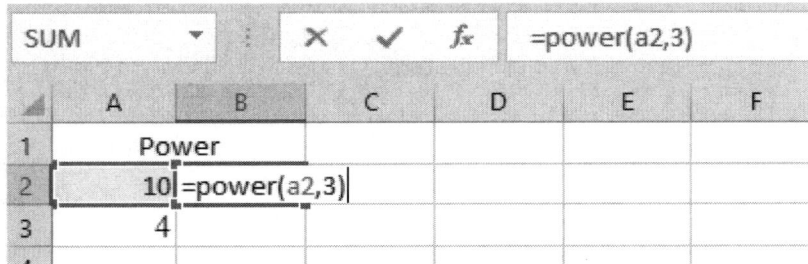

Image 140: The Power formula in action

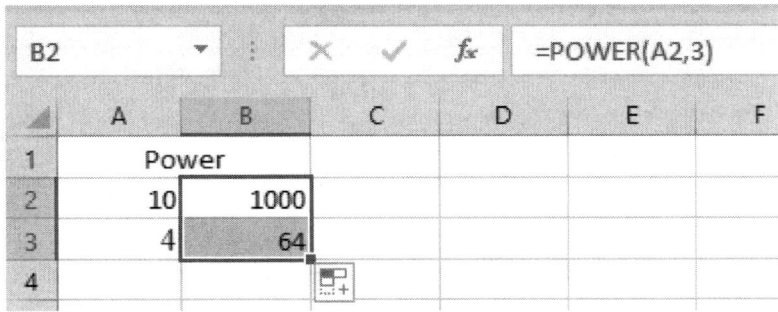

Image 141: Power formula results

As you can see, we need to enter "= POWER (A2,3)" to discover its power of 10 contained in A2 increased to 3. This is how Excel's power function works.

FLOOR

The floor function rounds a given number down to the nearest multiple of significance.

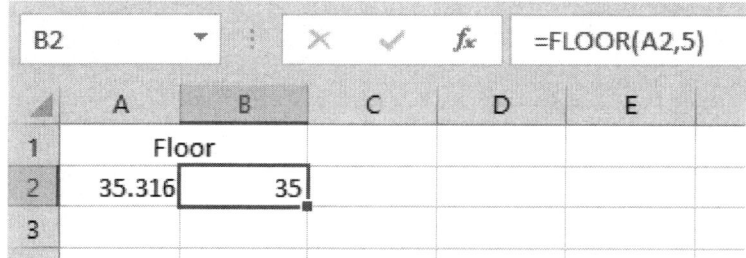

Image 142: Floor formula

Considering 35.316, the minimum multiple of Five is 35.

LEN

LEN() calculates the total quantity of letters in a file. As a result, the whole number of characters, comprising spaces and special characters, will be counted. An illustration of the Len method is shown below.

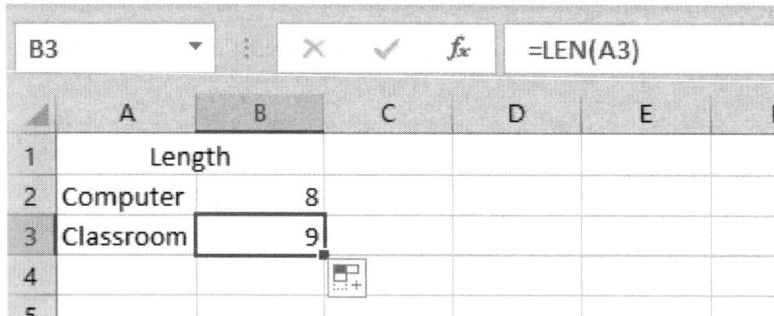

Image 143: LEN formula

CONCATENATE

This method connects or merges several text data into a single string. The many methods for performing this function are listed below.

- We have used the notation =CONCATENATE in this example (A2, " ",B2)

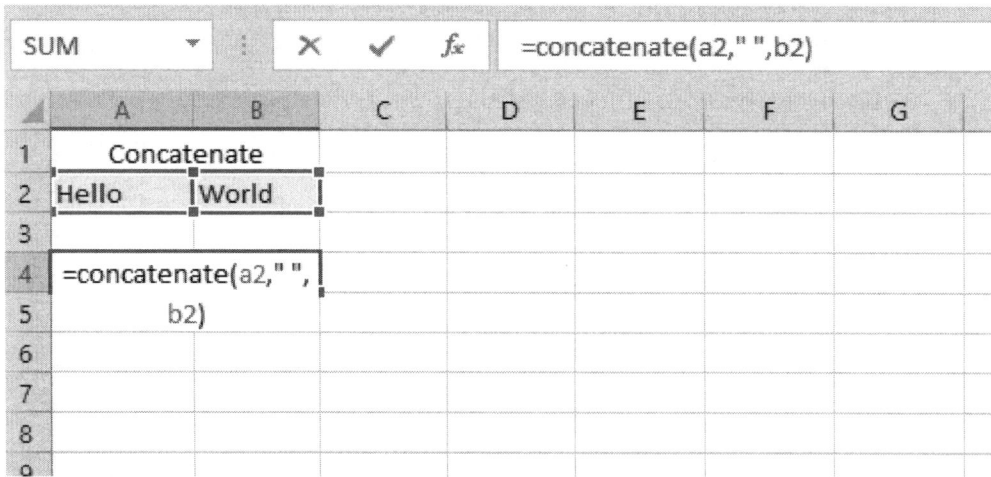

Image 144: Concatenate formula

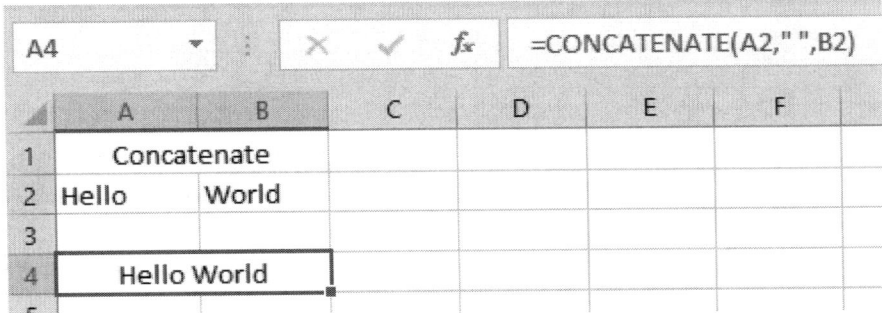

Image 145: Concatenate formula results

- We have used the notation =CONCATENATE in this sample (A2&" "&B2)

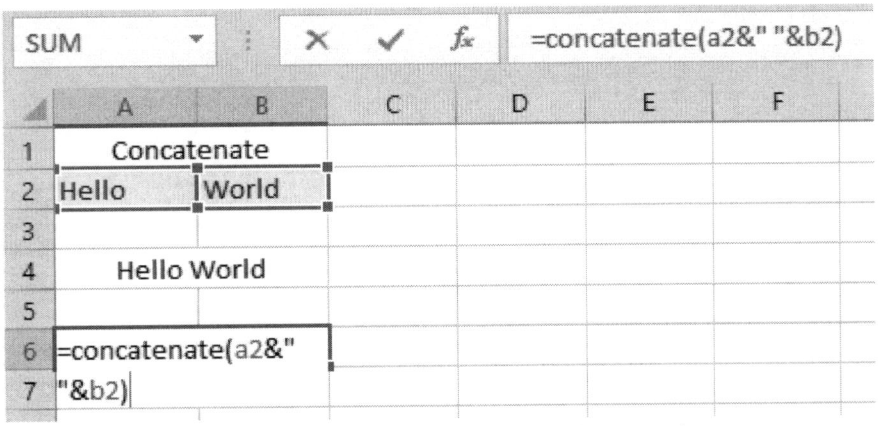

Image 146: Concatenate function using notation

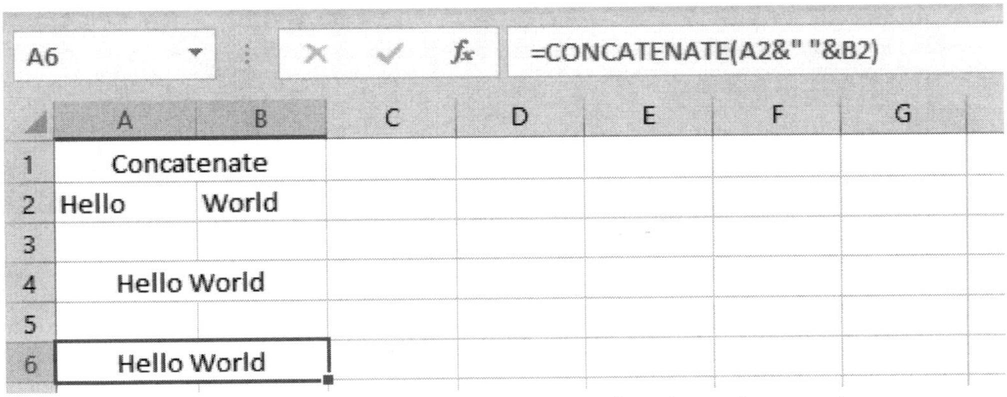

Image 147: Results of using Concatenate function using notation

The concatenation function in Excel may be done in two different ways.

REPLACE

The REPLACE() method replaces a section of a string of text with another text string, as its name implies.

"=REPLACE(old text, start num, num chars, new text)" is the syntax. The index point at which you wish to begin replacing the characters is denoted by start num. The amount of characters you wish to replace is indicated by num chars.

Let's glance at how we can take advantage of this feature.

- By entering "=REPLACE(A15,1,1,"B")" we are substituting A101 with B101.

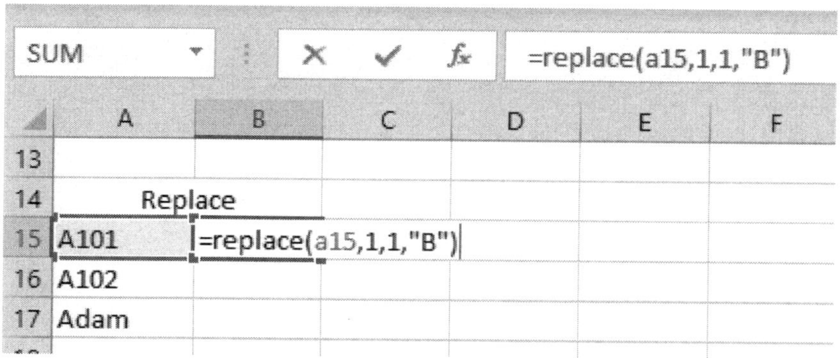

Image 148: Writing the REPLACE formula

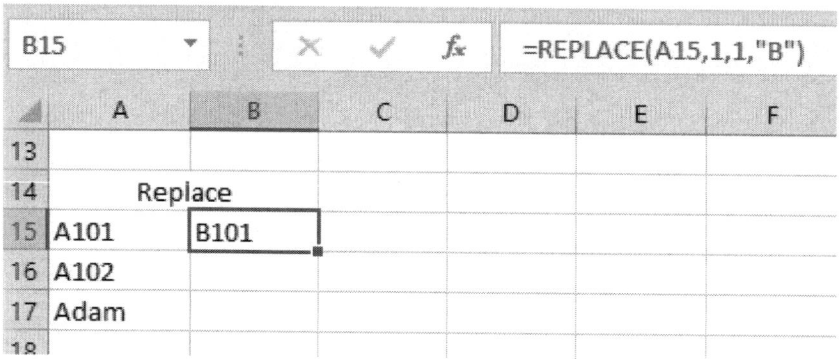

Image 149: Results of the REPLACE formula

- Next, we type "=REPLACE(A16,1,1, "A2")" to replace A102 with A2102.

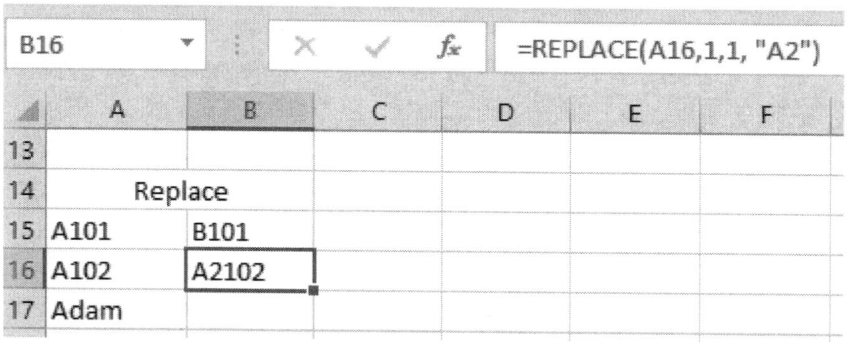

Image 150: Another way of using Replace

- Lastly, we type "=REPLACE(A17,1,2, "Sa")" to replace Adam with Saam.

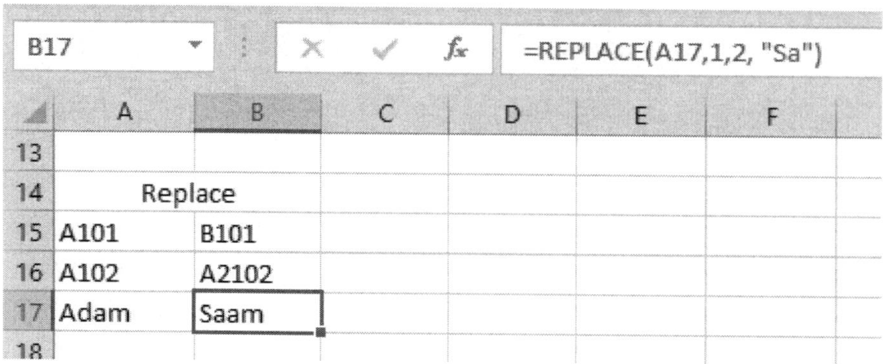

Image 151: Replacing first letter

After all this, we will move toward the following function.

LEFT, RIGHT, MID

The LEFT() method returns the set of characters in a text string starting from the leftmost character. Meanwhile, the MID() method, given a starting location and length, retrieves the words from the center of a text string. Finally, the right() method returns the number of characters remaining after a text string has been terminated.

Let's look at a few instances to comprehend these functions better.

- In the example below, we use the method left to get the leftmost item on the phrase in cell A5.

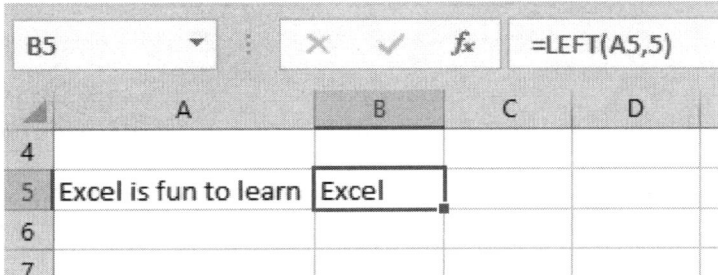

Image 152: LEFT formula

An example of how to use the mid method is shown below.

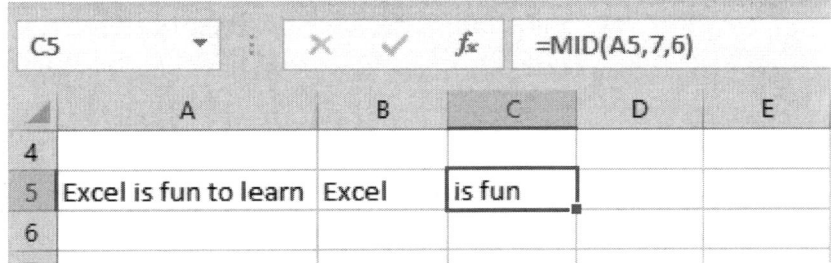

Image 153: MID formula

- Here's an illustration of how to use the correct function.

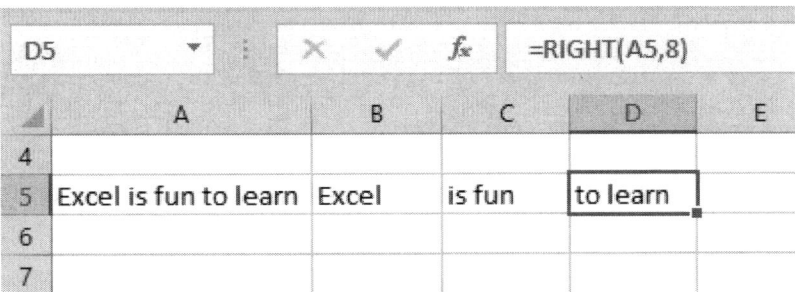

Image 154: RIGHT function

Trimming the Data (TRIM)

With the TRIM function, you can be confident that your routines will not cause errors due to disordered gaps in their input. It ensures that all empty spaces are filled in this manner. While other activities are capable of acting on many cells at the same time, TRIM is limited to working on a single cell, as opposed to other functions that are capable of acting on multiple cells at the same time. The drawback of this method is that it introduces duplicate data into your spreadsheet as a consequence of this.

- =TRIM (text)

Example:

Trim(A2) eliminates any blank spaces from the value in cell A2 by using the TRIM() function.

TODAY ()

The TODAY() method returns the current date and time on the system.

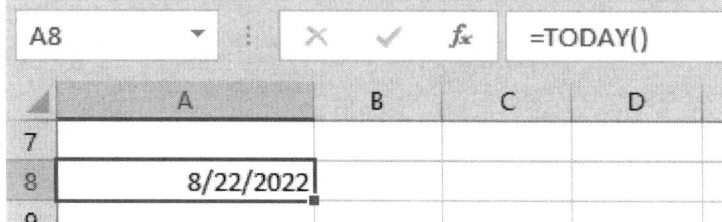

Image 155: Today () function

The DAY() method returns the current month's day of the week. It will be a number ranging from 1 to 31. The start day of the month is January 1, and the end day of the month is December 31.

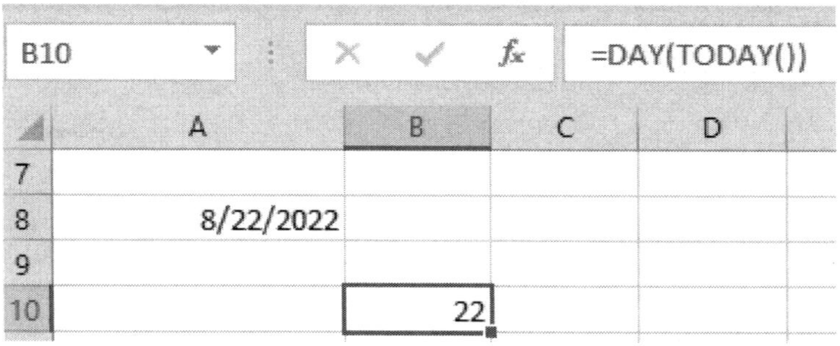

Image 156: The DAY() formula

The month is returned by the method MONTH() as a number between 1 and 12, with 1 representing January and 12 representing December.

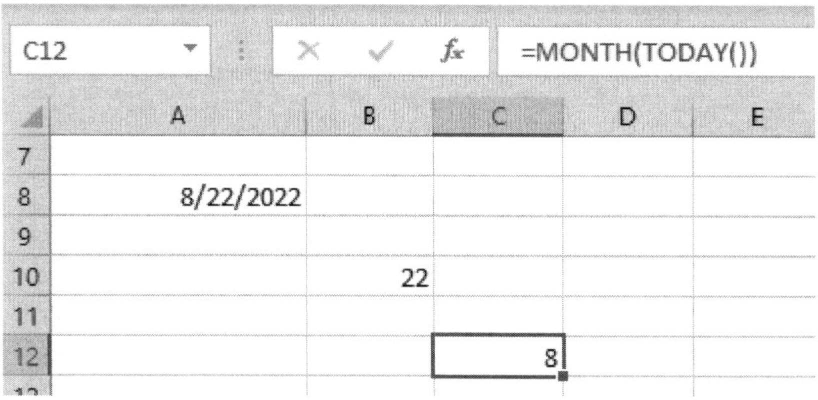

Image 157: The Month() formula

When a date value is provided, the YEAR() method returns the year, as the name implies.

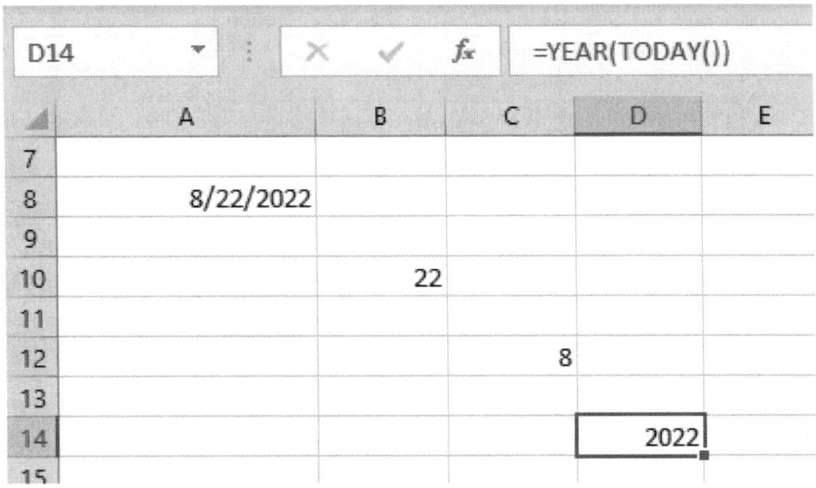

Image 158: The Year() function

DATEDIF

The DATEDIF() method calculates the difference in years, months, or days between two dates by comparing the dates in question.

A DATEDIF function, as seen below, calculates a person's current age from the person's birth date and the date of the current calculation.

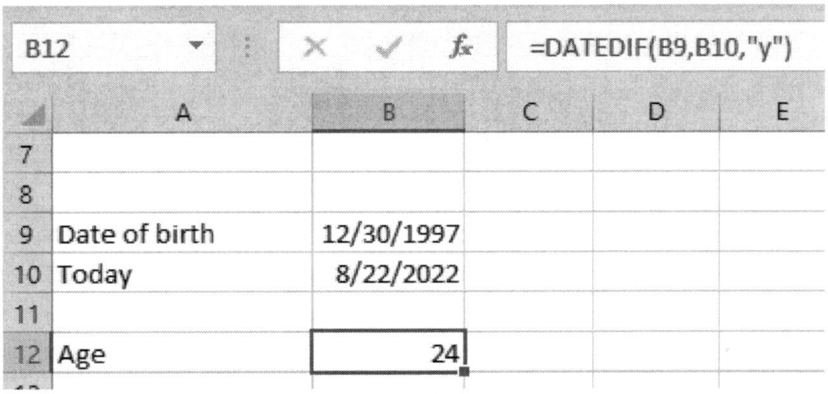

Image 159: DateIF() function

Now, let's look at a few of the essential advanced Excel functions often used to analyze data and generate reports.

VLOOKUP

The VLOOKUP() method is the next subject in this section. This is a vertical lookup function for searching a specific value in the table's leftmost column. The function returns a value from a column in the same row you specified. The following are the parameters of VLOOKUP function:

- The lookup value - It is the value you must search for within the table's first column to complete the operation.

- Table - This displays the name of the table from where you obtain the value.

- Col index - The index of the table column from which you retrieve the value.

- Range lookup – The TRUE = approximate match in the range (default).

- FALSE indicates that there is an exact match.

The VLOOKUP function will be shown with the help of the following table.

	A	B	C	D	E
1	**First Name**	**Last Name**	**Department**	**City**	**Date Hired**
2	Ben	Zamba	HR	Boston	10/11/2015
3	Stuart	Carry	Marketing	Chicago	9/8/2011
4	Jenson	Button	Operations	Ohio	7/3/2017
5	Lucy	Davis	Sales	New York	10/1/2019
6	Trent	Patinson	IT	Kansas	5/4/2020
7	Johnny	Evans	Sales	Houston	2/3/2018
8					

Image 160: Table to use for VLOOKUP

You might use the VLOOKUP function to determine which department Stuart is a member of, as seen in the following example:

Here, 0 represents the range lookup, A11 represents the lookup result, A2:E7 represents the table array, and 3 represents the column index number containing department information.

C11			f_x	=VLOOKUP(A11,A2:E7,3,0)		
	A	B	C	D	E	F
1	**First Name**	**Last Name**	**Department**	**City**	**Date Hired**	
2	Ben	Zamba	HR	Boston	10/11/2015	
3	Stuart	Carry	Marketing	Chicago	9/8/2011	
4	Jenson	Button	Operations	Ohio	7/3/2017	
5	Lucy	Davis	Sales	New York	10/1/2019	
6	Trent	Patinson	IT	Kansas	5/4/2020	
7	Johnny	Evans	Sales	Houston	2/3/2018	
8						
9			Vlookup			
10	**First Name**	**Last Name**	**Department**	**City**	**Date Hired**	
11	Stuart		Marketing			
12						

Image 161: Vlookup function in action

On pressing the Enter key, the program will return the word "Marketing," indicating that Stuart is a member of the marketing department.

HLOOKUP

HLOOKUP(), also known as horizontal lookup, is a function that functions similarly to VLOOKUP(). The HLOOKUP function scans the first row of a table or array of benefits to find a value. Then, it returns the value from a specific row in the same column that has been supplied.

The following are the parameters of the HLOOKUP function:

- This is the value to lookup in the lookup table.

- Table - This is the table where you must extract information.

In this case, the row index specifies the row number from which the data will be fetched. If the match is exact, this value is true; otherwise, it is false. Range lookups are Boolean value that shows whether the match is precise or approximate. The default result is TRUE, which implies that there is a good match in this case. Let's look at how to utilize the HLOOKUP function to locate the city of Jenson in the table above.

	D	E	F	G	H	I	J	K	L	M
=hlookup(H8,G1:M5,4,0)										
				First Name	Ben	Stuart	Jenson	Lucy	Trent	Johnny
				Last Name	Zamba	Carry	Button	Davis	Patinson	Evans
				Department	HR	Marketing	Operation	Sales	IT	Sales
				City	Boston	Chicago	Ohio	New York	Kansas	Houston
				Date Hired	10/11/2015	9/8/2011	7/3/2017	10/1/2019	5/4/2020	2/3/2018
				First Name	Jenson					
				City	=hlookup(H8,G1:M5,4,0)					

Image 162: Hlookup in action

In this example, H8 contains the lookup value, i.e., 4 represents the row index number, Jenson, G1:M5 represents the table array, and 0 represents an approximation match. Once you press the Enter key, the word "Ohio" will appear.

G	H	I	J	K	L	M	N
First Name	Ben	Stuart	Jenson	Lucy	Trent	Johnny	
Last Name	Zamba	Carry	Button	Davis	Patinson	Evans	
Department	HR	Marketing	Operation	Sales	IT	Sales	
City	Boston	Chicago	Ohio	New York	Kansas'	Houston	
Date Hired	10/11/2015	9/8/2011	7/3/2017	10/1/2019	5/4/2020	2/3/2018	
First Name	Jenson						
City	Ohio						

Image 163: Results of Hlookup

INDEX-MATCH

The INDEX-MATCH function matches a value in the left column to a value in the right column. On the other hand, the VLOOKUP function does not allow you to return an assessment from a column to the right. In addition, index-match benefits VLOOKUP in that VLOOKUP demands more processing capacity from Excel.

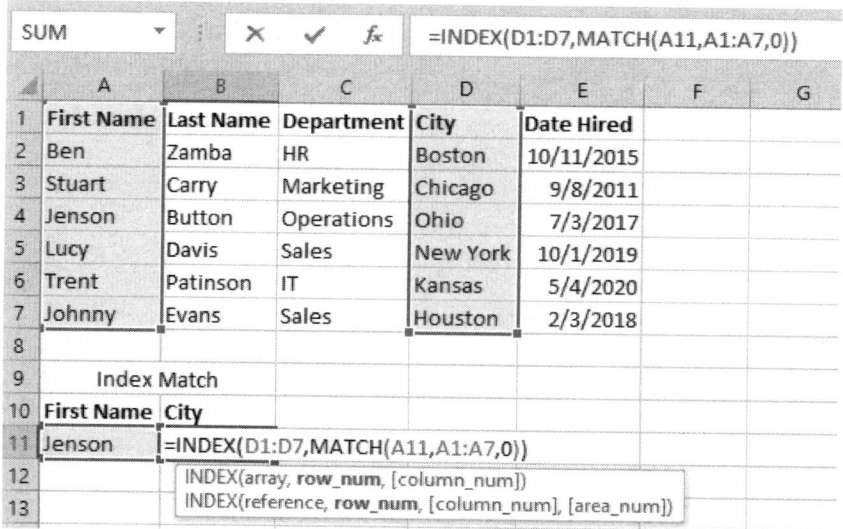

Image 164: INDEX-MATCH function

This is because it must assess the whole table array you picked, which is time-consuming.

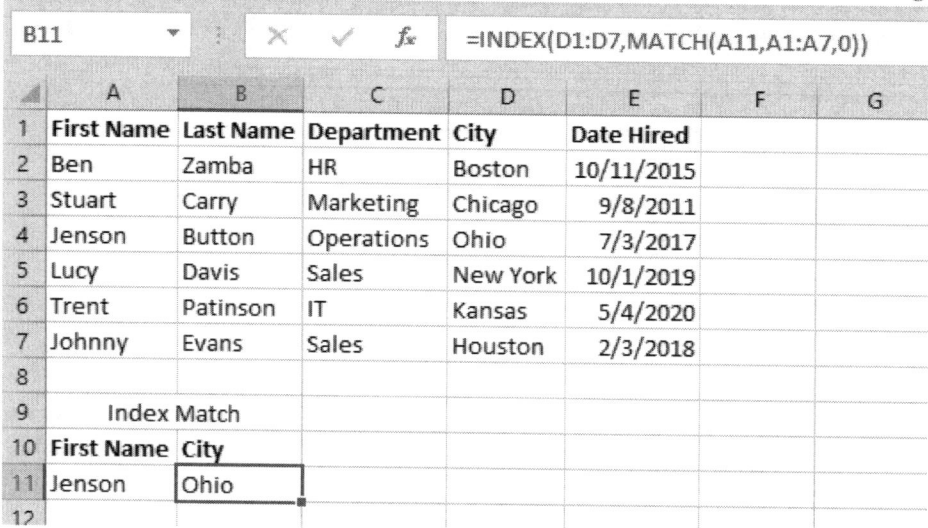

Image 165: Results of INDEX-MATCH function

With the INDEX-MATCH function, Excel has to take into account the return column and the lookup column.

COUNTIF

COUNTIF() is a function that counts the total number of cells in a range that meet a condition. It counts the total number of cells in a range that satisfies a condition.

SUMIF()

SUMIF() is a function that adds cells specified by a criterion or condition to the total.

SUMIFS() is a function that adds the cells indicated by a set of criteria or conditions to the end of a string.

13 Writing Text in Microsoft Excel

To write text in Microsoft Excel, you can take a few steps to format your data. Before entering data, you can format the cells with text or numbers. To format the entire column, you should right-click and select Format Cells on Number tab. Then, on the Home tab, choose Text format. The default text format is Number, so you can change it to another type to make it easier to sort. You can also change a single entry to text format by typing an apostrophe (') in front of the data.

Aligning text to the left

To align text to the left in Microsoft Excel, select the Helper column of the cell you'd like to align. Type the original string in the helper column. If necessary, add leading spaces to it. To calculate the number of spaces to align text, subtract the position of the aligning character from the maximum number of characters before it. Then, click the Align Text button to apply the change. Using the Format Cells dialog box, you can also choose to align numbers and text to the bottom-left corner of cells. First, click on the Align Text or Align Numbers option. Next, select the desired option and then click OK. The options for alignment will change. To align text, you can also adjust the indentation of the cell by using the Format Cells dialog box or the shortcut keys Alt+H.

Formatting text

You're not alone if you're looking to format text in Microsoft Excel. Many people struggle with this task. Fortunately, you can take some easy steps to make your work much easier. You can choose from several preset styles to make formatting your text a breeze. Listed below are a few tips for formatting text in Excel. Once you've learned them, you'll be on your way to writing effective and professional documents in no time. The first step to formatting text in Excel is selecting the text you want to format. Use the font group on the Home tab and click the arrow in the bottom-right corner of the text group. In the Font tab, you can change the font style and color of your text. After you've made your selections, click the "Apply" button to save the changes. You can then format the text by right-clicking the cell.

Checking for errors

One way to detect errors when writing text in Microsoft Excel is to use the IFERROR function. The IFERROR function checks for errors in a VLOOKUP formula and returns user-friendly error text when there is a problem. You can also use the IFNA function to trap #N/A errors if an error is detected. The IF ISNA formula traps only #N/A errors. The warning icon or green triangle in the upper left corner of a cell indicates an error. The error is caused by a faulty formula or a reference to a cell that does not exist. However, some errors are more serious and may even break the fundamental laws of mathematics. An example of an error in a formula is that the column is too narrow to fit the data. If the column width is too small, you can simply resize the column, and the error will go away automatically.

Changing the font type

You can change the font type in Microsoft Excel to any other font you want. The fonts available in Excel typically range from 8 to 72 points, but you can change the size of each font by selecting "Custom." To revert to the default font, you must restart Excel. Otherwise, you can change the font size by clicking "No Formatting."After you change the font, Excel will revert to the default settings for the font used for cell entries. You can change this setting in Excel 2010 without affecting your existing workbooks. Before making a change, you may want to preview the fonts in a worksheet first to ensure they look right. For accessibility purposes, you may want to use a larger font size. Changing the default font is a simple way to add style to your spreadsheet and give it a professional appearance.

Changing the font size

If you're writing text in Microsoft Excel, you may wonder how to change the font size. Excel specifies font size in points equal to 1/72 of an inch. To change the font size, use the toolbar. Next, click the point size tool to the left of the text-attribute tools. From there, select the font size you'd like. Excel will then display a drop-down list of options.

You can also change the font size by using the arrow keys. In the arrows, you can scroll through the font size list and change the size of your text. By increasing the font size, you'll get a bolder font, while decreasing it will result in a smaller font. Changing the font size can be tricky, but if you follow a few simple steps, you'll have no trouble making changes.

Changing the color of the text

The first step to changing the font color in Microsoft Excel is to select the cell in which you want to change the font. On the 'Home' tab, click the 'Font' button. From the dropdown menu, select a font size from the color palette. Click OK to apply the change. You will then be able to select a new font color. Changing text color in Microsoft Excel is easy once you know how.

The next step is selecting the text's color in the cell. Click the Format button in the lower section of the formula, which contains cell A1. Then, click the Font tab, where you can select a color. Click OK to apply the selection. The formatted text in Figure A is now red. In Figure B, you can see the formatted text and formula. After this, click the Font tab again to choose a color for the font.

FUNCTIONS FOR TEXTS IN EXCEL

These functions are used in text data. Their presence in your formula allows Excel to concatenate, switch text cases, find and extract specific parts of the indicated text, etc.

Function to Combine Strings of Text

The **CONCATENATE** function is used for combining multiple strings of texts in Excel. An example is **=CONCATENATE(D1, F1).**

The operator to perform a similar operation is the ampersand (**&**) symbol.

Switching Texts to Sentence Cases

The function **PROPER** is used for this operation. Other functions to switch text cases are the **UPPER** function for capital letters and the **LOWER** function for small letters. Examples are:

=LOWER(A2)

=UPPER(A2)

=PROPER(A2)

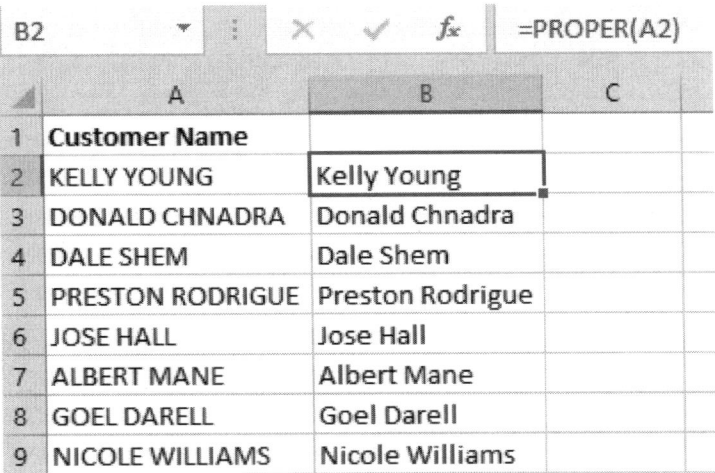

Image 166: Proper function in text

Deleting Excess Spaces in Strings of Text

Excess spaces can be removed from your texts using the **TRIM** function. E.g. **=TRIM(C2)**

Image 167: Trim Function

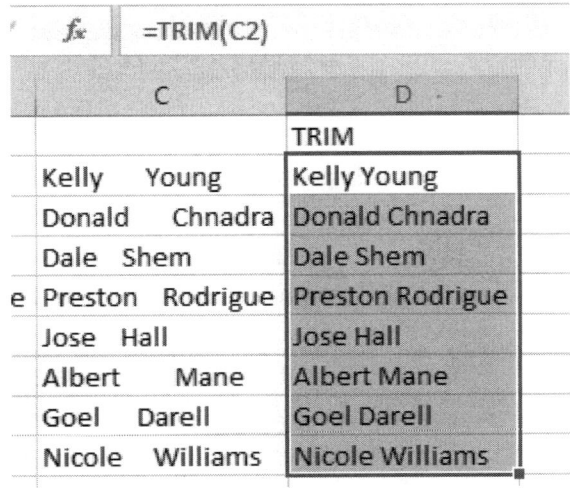

Image 168: Trim results

Discovering Parts of a String of Texts

Various functions are available to extract specific parts of your texts. These include:

- **The LEFT Function**

This function finds characters starting from left side of your text. The syntax for the formula is as follows:

=LEFT(cell_text, num_chars)

cell_text argument denotes the cell holding the text, and **num_chars** denotes the number of characters to be extracted. E.g: **=LEFT(B2,4)**

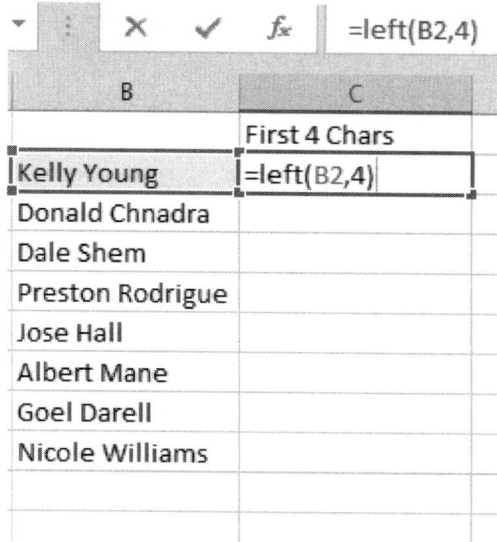

Image 169: Left function for text

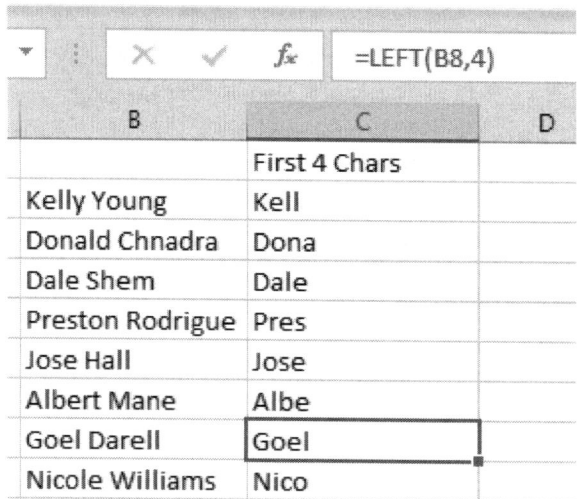

Image 170: The Left Function results

- **The RIGHT Function**

This function finds characters starting from your text's right side. The syntax for the formula is as follows:

=RIGHT(cell_text, num_chars)

E.g: **=RIGHT(B2,4)**

Image 171: Right function in text

- **The MID Function**

This function holds an addition argument to tell Excel where to start and end its extraction operation.

=MID(text, starting_num, num_chars)

E.g: **=MID(B2,6,3)**

This formula above tells Excel to start its extraction from the 6th character and then extract the next three characters.

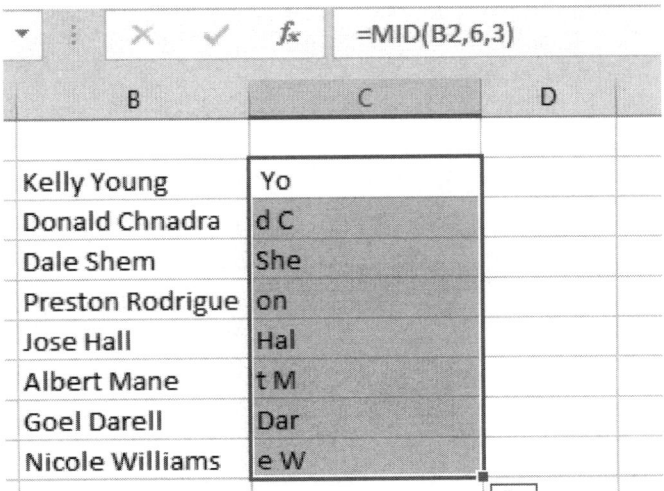

Image 172: MID function in text

Extracting Texts Before and After Particular Characters

The **LEFT/RIGHT** functions and the **SEARCH** function are used as suitable.

For extracting texts before the character, use the following syntax for your function:

=LEFT(cell_text, SEARCH("char", cell_text)-1)

The **char** argument denotes the character to be used as the reference point. Example includes:

=LEFT(C2, SEARCH("-",C2)-1)

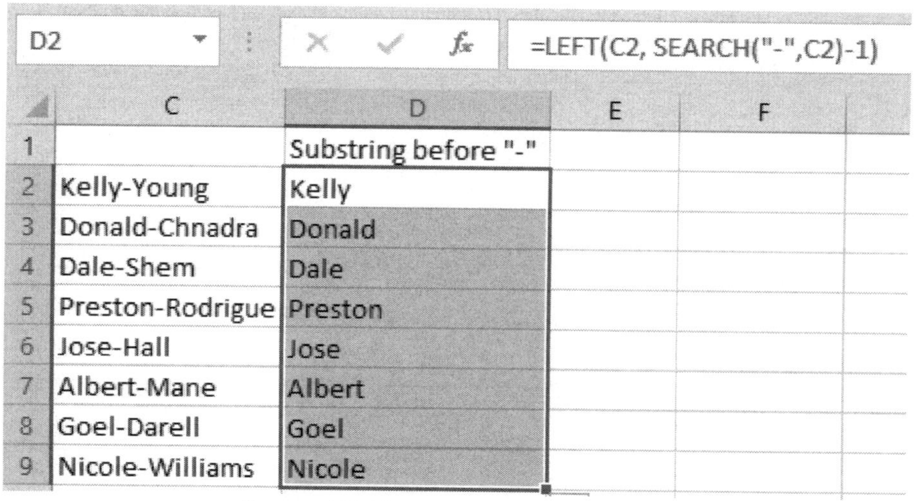

Image 173: Extracting the text before

For extracting texts after the character, use the following syntax for your function:
=RIGHT(cell_text,LEN(cell_text)-SEARCH("char", cell_text)).
Example includes: **=RIGHT(C2,LEN(C2)-SEARCH("-",C2))**

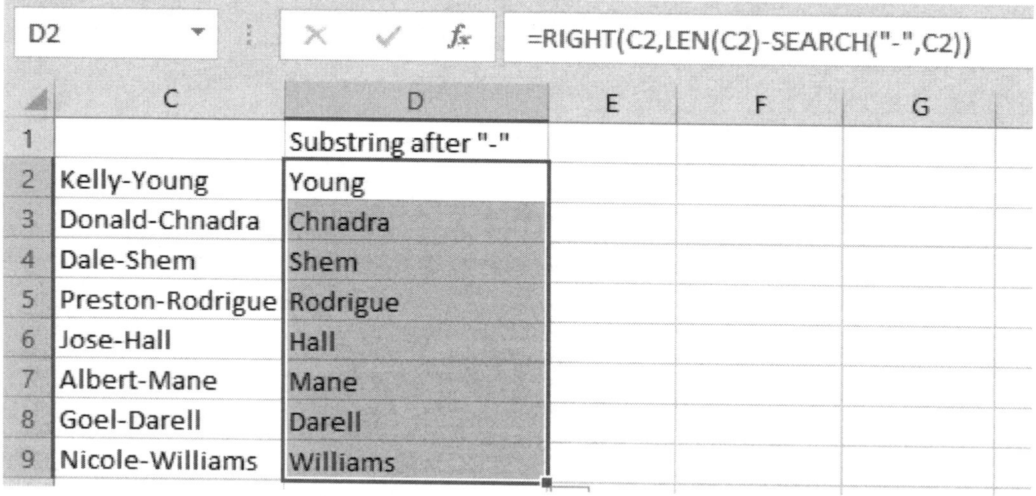

Image 174: Extracting the text after

Searching for Specific Text Characters in a String

The **SEARCH** or **FIND** functions are used for this operation. The syntax is as follows:
=FIND(find_character, within_text) or
=SEARCH(find_character, within_text).

For example: **=FIND("e", "fine")** or **=SEARCH("wash", "carwash")**

Searching for Second Occurrence of Specific Text Characters in a String

This operation uses the **FIND** function. Where the specific character is first found is indicated in the formula. E.g: **=FIND("-","POWER-2-BIG", 7)**

This formula tells Excel to search for the **"-"** character and begin its search from the 7th character since the character is first found in the 6th character.

Replacing Content of Texts

The **SUBSTITUTE** function is applied with the following syntax:
=SUBSTITUTE (cell_text, old_text, replacing_text).

E.g: **=SUBSTITUTE(D5,"c","b").** This formula replaces every "c" character with "b."

If you want only to replace specific characters, you can add another argument to denote this:
E.g: **=SUBSTITUTE(D5,"c","b", 2).** This tells Excel to only replace the second "c" character with "b."

Calculating Number of Times a Given Character Appears in a Certain Text

This operation uses the **LEN** and **SUBSTITUTE** functions. Example includes:
=LEN(D2)-LEN(SUBSTITUTE(D2,"A","")).
This formula calculates the number of times the character **"A"** appears in the text.

Starting Lines of Formulas on New Lines

- Place your mouse blinking cursor at the start of the argument where the new line would begin

- Press key **Alt** and press **Enter**

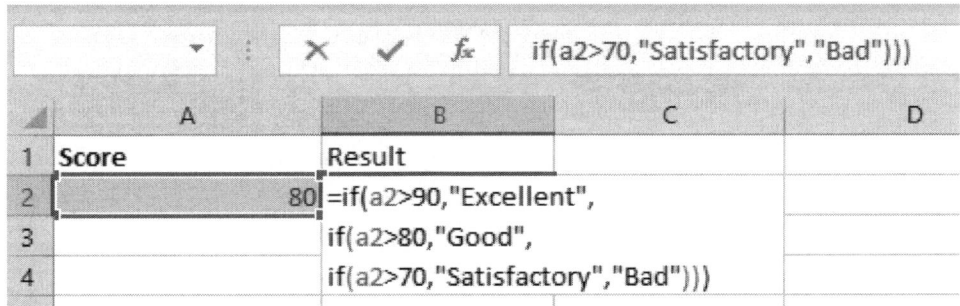

Image 175: New lines in a formula

Erasing Unwanted Characters from Fields for Text

Follow this syntax to clean up unwanted characters in your texts:
=SUBSTITUTE (Cell_Text , "char_to_be_removed", "replace_with").
E.g: **=SUBSTITUTE(D3,"!"," ")**
This formula replaces the "!" character in cell D3 with a space.

Formatting Numbers by Adding Zeros

The **TEXT** function is used in this case. E.g. **=TEXT(B2,"0000000000")**
The dialogue box for customizing numbers can also be used.

- Highlight the cells to be formatted

- Right-click on these cells and select the option to format them

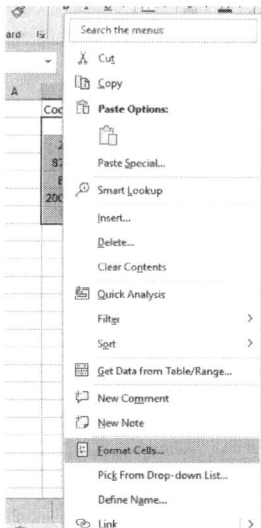

Image 176: Steps for formatting text

- Navigate to the option for **Custom** in the dialogue box

- Type in multiple zeros as desired and select the **OK** button

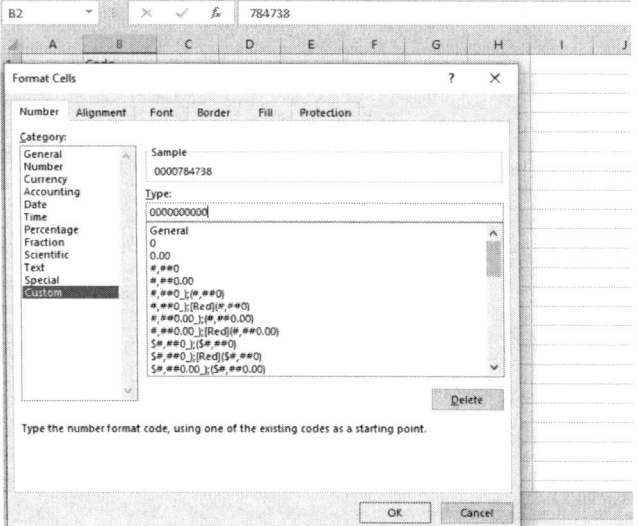

Image 177: Multiple zeros

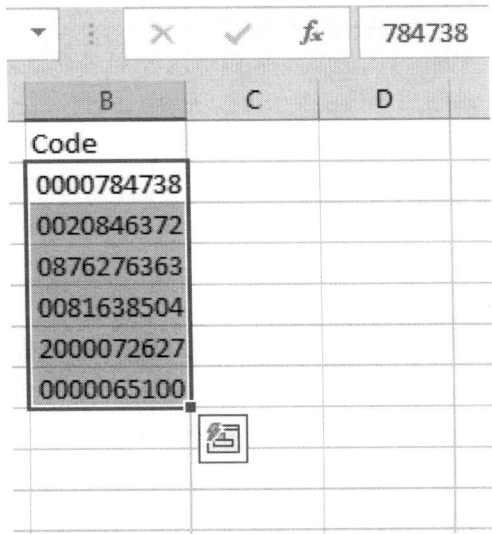

Image 178: Results of adding multiple zeros

Formatting Numeric Values in Strings of Text

This operation includes the concatenation operator and the **TEXT** function for combining text and numeric values. Formatting the numeric values follows the syntax:

=TEXT (cell_reference, required_formatting)

E.g. **=B5&": "&TEXT(C8, "$0,000")**

This formula combines the text in cell B5 and the formatted currency value in cell C8.

Applying the DOLLAR Function

This function changes numeric values to text, as mentioned in the previous section for formatting numbers in texts. Example includes:

=DOLLAR(259.99) that gives a result of **$259.99**

Combined with text, for instance,

="Radio price is "&B6 would give a result of **"Radio price is 99."**

Including the **DOLLAR** function:

="Radio price is "&DOLLAR(B6) would give a result of **"Radio price is $99.00."**

14 Using Images and Shapes in Microsoft Excel

If you're unfamiliar with using Images and Shapes in Microsoft Excel, then you've come to the right place. Learn how to add clip art or shapes to a document, worksheet, or spreadsheet. Using these tools is quick, easy, and will help you make your documents and spreadsheets stand out from the crowd. This section will walk you through the process from beginning to end. Using Images and Shapes in Microsoft Excel will make your documents look stunning and enhance your data entry efforts.

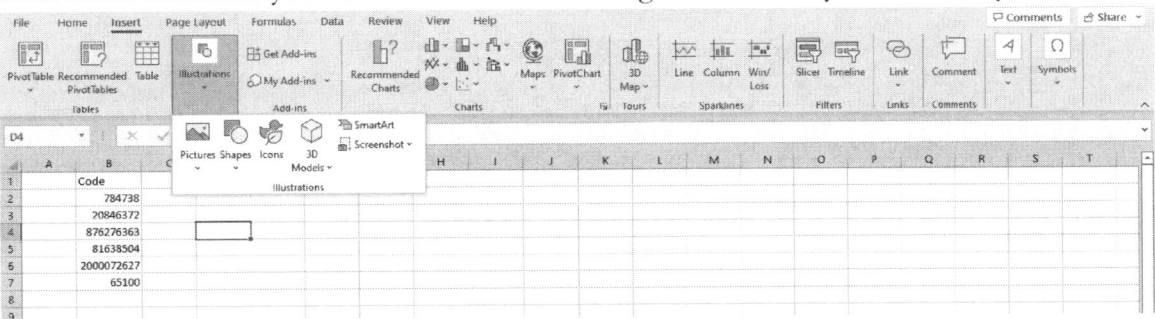

Image 179: Pictures and shapes under Insert tab

Formatting images and shapes in Microsoft Excel

There are several ways to resize and format images and shapes in Microsoft Excel. Most images and shapes move with the cells in the spreadsheet. However, your images and shapes can stay in place by locking their size. To do this, right-click on your object and choose the "Size and Properties" category. The Properties menu is located on the left side of the window. After formatting the objects, you can click the Save button.

Select a picture in your Excel spreadsheet. You will then see a text box over the image. It is possible to alter font, size and color of the text. You may click "Picture" button as well to change the shape's appearance. The task pane also allows you to resize and reposition the object. It will remain centered when you reposition the image.

Adding clip art to a spreadsheet

Adding clip art to a spreadsheet in MS Excel is a simple process, as long as you know how to use the program. The clip art is a collection of readymade illustrations that can be used within Microsoft Office programs. The clip art is divided into several categories, and you can easily insert them into your spreadsheet by using the tool that comes with Microsoft Excel. To insert clip art, simply type the name of the image into the search field and click "Insert." This will show you a list of results, and you can then select the image you want to insert into your document.

There are two ways to insert a picture into your spreadsheet. First, you can insert a picture by dragging it into your spreadsheet or selecting a picture and inserting it. Once you have the picture, you can move it to another location. If you move the picture, you must recreate the link. The second way is to browse the file that contains the picture. In the "File name:" field of the Insert Picture dialog, type the picture's name. Then, choose the option of Paste to paste the picture into the sheet.

Adding a shape to a worksheet

In Microsoft Excel, adding a shape to a worksheet is a fairly straightforward process. To add a shape, select it and right-click it. Then, you can choose from the shape's Styles options to choose a style for your shape. The Intense Effect style will add a shadow to your shape and gives it a 3D look. You can also change the Theme setting to choose a beveled effect instead.

Adding a shape in Microsoft Excel is easy - just select the Insert tab and the Shapes or Illustrations option. You'll then be able to click on the desired shape and drag it to the desired location on the worksheet. Shapes can be tied to cells in the worksheet, updating the text as the worksheet is calculated. They can also be drawn with the mouse pointer. To use shapes in Excel, you need to know that you can add several shapes to a worksheet.

Adding a shape to a document

Adding a shape to a document is an excellent way to add visual appeal and clarity to your work. You can use it to create graphs, charts, and maps and add them to email correspondence or slide shows. Shapes are also great for separating names and addresses. In addition to adding visual appeal, shapes can help you organize your work by making it easier to read. The shapes you can add are called SmartArt graphics, and they can be used in various ways.

You can also use the Shape tool to add text to your shape. You can type text inside a shape and change the font and color to suit your document. You can use the Text tool to add meaningful text when adding text to a shape. You can find text formatting options on the Home tab. In addition, you can lock the drawing mode to resize and position the shape easily.

14.1 Using Smart-Art in Microsoft Excel

If you want to add visual flair to your spreadsheets, you can use SmartArt in Microsoft Excel. Here are some tips and tricks. You can also add text or bullet lists to SmartArt. First, let's take a look. Using SmartArt in Excel is easy once you understand how they work. Once you've mastered the basics, you can start creating your SmartArt! You can even change the look and feel of your SmartArt by adding different shapes.

Adding a shape to a SmartArt

To add a shape to a SmartArt in the text pane, select the graphic. You'll notice two contextual tabs at the bottom of the window. Select the Design tab and click the Add Shape button. This brings up a drop-down gallery of shapes to add to the graphic. Then, you can select a shape and click OK to make it the new default one.

You can also change the colors and styles of your SmartArt graphic. Click the "Change Colors" button on the "SmartArt Tools" ribbon. Hovering over the options gives you an idea of which colors you want. Click OK to commit your changes. Now, you can add text inside the shape or beside the bullets in the pane. You can also change the shape and fill color.

Here is the step-by-step guide:

Go to INSERT tab.

Select illustrations then SmartArt.

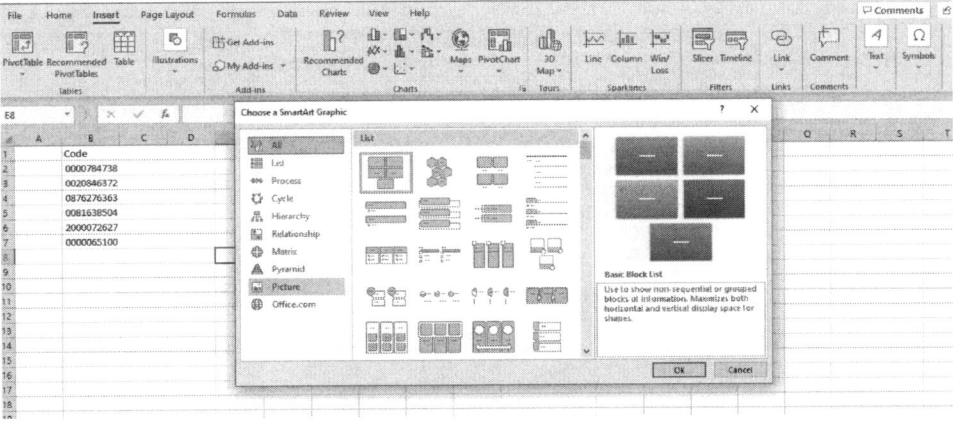

Image 180: SmartArt in Excel

Choose your preference the list then click OK

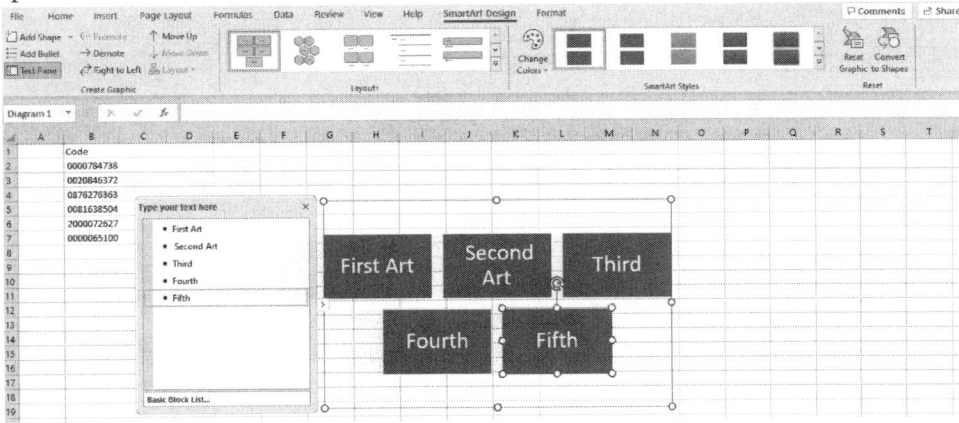

Image 181: SmartArt in Action

Modifying the look and feel of a SmartArt

In Microsoft Excel, the SmartArt object starts as a simple blue diagram. In the Design tab, you can customize the look and feel of the SmartArt with one of the several available color styles. SmartArt also has a color palette and supports adding pictures and text. In addition, the Colors and Styles group contains more than 30 color schemes. To choose a style, click the Change Colors or SmartArt Styles button. You can change the look and feel of a SmartArt by changing the shapes and text. Changing the font, color, and size of a SmartArt is simple. To change the layout, click on the Shape toolbar and select a different color. You can also change the look and feel of a SmartArt by ungrouping it. Creating separate SmartArts is also a great way to make the graphics look more professional.

Adding text to a SmartArt

The first step in adding text to a SmartArt is to insert a new shape. You will notice that as you add more shapes, the size of the SmartArt will decrease. To resize the SmartArt, simply drag the border out of the shape's borders. Excel will adjust its dimensions to the new dimensions. You can then add text inside the shape or beside the bullets in the pane. If you're using a SmartArt, it's vital to note that you can add multiple shapes and text to the graphic. The shapes can be of any shape, such as a line, a triangle, or a circle. This makes it easy to make the SmartArt graphic look more professional. The text boxes can be resized, rearranged, or formatted in any way you desire.

Adding a bullet list to a SmartArt

You will need to find the right one to add bullets to a SmartArt graphic. First, click on the Insert tab and select the SmartArt Illustrations group. From the list, select the SmartArt Graphic you want to use. Then click OK. Once inserted, you can change its color or shape using the Format tab. In the following steps, you will learn how to add a bullet list to a SmartArt graphic. The next step is to copy the bullet symbol and paste it into the text box. If you do not have a numeric keypad, you can activate Num Lock by pressing Shift + Fn. Alternatively, you can simply click and drag the fill handle to the desired location. If you want to repeat a list of bullets, you can repeat the steps above. You can also copy the bullet symbol and paste it into another cell.

15 Basics of Data Validation in Microsoft Excel

If you are creating a report in Microsoft Excel, you may be interested in knowing more about data validation. This feature is used to specify which types of data and values are allowed. Depending on the data you are calculating, data validation may restrict the values you can enter in fields such as drop-down lists, whole numbers, decimal numbers, lists, and text length. This section will cover the basic types of data validation and how you can apply them to your report.

List validation

There are many ways to use list validation in Microsoft Excel. First of all, you need to know that list validation is not foolproof, and you can get around it by pasting data into a cell or selecting Clear>Clear All on the Ribbon's Home tab. The easiest way to keep a list of options is to type them on the worksheet. You can create a drop-down list on the same worksheet if you need to have several options at once. It is possible to specify an optional message for users when using drop-down lists. This message will appear when a user selects a cell having a drop-down list. This message will be displayed on the user's screen and will inform them to enter valid data. You can also use the Input Message tab to customize the error message. Once the message has been created, click OK. Then, close Data Validation window.

The Drop Down List within a Cell

You may name an item based on a specified Excel table to build a drop-down menu in Excel. And use that item as the Data Integrity drop-down list's source. If you don't wish to build a named table, see the named range paragraph below for details.

Creating a Drop-Down List

You may build a drop list of choices in a cell with the use of Data Validation. There are three simple steps to follow:

- Make a table of contents OR a list

- Give the List a Name

- Make the drop-down menu

Make a title for the list — In this case, the employees. Type the items you wish to view in the drop-down list in a single column immediately below the header cell. Between the entries, do not leave any blank cells.

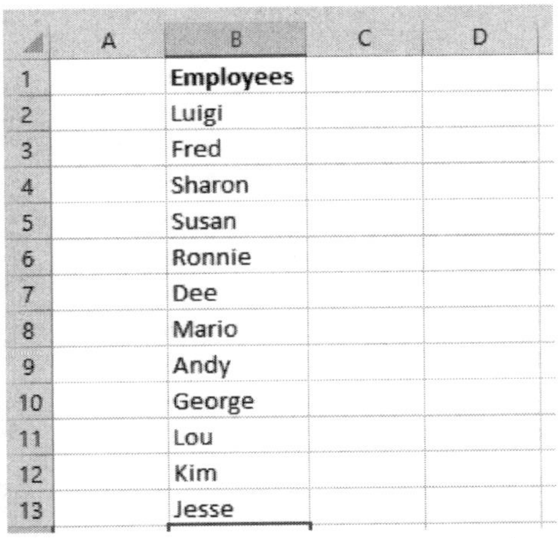

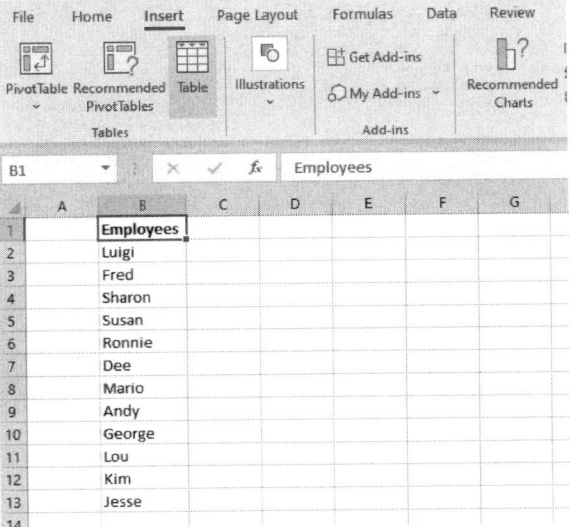

Image 182: Table to use in creating drop-down list

- Click on the insert and then click on the table

Image 183: Click one cell in the table

- Check the box

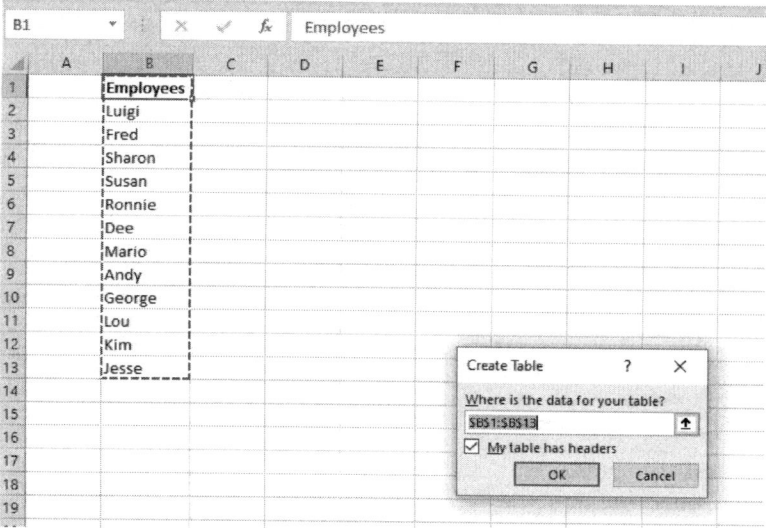

Image 184: Creating table with headers

In this way, you can name the table.

You may use a named range to construct a list inside one or even more cells now that you've generated one. Choose the cells where you would like this same drop-down list to appear.

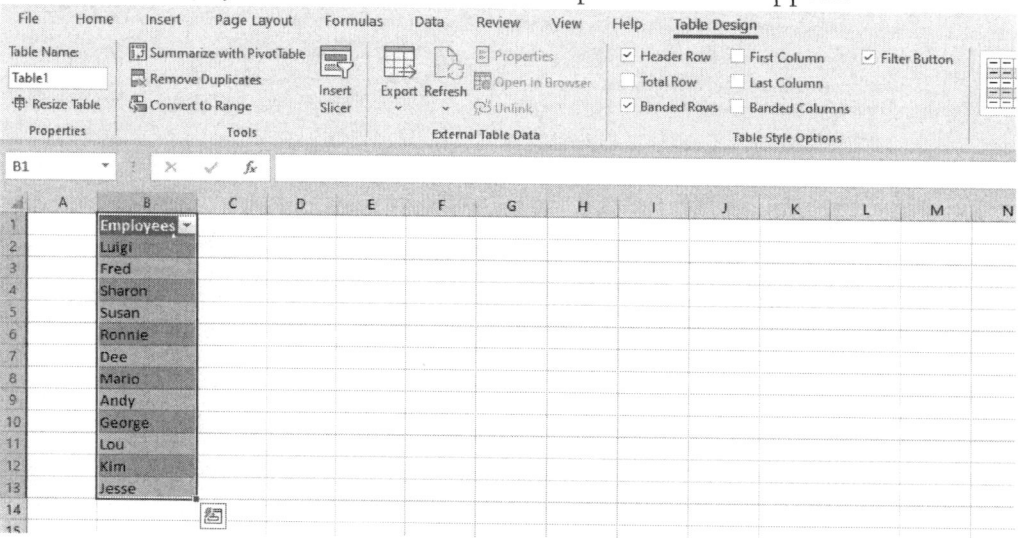

Image 185: Drop-down list

Checking for duplicates

You might have trouble finding duplicate values in your data, but you can easily filter the data by using the "Check for Duplicates" tool in Microsoft Excel. This feature helps you identify any row, column, or cell with duplicate data and displays a duplicate symbol if it exists. You can also delete duplicates, copy them, or move them to another row or column. Read on to learn how to operate.

You can check for duplicates in a data table by applying a formula to the data. Then, depending on the data set, you can apply a filter on a cell header or column content to find duplicates. Once you have the formula applied, you can delete the duplicate data. To perform this operation, select the data set and the range that includes the duplicate data. You can then use the COUNTIF function to get the number of duplicate values in each cell.

Checking for intersections

There are several ways to check for intersections in Microsoft Excel data validation. The intersect operator returns the intersection of two lists. This operation can be performed on single or multiple rows. In the example above, the intersect operator returns the value 11 if cell E4 is the only cell in both ranges. Differently, you can check for intersections using named ranges. For example, if you want to test whether a product is available during a particular month, you can use the intersect operator. Using the intersecting reference is a much simpler way to check for intersections in your Microsoft Excel data. You can create a rule that will filter all intersections of two ranges based on their labels. You can also use an intersection reference to specify a specific department or period for combining the cells. Using an intersection reference makes the consolidation process faster and helps you maximize the amount of information available.

Creating a rule for data validation

Creating a rule for data validation in MS Excel requires some technical knowledge. To get started, create a named range. Named ranges are always absolute, so the names of cells in that range will never change. To create a named range, simply enter the name of the range in the Names field of the workbook and then click the Add button. Once you have created the rule, you should click the Data - Validation tab to open the Settings tab. In the List, select Allow, and then enter your criteria for data validation. It's important to remember that Excel does not differentiate between uppercase and lowercase names, so make sure you enter the correct name. Data validation rules are a useful feature of Excel 2016. They prevent data entry errors by telling users what to enter and what not to enter. Data that does not meet these rules will be flagged as incorrect. This helps keep the data clean and prevents it from being contaminated by mistakes. In addition, data validation rules help prevent sloppy data entry and itchy feelings. For example, you can create a date-validation rule that requires the date of birth to be within a specific range. You can also create a numeric rule to check if a number falls within a specific range.

16 Using Pivot Tables in MS Excel

If you are working with data you want to analyze in a pivot table, you will need to organize it. Separate data into columns and rows and group similar data together. Make sure to format column headings differently from the data. Bolding and centering them can help differentiate data. Create data islands if necessary to separate data. You can choose a Pivot Cache or Report filter for more advanced users.

Advanced Pivot Tables

There are several ways to use advanced pivot tables in Microsoft Excel. First, you can sort items by descending or ascending values by clicking the More Sort Options button. This will open a filter menu and display options to sort values by columns, rows, or totals. The values in the data table are default sorted by column headings. For example, to sort by percent, choose % Difference From or % Sum of Columns. You can also add color scales to your pivot tables. Select Styles > Color Scales to add them. Then select or choose color option that you wish to use. You can create your own if you don't find one you like. You can also add icon sets to indicate changes in your pivot table. For example, if you wanted to show how many sales increased or decreased in a particular quarter, you could create a color scale for the entire range.

Report filter

There are a few ways you can customize your report filter in Microsoft Excel. One of the most powerful options is the ability to sort items by descending values or ascending values. This option is found in the filter menu. You can choose to group or ungroup items by using the options on the right. To sort an item by descending value, click on the More Sort Options button. Then, select the value field you'd like to sort by. To use the Report filter, drag the Region cell to the filter area. Then, you can choose Northeast as the criteria. After this step, the filter will be added to the pivot table. This option works like any other filter but is easier to use. The following section will show you how to make your filter more intuitive. However, before using it, ensure you understand how the report filter works. If you're using the Report Filter to create a report, you should make sure you understand the limitations of the Report filter.

Show Values As

If you have calculated fields with division operations, you may see errors such as "#DIV/0!." The value will appear in the value field as "0," but the error message will not be helpful for your audience. To correct these errors, you can change the value field settings by clicking "Analyze" on the ribbon and then selecting the little down arrow in the Value Field settings. The default value for column A/row 1 is "A." This is the top-left-most cell of your sheet. Click this cell to select the value of that column. After you've made your changes, you'll see a new table with the values you want. You can also change the columns and rows by rechecking the "Edit" button at the top of the new window. This is the default value for columns in Microsoft Excel pivot tables.

Pivot Cache

To create separate caches in Microsoft Excel, you can use a table. Simply click on the Table button on the Ribbon. Select your data source you wish to work with. Once you have chosen the data source, Excel will open the Design tab and prompt you to name the table. Type a descriptive table name and click OK. Your table will then be saved as a separate cache. You can remove the cache if you want to reduce the size of your Excel file. You must have a calculated field in your workbook to use a calculated field in your pivot table. Creating a pivot table from this field is easy - open the data source and select it from the list of options. You can then sort the data by ascending or descending values. In the Value Fields tab, click on the drop-down menu to ascend or descend.

16.1 How to create your first pivot table

Pivot tables work best with transactional data. Raw data files are obtained straight from your company's IT department. To generate the greatest pivot tables, make sure your data adheres to the following guidelines:

- Make certain that each column has a one-cell header. Use different headers for each column; don't use the same heading for two columns. If you want your headers to display in two rows, enter the first word, press **Alt+Enter**, and then write the second.

- If a column should include numeric data, no blank cells should be allowed in the column. Instead of blanks, use zeros.

- Avoid using blank rows or columns.

- Remove any totals that are incorporated in your report.

- Make sure the worksheet is not in Compatibility mode. When the worksheet is in Compatibility mode, several pivot table capabilities from Excel 2007–2019 are disabled.

- When you add any new data to bottom of your monthly data set, you should consider converting it to a table using **Ctrl+T**. After a refresh, pivot tables generated from tables instantly take up new rows copied to the bottom of the tables.

- Whether your data contains months split over multiple columns, return to the source software program to check if an alternative representation of the data with months running down the rows is available.

This data collection contains two years' worth of transactional data. The customer has a single text column. There is just one date column. Quantity, Revenue, COGS, and Profit are all numerical columns.

	Region	Product	Date	Customer	Quantity	Revenue	COGS	Profit
1	Region	Product	Date	Customer	Quantity	Revenue	COGS	Profit
2	East	XYZ	1/1/2022	Microsoft	954	22810	10220	12590
3	Central	DEF	2/3/2022	TellTale Fi	118	2256	948	1308
4	East	XYZ	4/4/2022	Design So	426	9140	4070	5070
5	East	DEF	4/7/2022	Compuy F	773	18502	7987	10515
6	East	ABC	8/5/2022	Oxygen Lt	407	8470	3589	4881
7	East	DEF	9/2/2022	Fotr Logist	1067	21800	9978	11822
8	Central	ABC	1/7/2022	Data Solve	355	46800	6653	40147
9	West	DEF	4/4/2022	Amazon	1820	33091	2200	30891
10	East	ABC	3/9/2022	Oxford	809	8809	3492	5317
11	West	XYZ	8/3/2022	Cambridge	649	9003	2820	6183
12	West	XYZ	2/6/2022	Jade	998	7323	1729	5594
13	Central	DEF	6/6/2022	Rux	849	8661	1309	7352
14	West	ABC	9/2/2022	Juke	1289	13892	3309	10583
15	Central	DEF	3/7/2022	Wetin	1354	36781	6720	30061
16	East	XYZ	9/1/2022	Oficia	1098	14602	4679	9923
17	Central	DEF	10/10/2022	Dolce	1134	22589	11980	10609
18	West	ABC	11/2/2022	Sdata Vad	682	67227	28928	38299

Image 186: Table to use in creating Pivot table

Begin with a blank pivot table

The typical way to make a pivot table is to start with a blank one. Select one cell from your data. From the Insert tab, choose PivotTable. The Create PivotTable dialog box appears in Excel.

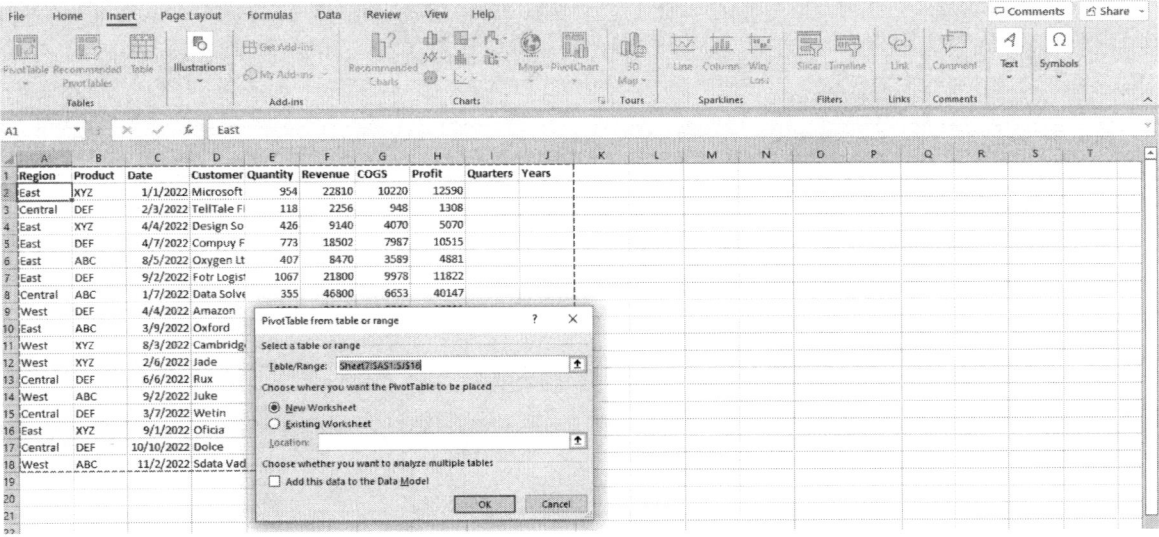

Image 187: Starting a blank table

This dialog box validates the data range. Excel usually does this properly if there are no blank rows or columns.

You can create the pivot table on a new blank worksheet or in an existing place by using **Create PivotTable dialog box**. For instance, if you want to create a dashboard with many pivot tables, you may place the pivot table in J2 on this worksheet or adjacent to another existing pivot table or pivot chart. You can create a pivot table from a relational model by clicking the Add This Data to The Data Model check box.

Using the field list to add fields to your pivot table

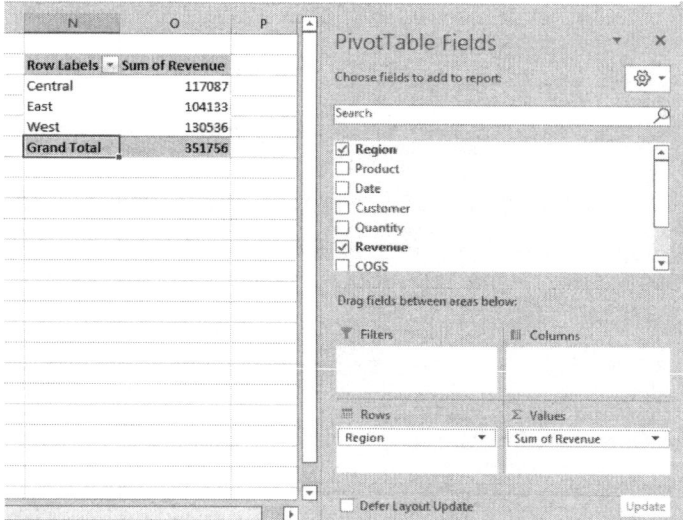

Image 188: Using the field list

If you begin with a blank pivot table, you will see PivotTable Fields. At the top of the PivotTable Fields section is a list of fields from your original data collection, and at the bottom are four drop zones. To create your report, drag and drop fields into the drop zones at the bottom.

Using the field list to modify the pivot table report

Examine the Region, Product, and **Revenue sections**.

When you choose a text or date field, it goes to the Rows drop zone in the PivotTable Fields list. When you check a numeric field, it goes to the Values drop zone, and the field type is changed to Sum of Field. You can view the Sum of Revenue by Region and Product by selecting **Region, Product, and Revenue**. You may further personalize the pivot table by rearranging the fields in the drop zones. Drag the Region field, for example, below the Product field in the Rows drop zone.

How to rearrange a pivot table

The following are the drop zone parts of the PivotTable Fields list box:

- **Filter:** This part is used to filter the report to just specified criteria. The slicer function effectively replaces this part.

- **Rows:** This part contains fields that display on the table's left side. When you pick the check boxes at the top of the field list, all text fields are moved here by default.

- **Columns:** This part contains fields along the top rows of your table's columns. *(NB: This is a crosstab report by old database experts)*.

- **Values:** This section contains all the numeric fields summarized in the table. Most values are automatically summed by default, but you may modify the computation to an average, minimum, maximum, or other calculation.

(NB: You can add fields to a drop zone by dragging them from the top of the PivotTable Fields list or from one drop zone to another. Drag a field from a drop zone to the outside of the PivotTable Fields list or uncheck it from the field list to remove it from the drop zone).

Calculating and roll-ups with pivot tables

Pivot tables provide many more calculation choices. One of the most fantastic features is the ability to roll daily dates up to months, quarters, and years.

Daily dates are organized into months, quarters, and years

Good pivot tables begin with high-quality transactional data. That transactional data is almost always recorded with daily dates rather than monthly summaries.

Follow these steps to create a summary by month, quarter, and year:

1. Begin with data, including daily dates. Next, create a pivot table with daily dates in the row field, regions in the columns, and the sum of revenue in the value area.

2. Choose a cell that has a date. Select **Group Field** from the PivotTable Analyze tab.

3. Select Months, Quarters, and Years from the Grouping dialog box. Click the OK button.

Follow these steps to create an intriguing alternative to the report:

1. To eliminate the **Region and Quarter fields** from the report, uncheck the boxes next to them.

2. Move the **Years field** from the Rows to the Columns area by dragging it from the Rows to the Columns area.

You now have a pivot table that displays totals by month and quarter and compares years throughout the report. You'll see that your pivot table field list contains three date-related fields: The years and quarters fields are both virtual. The months are included in the original Date field. Microsoft made a good design move by allowing years and months to be pivoted to various areas of the pivot table.

Adding calculations outside the pivot table

However, after you've grouped the dates in the pivot table, you won't be able to add a calculated field inside the pivot table. Thus you'll have to use ordinary Excel to give the percent Growth column. The most common stumbling block is step three. Take the following steps:

1. In D4, right-click the **Grand Total** and choose to **Remove Grand Total**.

2. In D4, create a heading called percent Growth.

3. Enter =C5/B5-1 in cell D5. If you utilize the mouse or arrow keys while creating the formula, you will get stung by the GetPivotData issue.

4. Cell D5 should be formatted as a percentage with one decimal point.

5. In D5, double-click the fill handle to copy the formula to all rows.

Changing a field's computation

By default, a numeric column with the default calculation of Sum will be added to the pivot table. Excel has ten more computations, including Average, Count, Max, and Min.

The figures in this part begin with an entirely new pivot table. You may follow along by doing the following:

1. Remove the pivot table from the previous examples' worksheets. This memory clears the pivot cache.

2. Choose one cell from the Data worksheet.

3. Select **Insert > PivotTable**.

4. Mark the Region, Product, and Revenue fields with a check.

5. Move Revenue to the Values section two more times. *(**NB: They will display as Sum Of Revenue2 and Sum Of Revenue3 in the pivot table**).*

6. Select **Report Layout > Show In Tabular Form** from the Design tab.

7. Select **Report Layout and Repeat All Item Labels** from the Design tab.

How to sort a pivot table

Customers are displayed alphabetically in all pivot tables in this chapter thus far. In each case, the report would be more interesting if it were provided and arranged by revenue rather than client name. When you click the AZ or ZA icons on the Data tab, Excel creates rules in the Sort and More Sort Options dialog boxes.

*   Open a row field drop-down box and choose **More Sort Options** to retrieve these choices later. More Sort Options may be accessed by clicking the **More button** (Customer).

How to filter using slicers

Slicers are visual filters that make it simple to do a variety of ad-hoc analyses. While slicers are simpler to use than the Report Filter, they have the advantage of filtering numerous pivot tables and charts built from the same data source.

Adding slicers

Follow these procedures to add default slicers:

1. Choose one cell from your pivot table.

2. Select **Insert Slicer button** on PivotTable Analyze tab.

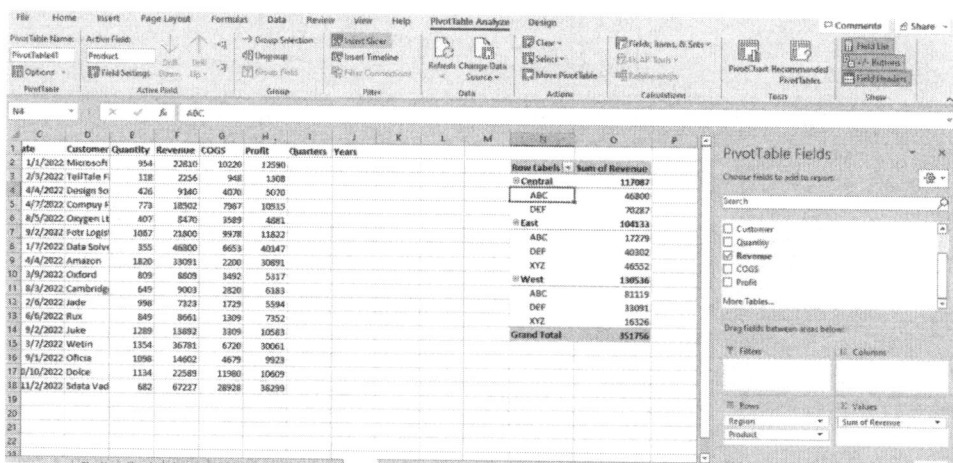

Image 189: Inserting slicers

3. Select any fields that would make good filter fields. The region, product, and years are chosen. Months, quarters, and dates would also work.

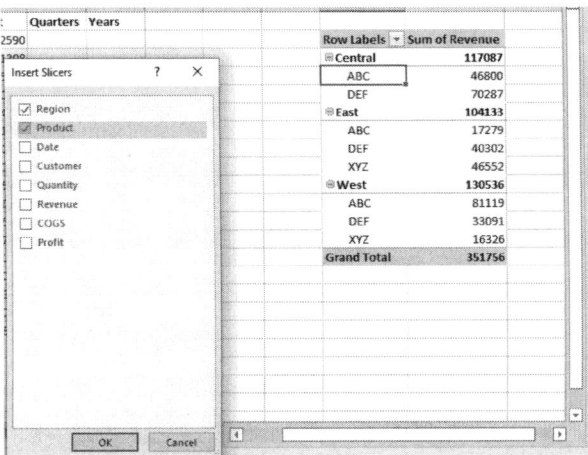

Image 190: Fields to add to pivot table

4. Click the *OK button*.

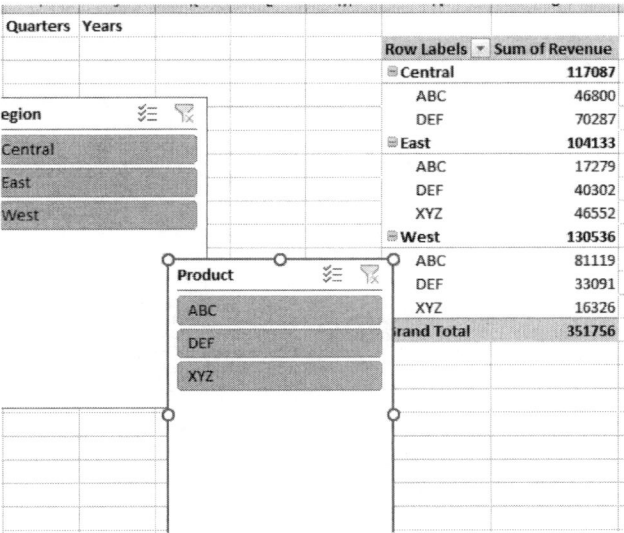

Image 191: Slicers added

Arranging the slicers

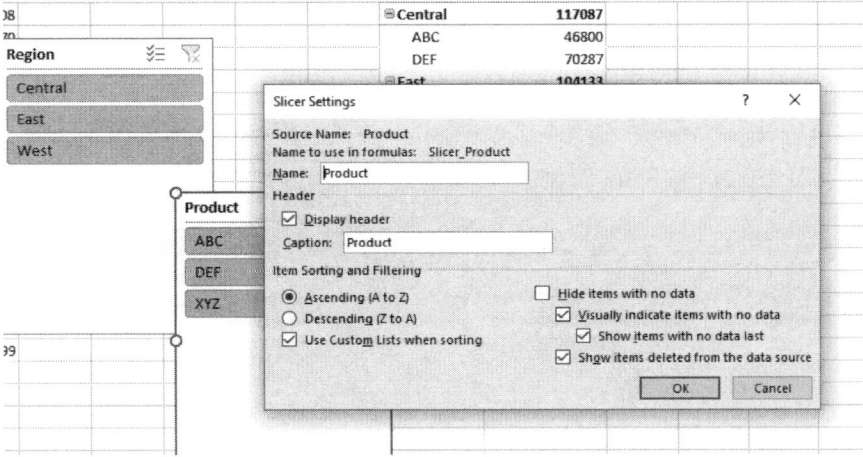

Image 192: Arranging the slicers

The slicers may be repositioned and resized. Choose a logical configuration for the slicers. Here are a few instances.

Short entries can be found in the Region and Product slicers. Extend the width of each slicer and then use the Columns option in the **Slicer Tools Options panel** to increase each slicer to three columns. The Year slicer is broader than necessary. There are also two more items in the slicer (1/1/2024 and >12/31/2025) that are Auto Group leftovers. These may be disabled in the Slicer Settings dialog box. Choose Slicer Settings after selecting the slicer. Hide Items With No Data is also enabled.

Using Excel's slicers

Choose that item to choose a single item from a slicer. Then, to multiselect in Excel, select the symbol with three check marks at the top of the slicer. Each item may now be selected by clicking on it.

You can also use the **Ctrl key** to pick several objects that are not adjacent or drag the mouse to select items that are nearby.

Items in other slicers may become inaccessible due to selections in one slicer. The items are pushed to the bottom of the list in this situation. This indicates visually that the item is not accessible based on the current criteria.

To remove a filter from a slicer, click the **Funnel-X symbol** in the slicer's upper right corner.

Slicers can be set up to filter many pivot tables and pivot charts at once. For example, if both pivot tables use the same data source, the slicers will affect both pivot tables.

If there are numerous pivot tables, proceed as follows:

1. Choose a slicer.

2. Select **Report Connections** from the ribbon's Slicer Tools Options menu.

3. Choose which pivot tables should be filtered by the slicer.

Using the row label filter to filter

To proceed, open the 16-Slicers.xlsx file and create a new pivot table. Examine Customer, Date, Quantity, Revenue, COGS, and Profit fields. Next, open the Report Layout drop-down menu from the Design tab. Select Tabular form, then Repeat All Item Labels. On the Design tab, tick the Banded Rows box. You will get the pivot table as a result.

This drop-down menu has four distinct filter mechanisms:

- For fields with text values, the Label Filters fly-out menu shows. You may use this fly-out to find client names that include specific words, begin, end, or fall between letters.

- The Value Filters fly-out menu lets you filter consumers based on values in the pivot table. Use the Value Filters fly-out if you only want orders above $20,000 or if you only want to view the Top 10 clients.

- Excel 2010 introduced the Search box, which is comparable to Label Filters but quicker.

- Use the check boxes to exclude specific consumers, or use Select All to clear or select all customers.

Clearing a filter

To clear all filters in the pivot table, click the **Clear button** in the Data tab's Sort & Filter group. To remove filters from a single field in the pivot table, enter the filter drop-down menu and pick Clear Filter from **"Field."**

Using check boxes to filter

The Customer drop-down menu lists all of the customers in the database. Clear their check boxes in the filter list if you need to exclude a few particular consumers.

The **(Select All) option** restores any previously cleared boxes. If all boxes are already checked, selecting **(Select All)** clears them all.

Because it is simpler to choose three clients than it is to clear 27 if you need to delete the majority of the items from the list of customers, you can do it by following these steps:

1. If any customers have been cleared, choose Select All to reselect all of them.

2. Tap **Select All** to delete all clients.

3. Choose which consumers you wish to see.

17 How to Use a Microsoft Excel Named Range in Formulas, Cells, and Formulas

If you've ever used a Microsoft Excel Named Range, you've probably wondered how to use it. But you're not the only one. You can use it in Formulas, Cells, and even Formulas! Here are a few tips to get you started. The name of a named range will always be case-sensitive, so it's crucial to know how to type it correctly. You can also find the range's name in the Name Manager and use it in your formulas.

The dynamic named ranges

You may create a dynamic named range by using a formula. It works just like a column or row. Firstly, you need to define the width and height of the range. Height and width determine the number of columns and rows you wish to include. After that, you simply need to define the first_cell. Similarly, the offset_cols will tell the function where to place the upper-left cell.

If the data you wish to add to a named range is changing in a short period, you can create a dynamic named range. If you don't wish to edit the formula, use the OFFSET function instead. However, you should note that this volatile function will slow down your Excel workbook. A better option is the INDEX function, which is semi-volatile and will not affect the speed of the workbook.

Case-insensitive names

If you're trying to use a named range in Excel, you might wonder how to specify a case-insensitive name. First, it is a good idea to remember that your name can contain up to 255 characters, but it can't be longer than that. Second, Microsoft Excel also doesn't distinguish between lowercase and uppercase letters, so if you enter the first name incorrectly, Excel will automatically replace it with the second. What are the steps of creating named ranges using Excel?

1. Go to the formula bar and select Define Names
2. A dialogue box will pop up where you will type your desired range name. a scope dropdown will always be set to a given workbook.
3. Select cell range in the other field
4. Click OK to finalize the changes and save.

Note: If you choose an absolute reference, Excel creates a name with the range scope of the workbook. If you want a relative name, remove the $ sign.

Formulas that can be created with named ranges

There are many advantages to using named ranges in your Excel workbooks. First, they make it easier to navigate the workbook. Using a named range will make navigation easier, as you can click the range's name and go to it. This makes it easier to type formulas and troubleshoot errors when creating or editing ranges. In addition, named ranges are easier to understand and write, making them easier to use. When creating a new named range, you can give it a descriptive name that refers to its contents. Named ranges are often used for multiple Worksheets, such as quarterly figures or annual reports. Named ranges can make it easier to remember which cell ranges are involved in formulas. Creating a named range is as simple as typing a descriptive name in the Name box.

Creating a named range in Excel

Creating a named range in Excel is easy. Simply navigate to the Formulas tab and click the Define Name button. In the Name box, enter a name for the range. This name will appear in the cell reference box. After entering the name, click OK. The Name box will contain the cell reference and the name. Type in any other name for the range if necessary. The Name Box will appear in the upper-left corner of the spreadsheet. The default scope is the workbook or worksheet.

Creating a named range in Excel makes it easy to manage and change the contents of your workbook. Named ranges are particularly useful in conditional formatting. Advanced and intermediate Excel courses cover the topic extensively. By creating and naming a range, you avoid physically selecting the cell range. The Name Box feature makes it easy to navigate to named ranges. Names must not be longer than 255 characters and contain no spaces.

18 How to Use the Microsoft Excel Lookup Function

If you've tried using the LOOKUP function in Microsoft Excel, you probably wonder whether it works. There are several reasons why it may not. For one thing, you may be asked to specify an exact or approximate value. Either way, Excel will automatically return the value closest to what you're looking for. The more advanced XLOOKUP function is another way to use the LOOKUP function.

LOOKUP function

You can use the LOOKUP function when you want to perform a lookup in Microsoft Excel. This function finds data that matches a value in a particular cell. There are a couple of different types of lookups. First, VLOOKUP searches for values in a column that matches a specific value. This function is best used when the data is organized by time and is large. Otherwise, you can use the HLOOKUP function. Excel will use the lower value if the lookup value is between two values. If the value is smaller than the first column, it will return an error message. A table array is created with the Price column. The cell value in the second column is the Price. Therefore, Excel uses the Price table in cells A17 to B24. Using this table array, the LOOKUP function in Excel will return the value of the Price from column A17 to B24.

Range_lookup

The Range_lookup function in Microsoft Excel allows you to look up data in a column by cell reference. You can use this function in all versions of Excel. The lookup_value argument can be a number, cell reference, or text string. In either case, you must include the column index number to get a match. If you don't include it, an approximate match will be returned. The Range_lookup function can only look at the first column in an array, so you will need to use an index or match formula to find a value in the left column.

The VLOOKUP formula has an optional argument for range_lookup, which matches two values based on the range. In this case, the function will find the closest match value. Otherwise, it will look for the next largest value less than the lookup value. The lookup column will return a #N/A error if the match does not exist. Alternatively, the VLOOKUP function can apply range lookup to larger tables.

Returns 0

If you receive an error message like "Microsoft Excel Lookup Function returns 0," it is likely that your data is incorrect. The reason is fairly simple. The Lookup function looks up a cell value that matches a specific text string. You should type the value in cell D14 in the first column. In the second column, type the word "cereal" to search for the value of "cereal." This function searches a specific cell's value, either an exact or relative match. The default match mode is exact, which returns a #N/A error if no matches are found. The match_mode argument can be any number between 0 and 1 (exact match).

Errors

Sometimes a VLOOKUP formula will fail to work, and you're not sure what the problem is. In such cases, you can try using the INDEX or MATCH functions. These functions will work similarly but search for values to the left of the range. For example, Microsoft Excel Lookup Function errors occur when numbers are formatted as text, such as when you import data from an external database or type an apostrophe before a number to show the leading zeros. The most common error in the VLOOKUP formula is the space character, which is a common occurrence. You will receive an error message with the code #N/A if this happens. You can use the TRIM function to remove spaces from the lookup values and VLOOKUP, which works similarly. The ISERROR function will detect errors and render output based on a logical test.

Using it to retrieve a value from a list or table

To use the lookup function in Excel, you need to create a formula containing a cell with a value present in the list or table you wish to find. This function is called a VLOOKUP. It looks for a value based on a unique identifier in the list and table. This information can be a product code, stock-keeping unit, or customer contact. Using the VLOOKUP function can be tricky. The problem can arise from the formula's syntax and the value referenced. When a VLOOKUP fails to locate a value in a column, it returns a #N/A error. If you have a table where the columns are sorted in alphabetical order, ensure you align the values vertically.

19 Macros In MS Excel

A macro in Excel is nothing more than a set of instructions that are repeated over and over. Following the creation of a macro, Excel will step-by-step carry out the instructions on whatever data you supply. Let's consider this example. We create a macro for giving instructions to the program where it picks a number, adds 3, multiplies by 5, then returns the modulus of the number.

- Now, whenever we instruct Excel to carry out the macro execution, it becomes an automatic process by Excel without the manual step by step.
- A macro can be used to record almost any type of information. As a result, it's possible to perform numerical computations, text operations, formatting, and cell movement in any way you can.
- When you continuously repeat the same steps, you save time when you use macros. While this may not seem like much initially, it can add up over time.

- If you're formatting raw data, filtering and sorting data, or simply repeating a sequence of functions and actions on your sheets, you're on the right track.

- You can easily share macros across your colleagues to carry on with the project since they are stored within a spreadsheet.

How to create a macro in Microsoft Excel

- Before you can utilize Excel macros to automate your chores, you must first "record" a macro in Excel.

- Excel should take steps when the macro is executed can be specified by recording the macro.

- Additionally, whereas Visual Basic for Applications (VBA) can be used to construct a macro, Excel allows you to record an Excel macro using standard commands rather than Visual Basic for Applications (VBA).

Consider the following straightforward example. We have a list of names in our spreadsheet, as well as a list of their monthly sales:

	A	B	C	D	E
1	Name	Sales			
2	Luigi	$ 12,967.00		Highest sales:	
3	Fred	$ 17,526.00		Name:	
4	Sharon	$ 14,625.00			
5	Susan	$ 14,088.00			
6	Ronnie	$ 11,973.00			
7	Dee	$ 10,726.00			
8	Mario	$ 18,923.00			
9	Andy	$ 15,636.00			
10	George	$ 10,819.00			
11	Lou	$ 13,728.00			
12	Kim	$ 16,514.00			
13	Jesse	$ 19,382.00			
14					

Image 193: Creating a macro

- Let's create a macro to rate the sales from the highest to lowest and goes through the information to come up with name of salesperson who beats the record with the most highest sales.

- Customizing the ribbon requires one to select File > Options. From the sidebar appearing, choose Customize Ribbon. Ensure you check the Developer Add-in in the Main Tabs:

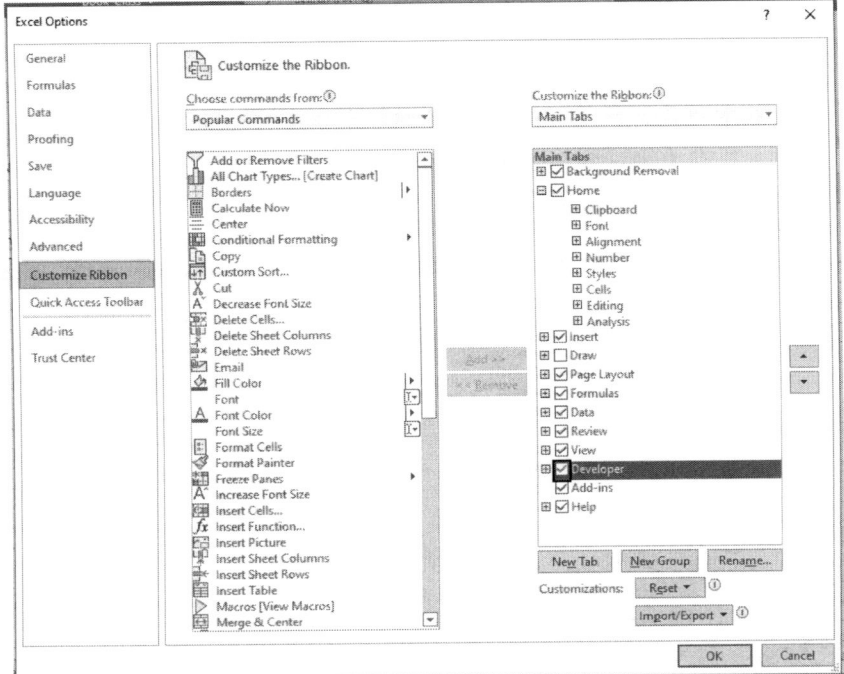

Image 194: Customizer ribbon in action for macros

- Click OK to ensure the tab shows in main window. You'll notice a Record Macro button.
- Simply click that button to begin recording a macro.

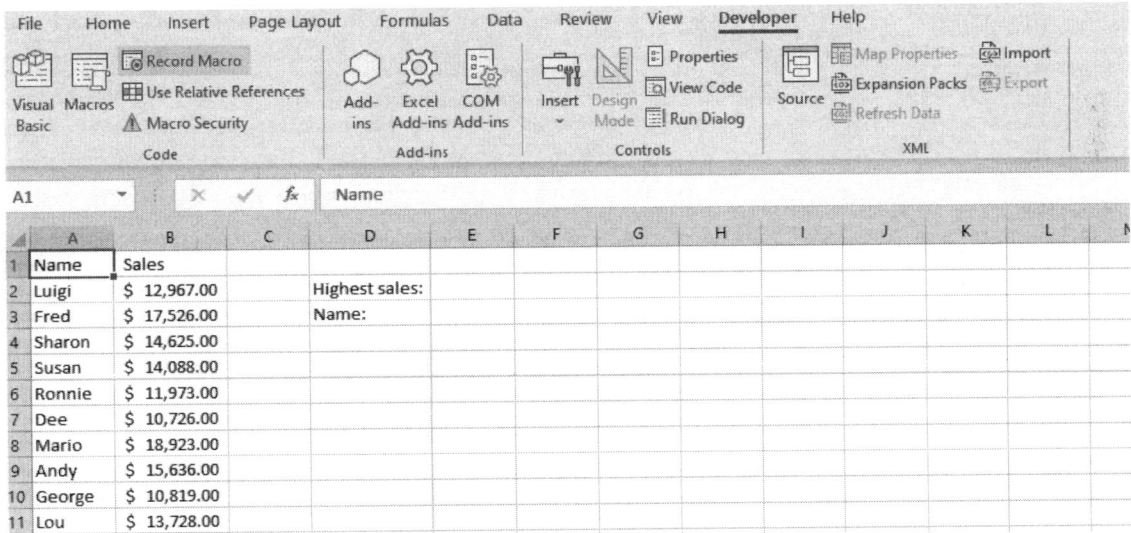

Image 195: Record Macro

- If you wish to provide a name to the macro (for this case we used "HighSales") and come up with a shortcut key, there will be a prompt requesting for that information.
- Avoid overwriting the default Ctrl-based shortcuts that people use on a frequent basis.

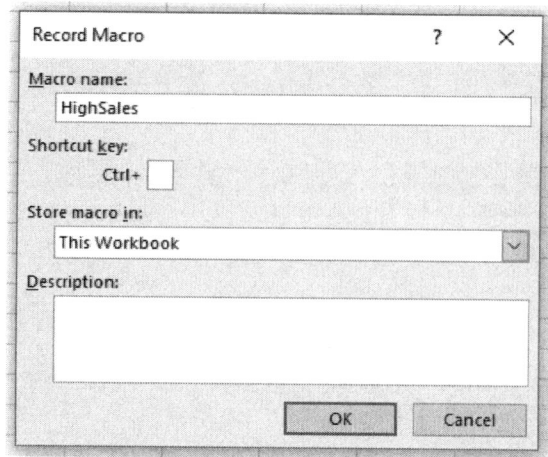

Image 196: Giving a name to the macro

- 3 options are available where one can store their macro: store in new workbook, current workbook, or in an existing macro workbook.

- This workbook (Book_Class.xlsx) contains macros that can be executed on any workbook that you can access in Excel.

- You can use it to store all of your Excel macros in a centralized location for easy access.

- If you're building a macro that will only be used in this spreadsheet, save it there. If, on the other hand, you believe you may need to reuse the macro in another worksheet, save in a macro workbook.

- Click OK and Excel will always execute as per the steps.

Let's follow these steps:

Apply filters to your columns

For column B, we sort it from highest to smallest figures

Copy cell B2

Click cell E2 and paste the copied content

Copy cell A2

Click cell E3 and paste the copied content

Make E2 & E3 **bold**

- To record a macro, simply click Record Macro, follow the on-screen instructions, before clicking Stop Recording.

- Once you start recording, Record Macro button is replaced by the Stop Recording button, which you can use to end the recording.

- Each of those activities is standard; for example, clicking Filter button, sorting using the dropdown filter arrow, and copying the cell with the Ctrl + C keyboard shortcut.

- This is what it will look like after we are finished:

	A	B	C	D	E	F
1	Name	Sales				
2	Jesse	$ 19,382.00		Highest sales:	$19,382.00	
3	Mario	$ 18,923.00		Name:	Jesse	
4	Fred	$ 17,526.00				
5	Kim	$ 16,514.00				
6	Andy	$ 15,636.00				
7	Sharon	$ 14,625.00				
8	Susan	$ 14,088.00				
9	Lou	$ 13,728.00				
10	Luigi	$ 12,967.00				
11	Ronnie	$ 11,973.00				
12	George	$ 10,819.00				
13	Dee	$ 10,726.00				

Image 197: End result of the macro

- A macro can be created using just this information! Press the record button, conduct some actions, and then press the stop button.

Running a macro

After saving your macro, you can execute it in various ways.

- To get started, you can launch it immediately from the Ribbon menu. A Macros button can be found on the application's View and the Developer tabs. To view the macros, click on corresponding icon.

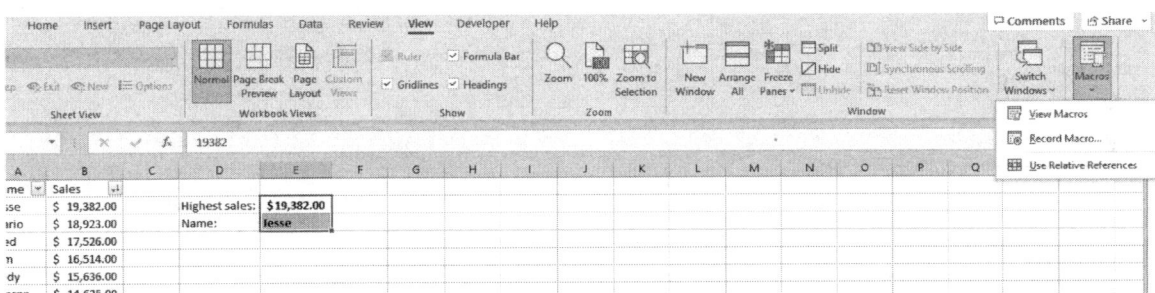

Image 198: Executing the macro

- The resulting window shows all saved macros. Select the one you need and click Run to execute.

- Excel will retrace the steps you took throughout the record-keeping session.

- To ensure it was successful, unbold E2 & E3 and delete them in the sample worksheet, and then arrange the names alphabetically in the new worksheet.

- Execute your macro and check if you get same results.

- The shortcut key that you used to save your macro can also be used to run it. For example, ctrl + the key combination you entered in the save box.

- Adding a shortcut key afterward is as simple as navigating to View Macros, selecting the macro, and selecting Options. Creating a new shortcut key will be an option when you log in.

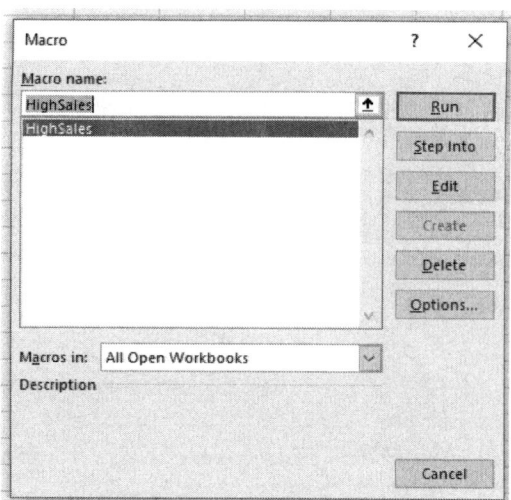

Image 199: Running the macro

- Add a shortcut key by heading to View Macros, choose your macro, click Options. Then, create a new shortcut key available to you after the installation is complete.

You can create a button to execute your macro if you regularly run a complex macro or share your spreadsheet with others.

This is how you do it.

- To begin, create a form; in this case, a rectangle with rounded corners will suffice.

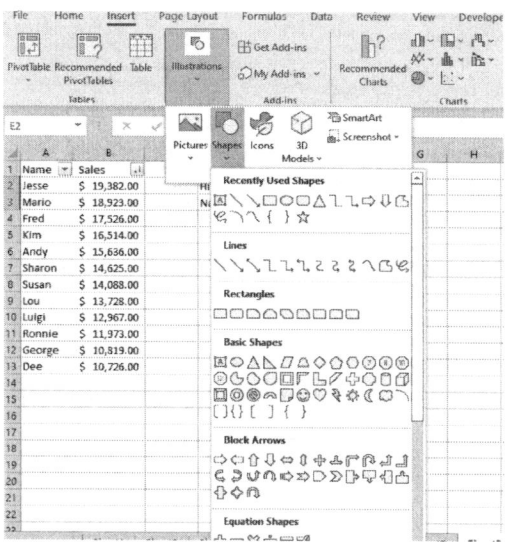

Image 200: Creating a button

- In the Shape Editor, right click and choose Edit Text to add describing text to your shape.

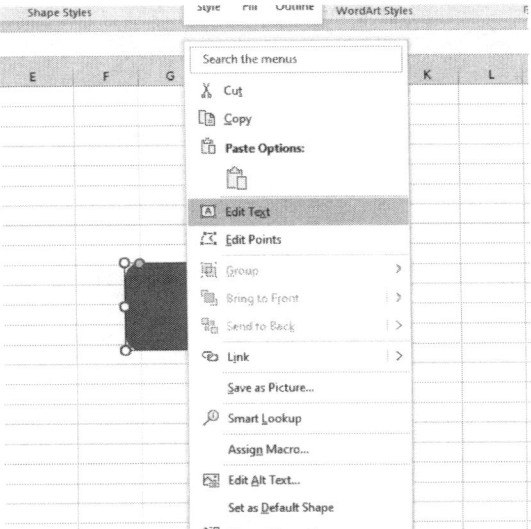

Image 201: Editing button caption

- Now, right-click the shape and choose Assign Macro from the context menu.

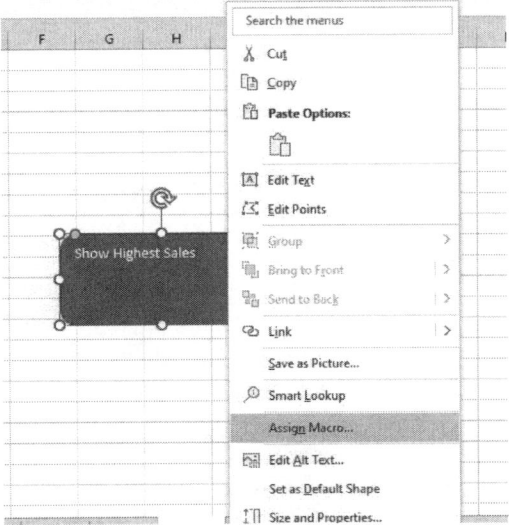

Image 202: Assigning macro to the button

- After selecting the corresponding macro from the subsequent window, click OK to confirm your selection.

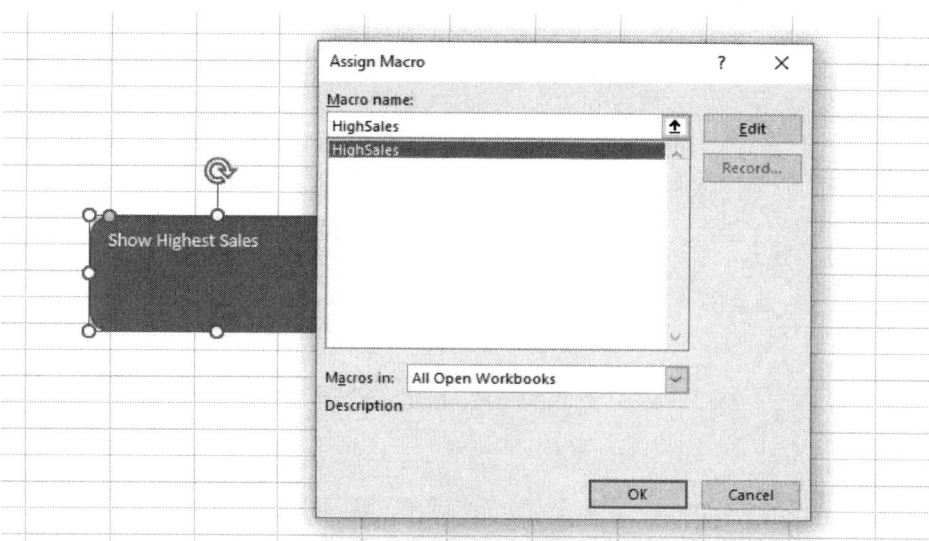

Image 203: Selecting the particular macro

- After that, clicking the shape will execute the pre-recorded macro.

Let's see how to directly run your macros using the QAT (Quick Access Toolbar).

- Before you can use the macro, add View Macros button to QAT.
- Select File > Options from the menu bar, and then Quick Access Toolbar from the left-hand pane:
- Scroll down and choose View Macros, followed by the Add >> button.

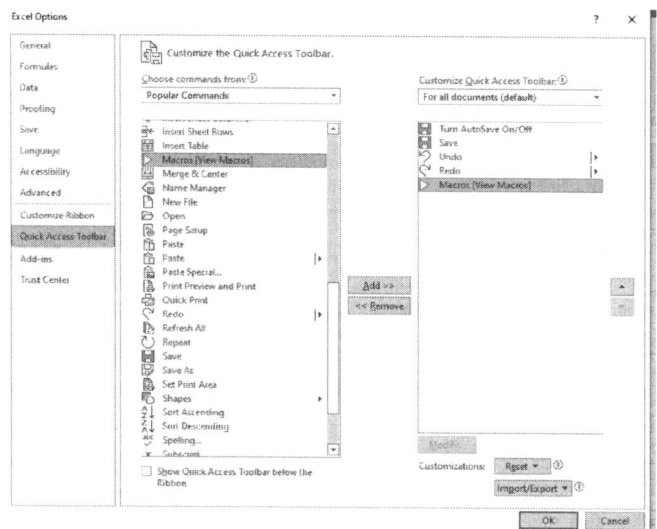

Image 204: Running macro added to QAT

- Click on the OK button.
- Simply click the macros button at the top of the Excel window to start a macro right away:

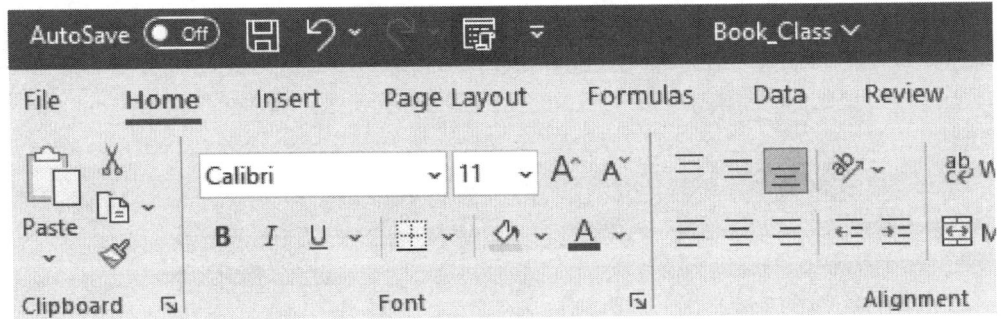

Image 205: QAT with the macro icon

20 Printing

How to work with page breaks

Page breaks fall into two:

- Automatic page break – Excel automatically goes to next page one it hits the bottom/right margin of your physical page.

These page breaks vary automatically when you modify the margins, add or remove rows, or change the height of specific rows on the page.

Initially, the spreadsheet does not display automatic page breaks. However, if you exit Print Preview and return to Normal view, automatic page breaks are shown in the document as a thin dashed line. Page Layout view and Page Break Preview mode both show automatic page breaks.

How do you disable page breaks? Click File then Options. Head to Advanced and select Display Options for This Worksheet. Ensure Show Page Breaks is unchecked. If you do this regularly, the shortcut keys **/fta** followed by **Alt+k** will bring you there.

- Manual page break

You can manually insert page breaks where you wish to start a new page in rows or columns. For example, at the beginning of a new part of a report, you may wish to place a manual page break. A manual page break does not alter in response to changes in the worksheet's rows.

Adding page breaks manually

Follow these procedures to insert a page break at a specific row manually:

1. Click the row number that should be the first row on the new page to choose a full row. Alternatively, choose the cell in that row's column A.

2. Select **Page Setup, Breaks, and Insert Page Break** from the Page Layout tab.

Follow these procedures to insert a page break at a specific column manually:

1. Click the letter above the column that should be the first column on the new page to choose a whole column. Alternatively, choose row 1 from that column.

2. Select **Page Setup, Breaks, and Insert Page Break** from the Page Layout tab.

Note: When you insert a page break when the cell pointer is outside row 1 or column A, Excel simultaneously inserts a row page break and a column page break. This is rarely what you desire. Make careful to insert a row break by selecting a cell in column A or a column break by selecting a cell in row 1.

Manual versus automatic page breaks

There is a small visual difference between manual and automated page breaks in Normal mode. The dashed line indicating a manual page break is more apparent than the line indicating an automated page break.

To have a clearer view of page breaks, go to **View, Page Break Preview,** and choose **Page Break Preview mode**. Automatic page breaks are shown as dotted blue lines in this mode. Solid lines represent manual page breaks.

Making adjustments using Page Break Preview

Page Break Preview mode allows you to move a page break by dragging the line connected with the page break. When you drag an automated page break to increase rows or columns on a page, Excel adjusts the Scale % for all pages.

Remove manual page breaks

To do away with a manual page break for a row, do the following:

1. Place cursor on the row below the page break.

2. Select **Page Setup, Breaks, and Remove Page Break** from the Page Layout tab.

To remove a manual page break for a column, do the following:

1. Set your pointer in the column to the right of the page break.

2. Select **Page Setup, Breaks, and Remove Page Break** from the Page Layout tab.

(NB: Select Page Setup, Breaks, Reset Any Page Breaks from the Page Layout tab to eliminate all manual page breaks. It's worth noting that removing the page breaks returns the scale to 100%).

How to find print settings

It is possible to alter the print settings or page setup in Excel at least nine times. The most frequent duties may be found in a variety of areas. You may, for example, modify the margins in five of the nine spots. In addition, four of the nine locations allow you to adjust the paper size and orientation. When you get to the more esoteric settings, you may only be able to discover them in one or two locations. You can find out where you may be able to adjust the setting for every specific job.

Here's where you can locate each location:

- **File > Print:** To show the **Print panel**, open the **File menu** and choose **Print**. This panel contains Printer and Page Setup options in the middle and a huge Print Preview on the right.

- **The Ribbon's Page Layout Tab:** Choose the Page Layout tab in the ribbon. Printing is divided into three categories: **Page Setup, Scale to Fit, and Sheet Options**.

- **Page Setup Dialog:** To open the classic **Page Setup dialog box**, click the **diagonal arrow** icon in the lower-right corner of the three groups in the **Page Layout ribbon tab**. There are four tabs in this dialog box. The tab is identified by the superscript next to each bullet: 1 for Page, 2 for Margins, 3 for Header/Footer, and 4 for Sheet. This dialog box may also be accessed by selecting the Print Titles button in the Page Layout tab of the ribbon.

- **Page Layout View:** On the View tab, choose **Page Layout**. This indicator may also be seen in the bottom right corner of the Excel screen.

- **Header & Footer Tools Design Tab:** On the **Page Layout view**, select one of the three header or footer zones on any page to bring up the **Header & Footer Tools Design tab** in the ribbon. It is important to note that to leave the Page Layout view, you must first click outside of the header or footer zones. Although this is the most concealed option, it provides a more convenient approach to adjusting headers and footers.

- **Preview of Page Breaks View:** On the **View tab**, choose **Page Break Preview**. This symbol may also be seen in the bottom right corner of the Excel window.

- **Printer Properties Dialog:** To open the **Print panel**, use **Ctrl+P**. Just below the printer name, a link to Printer Properties appears.

- **Excel Options:** Select **Options, Advanced from the File menu**. After you've done a Print Preview, this is the sole area where you may disable the display of automatic page breaks.

- **Print Preview Full Screen:** Drag this icon to the **Quick Get Toolbar** to access a full-screen version of Print Preview akin to prior Excel versions.

Printing with a single click

If you're a keyboard fanatic, you may be annoyed that **Ctrl+P** in Excel brings you to the Print panel rather than completing a rapid print. However, Quick Print can be restored to Excel in a few simple steps.

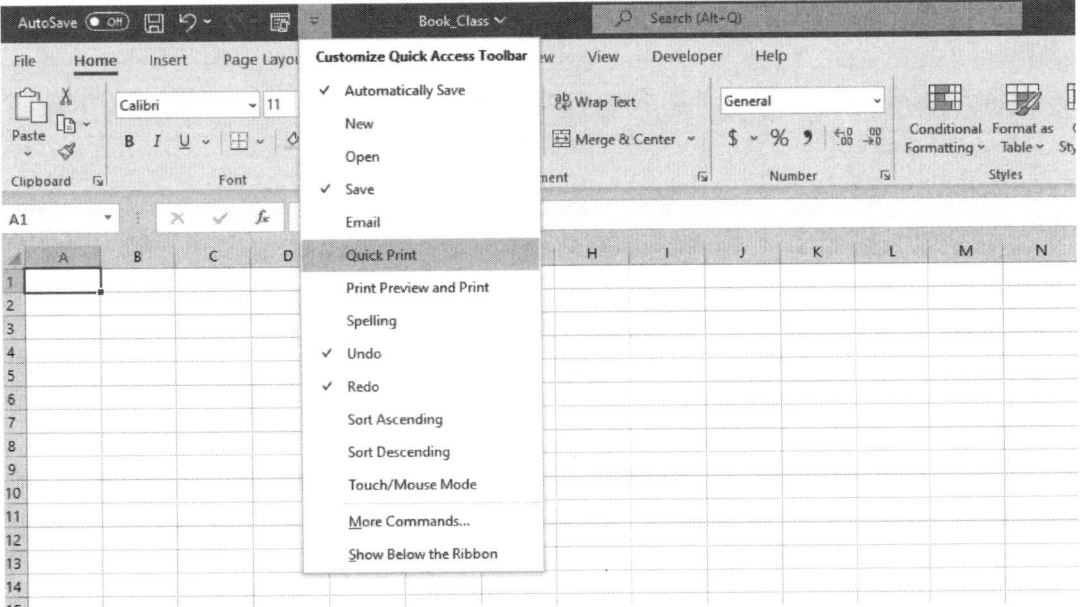

Image 206: Printing using the QAT option

The Quick Access Toolbar (QAT) is a row of tiny icons immediately above or below the ribbon. A drop-down menu appears to right side of this toolbar. To show a brief list of common commands, use the drop-down menu at the right edge of the Quick Access Toolbar. Select **Quick Print**.

When you click the **Quick Print button**, Excel sends one copy of the current worksheet to the last printer you used. The worksheet is sent to the default printer if you have not previously printed it in this Excel session.

Although this restores Quick Print as a mouse click, it is still inconvenient for keyboard-centric users. On Excel, pressing and releasing the **Alt key** displays a row of shortcuts for the first nine items in the Quick Access Toolbar.

Using the File menu to print

To reach the Print panel, select **File > Print, or you may press Ctrl+P**. The resulting panel combines options from the Print and Page Setup dialog boxes in the screen's center and Print Preview on the right. As you change the settings in the screen's center, Print Preview changes, allowing you always to see the most recent preview.

Image 207: Print under the File option

A huge Print button dominates the screen's left side. To print your document, click this button. You can adjust the number of copies printed by spinning the spin button next to the Print button.

(NB: The remainder of the left panel is devoted to a new kind of gallery. Without opening the gallery, you may view the current selection. There is no need to access the drop-down menu if the relevant printer is already chosen).

Choosing a Printer

Excel shows all the existing printers and indicates whether or not the printer is presently online and accessible when you enter the Printer drop-down menu. This useful enhancement lets you identify whether the department printer is jammed and print to a new printer.

Viewing the Page Layout

The Normal view is the default view when you start Excel. The only options in previous versions of Excel were Normal view and Page Break Preview mode. However, starting with Excel 2007, Microsoft introduced the **Page Layout view**, which is useful when preparing a document for printing. *(NB: The three views in Excel may be found on the View tab or the right side of status bar).*

You have a fully functional worksheet in the Page Layout view. The formula bar, for example, works, and you can browse around the worksheet. However, the following are the distinctions between Page Layout and Normal view:

- On each page, white space appears to illustrate the margins. This is typically advantageous since you can see page gaps between columns or rows. If you wish to conceal the white space, right-click it and choose **Hide White Space**.

- A ruler appears underneath the formula bar, which you can use to modify margins by moving the ruler's gray regions.

- Areas are labeled **Add a Header and a Footer by clicking the Add a Header and Add a Footer buttons**. Whereas headers and footers are hidden in previous versions of Excel, they are visible in the **Page Layout view** of Excel.

- Click to **Add Data** is shown in areas of a worksheet that are not in the data area. One issue with the Page Break Preview mode was that sections outside the data area were grayed out. *(NB: The Click to Add Data Labels option enables you to continue adding pages to your spreadsheet).*

(NB: The sole downside of using Page Layout view is that it disables your Freeze Panes settings. Excel alerts you to the fact that this is occurring. Excel employs this to underline the distinction between Print Titles and Freeze Panes).

How to choose what to print

Active Sheets, Entire Workbook, and Selection options are available in the Print What gallery. You can further customize these options by selecting Ignore Print Area.

When you pick **Active Sheets**, the currently chosen sheet is printed. If you specify a print area, just that range is printed; otherwise, Excel displays the whole document's usable range. However, when you pick several sheets in Group mode, all of the chosen sheets print.

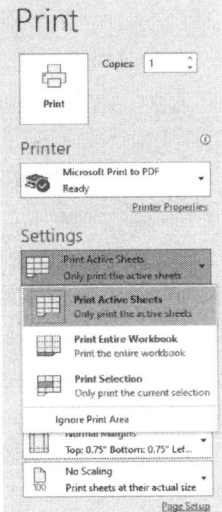

Image 208: Printing active sheets

When you choose the Entire Workbook option, all no hidden worksheets in the workbook are printed. One benefit of this choice is that the pages are sequentially numbered as the printing progresses from Sheet1 to Sheet2.

By selecting the Selection option, you can temporarily override the print area. For example, if you need to print a tiny portion of a huge report, choose that portion and then choose the Selection option in Print What gallery. *(NB: This saves you from changing the Print Area repeatedly).*

The **Ignore Print Area option** instructs Excel to disregard any previously set print zones. The full utilized area of the worksheet is printed as a result of this. Using the Pages spin buttons, you may print selected pages. Key in page number in both the Pages and To boxes to print a single page.

Changing Printer Settings

The remaining galleries on the left side of the Print panel are repainted once you choose a printer. Use the gallery to pick each choice if you print to an office printer that supports collating and stapling. Excel does not display the galleries if you print to a home printer that does not have these settings.

Changing a few of the Page Setup options

Despite their appearance, the final options on the left side of the Print panel are used to manage portrait vs. landscape, paper size, and margins. If you modify it here, it will be reflected in the Page Setup dialog box. If you're wondering why these settings are duplicated here, you may also be wondering why your preferred Page Setup options aren't. Although it is convenient to go from portrait to landscape mode here, it would be much more convenient to be able to modify the Page Scaling or **Rows to Repeat At Top options**. However, this is impossible since such adjustments need closing the **Print panel** and using the ribbon's **Page Layout tab**.

Exploring other page setup options

Other page layout options can be found throughout the various interface areas. Although some of these are obscure, you may need to use them in certain circumstances.

Printing gridlines and headings

Select **Sheet Options > Gridlines > Print from the Page Layout tab** to print the gridlines on a worksheet. You can also print the A-B-C-D column and 1-2-3-4 row headings. To do so, go to the Page Layout tab and select **Sheet Options, Headings, and Print**. This option comes in handy when printing formulas with the FORMULATEXT function and the need to see each cell's cell address.

Centering a small report on a page

Small reports printed in the page's upper-left corner may appear out of place. Instead of expanding the margins, you can center the report horizontally or vertically on a page.

To open the **Page Setup dialog box**, choose **Page Layout, Margins, and Custom Margins**. Two check boxes at the dialog box's bottom allow you to center the report on the page.

Replacing error values when printing

Excel computations may sometimes produce mistakes such as **#N/A! or DIV/0.** Although these error numbers assist you in determining how to correct the issues, they seem out of place on a printed page. You have the option of replacing any mistake cells with a blank or two hyphens.

To access the Sheet tab of your Page Setup dialog box, choose **Page Layout and Print Titles**. Then, select **blank> or — from the Cell Errors As drop-down option**.

Printing comments

Cell comments are often shown as a little red triangle in a cell. After your report, you can print a table with all the comments. Then, choose **At End Of Sheet** from the **Comments And Notes drop-down menu** on **Sheet tab** of Page Setup dialog box.

Excel produces your report and then opens a new page with each comment/note listed. The new page displays the cell and the comment/note content.

The other option for printing comments and notes is to print any visible ones that are currently visible where they are displayed. Select **Review, Notes, and Show All Notes** to see them all. You can drag them to a new location when visible so they do not obscure important cells.

Controlling the first-page number

You may be putting a printed Excel spreadsheet amid a printed Word document. If the Excel worksheet appears on the tenth page of the Word report, for example, you'd want the Excel page numbers to begin at ten rather than 1.

Select the **dialog box launcher** from the Page Layout tab at the bottom right of Page Setup group. The **Page tab** of your Page Setup dialog box is displayed in Excel. The last option is First Page Number, set initially to **Auto**. For instance, enter 10 in this field, Excel will print the Excel worksheet with page numbers 10, 11, 12, and so on.

21 Excel Shortcuts

There are so many shortcuts in Excel. However, I will be introducing you to some shortcuts that are mostly used in Excel

Editing Shortcut

Shortcut Keys	Functions
F2	For editing cell
Ctrl + C	For copying cell content
Ctrl + V	For pasting cell content
Ctrl + X	For cutting cell content to another cell
Ctrl + D	To fill down
Ctrl + R	To fill right
Alt+ E+ S	Paste special
F3	For pasting the name into a formula
F4	Toggle reference
Alt +Enter	For starting another new line within the same old cell
Shift + F2	For inserting or editing a cell comment
Shift + F10	For displaying a shortcut menu
Ctrl + F3	For defining the name of a cell
Ctrl + Shift + A	For inserting arguments names with parentheses for a function after typing a function name in a formula
Alt + I + R	For inserting a row
Alt + I + C	For inserting a column

Table 3: Table with editing shortcuts

Navigation Shortcuts

Shortcut Keys	Functions
Arrow	For moving from one cell to the next
F5	Go to
F6	For switching between the worksheet, the Ribbon, the task pane, and the Zoom controls
Home	To go to the beginning of a row
Ctrl + Home	For moving to the beginning of a worksheet

Shortcut Keys	Functions
Ctrl + End	For moving to the last cell that has content in it within the worksheet
Shift + Arrow	For selecting the adjacent cell
Shift + Spacebar	For selecting an entire row
Ctrl + Spacebar	For selecting an entire column
Ctrl + Shift + Home	For selecting all to the start of the sheet
Ctrl+ Shift + End	For selecting all to the last used cell of the sheet
Ctrl + Shift + Arrow	To select the end of the last used row/column
Ctrl + Left Arrow	For moving the word to the left while in a cell
Ctrl + Right Arrow	For moving the word to the right while in a cell
PageUp	For moving the screen up
PageDown	For moving the screen down
Alt + PageUp	For moving the screen to the left
Alt+ PageDown	For moving the screen to the right
Ctrl + PageUp/Down	For moving the next or previous worksheet
Ctrl + Tab	To move to the next worksheet while on the spreadsheet
Shift + Tab	For moving cell to the right
Tab	For moving to the next cell

Table 4: Table with navigation shortcuts

File shortcuts

Shortcut Keys	Functions
Ctrl + N	New
Ctrl + O	To open
Ctrl + S	To save workbook
F12	Save As
Ctrl + P	Print
Ctrl + F2	For opening the preview print window
Ctrl + Tab	For moving to the next workbook
Ctrl + F4	For closing a file
Alt + F4	To close all open Excel files

Table 5: File shortcuts

Formula shortcuts

Shortcut Keys	Shortcuts
Ctrl + Shift + Enter	To enter an array formula
Ctrl + /	For selecting array formula range
Ctrl + '	To copy a formula from a cell and edit
Ctrl + [	For selecting all precedents cells
Ctrl +]	For selecting all dependent cells
F4	For changing the type of cell reference from relative to absolute

Alt + =	Sum range
F3	For displaying the range of names

Table 6: Formula shortcuts

Paste special shortcuts

Shortcut Keys	Functions
Ctrl + Alt + V+T	Paste Special formats
Ctrl + Alt + V+V	Paste Special values
Ctrl + Alt + V+F	Paste Special formulas
Ctrl + Alt + V+ C	Paste Special comments

Table 7: Paste special shortcuts

Ribbon Navigation shortcuts

Shortcut Keys	Functions
Alt	To display the Ribbon shortcut
Alt +F	To go to the File tab
Alt + H	To go to the Home tab
Alt + N	To go to the Insert tab
Alt + P	To go to the Page Layout tab
Alt + M	To go to the Formulas tab
Alt + A	To go to the Data tab
Alt + R	To go to the Review tab
Alt + W	To go to the View tab
Alt + Q	To put the cursor in the Search box
Alt + JC	To go to the Chart Design tab when the cursor is on a chart
Alt + JA	To go to the Format tab when the cursor is on a chart
Alt + JT	To go to the Table tab when the cursor is on a table
Alt + JP	To go to the Picture Format tab when the cursor is on a picture
Alt + JI	To go to the Draw tab
Alt + B	To go to the Power Pivot tab

Table 8: Ribbon Navigation shortcuts

Clear shortcuts

Shortcut Keys	Functions
Delete	For clearing cell data
Alt+ h + e + f	For clearing cell format
Alt+ h + e + m	For clearing cell comments
Alt+ h + e + a	For clearing all data formats and comments

Table 9: Clear shortcuts

Selection shortcuts

Shortcut Keys	Functions
Shift + Arrow	For selecting a cell range
Ctrl + Shift + Arrows	For highlighting a contiguous range
Shift + Page Up	For extending selection up one screen
Shift + Page Down	For extending selection down one screen
Alt + Shift + Page Up	For extending, selection left one screen
Alt + Shift + Page Down	For extending selection right one screen
Ctrl + A	For selecting or highlighting all cells in the worksheet
Ctrl + Space	To select the whole column or row
Shift + Ctrl + Space Bar	For selecting table
Alt + ;	For selecting visible cells
Shift + Home	For selecting a range from the start cell too far left
Shift + End + Arrow	For selecting a range from the start cell to the direction of the arrow
Ctrl + *	For selecting a continuous range of data
Ctrl + Shift + 0	For selecting all cells with comment
F5 + Alt +S +K + Enter	For selecting all blank cells

Table 10: Selection shortcuts

Data editing shortcut

Shortcut Keys	Functions
Ctrl + D	To fill down from the cell above
Ctrl + R	To fill right from cell left
Ctrl + F	To find and replace
F5 + Alt + s +o	For showing all constants
F5 + Alt + s +c	For highlighting the cell with comments

Table 11: Data editing shortcuts

Data editing (inside a cell) shortcuts

Shortcut Keys	Functions
F2	For editing the active cell
Enter	To confirm a change in a cell before opting out of that cell
Esc	To cancel a cell entry before opting out of that cell
Alt + Enter	To insert a line break within a cell
Shift + Left/Right	For highlighting within a cell
Ctrl + Shift + Left/Right	For highlighting contiguous items
Home	To move to the beginning of the cell contents
End	For moving to the end of a cell content
Backspace	For deleting a character from left
Delete	For deleting a character from the right

Table 12: Data editing (inside a cell) shortcuts

Other shortcuts

Shortcut Keys	Functions
Ctrl + Z	To undo the last action
Ctrl + Y	To redo the last action
Ctrl + 9	To hide any selected rows
Ctrl + 0	To hide any selected rows
Ctrl + Shift + (	To unhide any hidden rows in a given selection
Ctrl + Shift +)	To unhide any hidden columns in a selection
Ctrl + ;	To enter date
Ctrl +:	To enter time
Ctrl + '	To show formula
Ctrl +]	For selecting an active cell
Alt	To drive menu bar
Alt + Tab	To open the next program
Alt + =	To autosum

Table 13: Other shortcuts

22 Conclusion

The new Microsoft Excel 2023 is equipped with a whole lot of new features and enhancements much more than its predecessor (Microsoft Excel 2022). This version of Microsoft Excel comes alongside Microsoft Office 365 and its collaboration makes Excel 2023 a very unique software. In this guide, users will learn the fundamentals regarding Excel like creating pivot tables, learn about worksheets and workbooks, creating links between worksheets, use formulas to join text use keyboard accelerators, using date math, how to use AutoSum and so much more. At the end of this guide, users will fully understand Microsoft Excel 2023 and get to begin using the software on their own and with their companies. Going further, this User Guide includes updated information and an up-to-date step-by-step guide to make your adventure of acquiring and learning Excel 2023 functionalities more enjoyable. If you are a business or individual worker who wants to learn how to create tables, organize, and manage data, you need to purchase this Guide and start your incredible journey.

BONUS: Take advantage of my bonus offer! Simply scan the QR code below to be directed to a special web page. Once there, provide your email and submit an honest review of my book on Amazon. In return, you'll get access to 17 exclusive bonuses, including online courses, Excel templates, and even a handy mobile app. Your feedback is incredibly valuable, and we can't wait to hear what you think. Get started now! Link: https://dl.bookfunnel.com/vxlkxjwlhz

Printed in Great Britain
by Amazon

26210221R00077